"Dr. Nathan Mellor in his book, *Sleeping Giants: Authentic Stories and Insights for Building a Life that Matters* inspires us with the stories of people who have made a tremendous difference in the lives of others through their remarkable accomplishments and great sacrifices. He challenges us to set our own successful journeys of life through faith, servant leadership, compassion, vision, determination and commitment."

—Mark A. Stansberry,
Chairman of The GTD Group,
& Former Chairman and Acting CEO of
People to People International

"Dr. Nathan Mellor is an astute student of human nature. His ability to refine the essence of everyday occurrences and interpret the behaviors and actions of individuals and situations into meaningful life lessons is extraordinary. This book is a powerful example of his ability to tell a compelling story and find the deeper universal meaning from the experience.

Dr. Mellor embodies the principles of his company, Strata Leadership, in providing leadership based on character. In my years of association with Dr. Mellor, he is consistently encouraging while honestly and realistically providing guidance to peers and those he mentors. His leadership and innovative ideas have provided guidance to companies and individuals in a wide range of fields and situations. His dedication to family as well as his spiritual commitments have provided him with valuable insights that provide illustrations and connections that go beyond the world of work to glean deeper lessons from real life experiences, which he readily shares in helping to guide corporations and individuals."

—Dr. Steve Eckman,
President, York College

"The stories and insights shared in Dr. Nathan Mellor's *Sleeping Giants* are as authentic as the man who has authored them. I have long been an admirer of Nathan's and an advocate of the work accomplished by the many Strata Leadership endeavors under his leadership. He is man of fine character. The core of his character is clearly rooted in faith and family, as evidenced in the heartwarming, eloquent lessons learned from his parents, his community, and fellow leaders, which he has penned in this book."

—Mo Anderson,
Vice Chairman of the Board, Keller Williams

"WOW! When I was a graduate student majoring in Administration and Leadership I wish my required reading had included this book! It is one thing to study Leadership models, and quite another to read about real people, in real situations who lived the kind of lives and made the kind of decisions that inspired the leadership models we study today. This book is a personal and historic account of our country's heritage. A heritage that includes everyday people who inspired, encouraged, taught and ultimately shaped the lives of the populace and future of our nation. As you read this book it will remind you that our heritage is one to be admired and respected. We, today, are truly standing on the shoulders of the "Sleeping Giants" of our ancestry."

—Dee Carson, ED.D.,
Retired Dean and Assistant Vice President,
Harding University

"If people respond to real stories, and I believe they do, this book should be a bestseller because it captures the true-life struggles and life lessons learned for the author, his family, friends and national leaders.

I have known the author since he was a student leader at Harding. I consider him a very close friend even though we live miles apart and seldom see each other. This doesn't really matter, because when we meet, it's as though we've never been apart.

He is a visionary and a dreamer with a plan. The consistent theme in the collection of stories that he shares in this book is the fact that service to others matters and makes a difference in relationships for individuals, for families, for communities, and for our nation.

I'm reminded of his leading a group of student volunteers while he was at Harding, to Georgia to clean up after a major flood. He did so as a student body President, but he really did it because it mattered to him, and this kind of leadership is simply part of his DNA."

—David B. Burks, Ph.D.,
Chancellor, Harding University

"Dr. Nathan Mellor is a master story teller who has the gift of painting with words the deeper truths that awakens the soul with a fire to change the world! All through telling the stories of giants, of those we all want desperately to be around and to do life with! Every generation must rediscover the truth about life, leadership, and service to others out of love.

I have known Nathan for the better part of a decade and his life has been in service to others through the teaching and speaking about leadership and character. He shares with us the tools and skills to building a life that matters. He has awakened and inspired many sleeping giants and his call to action is as clear as Ted Roosevelt's when faced with adversity and seemingly impossible odds, "we'll start the war from here."

Consider the lives and choices made by those within these pages and the impact they have had on those around them and then contemplate the principles being lived out and see how they can serve us in our present generation with the challenges we face today.

I count it as a great honor to have called Dr. Mellor professor, mentor, coach, Whistle Pig, and best of all friend."

—Shad Glass, MBA,
Executive Vice President, Kimray Inc.

"We constantly shuffle, reshuffle, and fight to develop working mental models to make sense of life. However timeless stories make the most impact in the process. Nathan uses both personal and well-known stories to set a stage and then like a microscope reveals the underlying values that make them great. We need to be reminded of ideals that bring true strength of character and service to others."

—Paul Crawford,
President/CEO, Ordermatic Corporation

"In his book and in his life, Nathan's storytelling ability is only surpassed by his desire to encourage others to realize how their day to day actions can change the people and the world around them. This book reminds you of how your gifts and opportunities impact others."

—Frank Smith,
President of Mosaic Personnel & Sr. Executive Coach

"Ever the consummate storyteller, Nathan Mellor takes us on a journey through his experiences with ease and simplicity. The vignettes are the type that you would imagine hearing as you sit around a campfire, sipping hot cocoa. Although they are a quick-read, the questions posed throughout the chapter cause moments of self-reflection that leads to the kind of deep thinking that might just awaken the giant in us all."

—Dr. Karen Dennis,
Assistant Professor of Education, University of Mobile

"This book is a treasure of inspiration wrapped in wisdom, humor, and humility. Virtue and optimism are conveyed on every page. As with his presentations, Dr. Mellor connects us with is sense of honor, family, and heroes from all walks of life—whether privileged or poor. He sparks a desire to ask more of ourselves and energizes us to take the next steps. His messages are a welcome respite in a world that tends to squelch the human spirit. My only question is this: how soon will he write another book? I'm eager to hear more!"

—Shannon Warren,
Founder/CEO, Oklahoma Business Ethics Consortium

"Throughout *Sleeping Giants*, Dr. Mellor invites leaders from all backgrounds and walks-of-life on a journey of transformation. Reading this book is an experience that encourages reflection, builds inspiration, and sparks action. In an ever-so-skillful manner, Dr. Mellor draws leaders to the point of exploring their own leadership journey through beautifully articulated stories of challenge, determination, and change. Whether you are a business professional, public or non-profit leader, or an educator, Dr. Mellor's words remind us of the exponential impact great leaders have on the world and the critical importance for today's leaders to step into their full potential."

—Bucky Dodd, Ph.D.

"Nathan is a master storyteller, whether it be in print or from a lectern. This book is best read over many cups of Guatemalan coffee as if you are listening to a friend reveal his heart one chapter at a time. The lessons and wisdom he shares are from a life filled with purpose...and purposely lived for God. Well done, Nathan."

—Rick Harper,
Executive Director, Health Talents International

"Dr. Nathan Mellor is an amazingly gifted teacher and mentor to people all over the spectrum of life—from the board room to the boiler room to the classroom. He has an ability to take the simple experiences of life and see in them the seeds of greatness and goodness. His strong faith, coupled with insight and genuine caring cause others to seek him out for advice and friendship. Not only has God gifted him with the proverbial 'five talents,' but he humbly acknowledges the source of those gifts as he continues to learn, to grow, and to multiply those talents each day. As he weaves these stories, may we, the readers, not to miss the profoundness of the daily human experience as a teacher and encourager."

—Mike E. O'Neal
President Emeritus of Oklahoma Christian University and
Former Chancellor of the University of Rwanda

"Count me among those most grateful that master storyteller, Dr. Nathan Mellor finally wrote this book. *Sleeping Giants* is rich with stories that will move and inspire you to awaken the sleeping giant within and then invest your life in awakening the potential in others. Full of poignant stories about people who make a difference, from local classroom teachers to world leaders, Mellor captures your imagination as to how you too can reframe your perspective, leverage your gifting, fulfill your purpose, and live a life that matters."

—David Whitlock, Ph. D.
President, Oklahoma Baptist University

"Aside from his excellent work in mentorship and executive coaching, Dr. Nathan Mellor is a captivating storyteller. In his book, *Sleeping Giants: Authentic Stories and Insights for Building a Life that Matters*, Mellor features numerous powerful narratives about the giants we have read about in history books and those he has encountered in his own life. In light of the incredible stories, Mellor challenges the reader to consider awakening the giants nearby and those within, on the courageous path of living life to its fullest."

—Susan DeWoody, Ed.D.,
Vice President for Academic Affairs,
Oklahoma Baptist University

"*Sleeping Giants: Authentic Stories and Insights for Building a Life That Matters* is a beautiful reminder everyone has a story to share and we can learn important life lessons when we listen with an open mind and heart. Dr. Mellor's debut book checks all the boxes - it's informative, educational, entertaining, and inspiring. I loved watching his personal journey unfold through stories of family, friends, mentors, colleagues and others. I wish we could put them all in a room and personally thank them for blessing so many with so much."

—Dot Rhyne,
Founder & President - Brand Talkers, LLC

"Dr. Mellor has the gift of seeing greatness in others and helping us see it in ourselves. *Sleeping Giants* is a journey through the the stories of people who embody an ability to reframe the world around them and exceed both their own expectations and the constraints placed on them by others. Dr. Mellor gets us close enough to these people to see the moments that mattered, and in doing so gives us the chance to see those same moments in our own lives. Give this book to anyone you wish true success fo Read this book to your children. Take these stories in and let them give you insight into your true potential. Dr. Mellor asks us, "Who do you want to be?" This book will help you decide."

—Thomas Hill III, CEO, Kimray, Inc.

SLEEPING
GIANTS

SLEEPING GIANTS

AUTHENTIC STORIES AND INSIGHTS FOR BUILDING A LIFE THAT MATTERS

DR. NATHAN MELLOR

FOREWORD BY MO ANDERSON
Vice Chairman of the Board, Keller Williams

MONOCLE
PRESS

This book is dedicated to my mother, Susan Mellor.

TABLE OF CONTENTS

FOREWORD

I cannot begin to express the honor and privilege I feel to have been asked to write the foreword to Dr. Nathan Mellor's *Sleeping Giants: Authentic Stories and Insights for Building a Life that Matters*. I first met Nathan in the summer of 2016. However, I was already familiar with Strata Leadership's mission to create character and competence-based solutions for businesses, communities, and individuals. In fact, Strata had been my role model for at least 10 years prior to that memorable introduction. Strata's *Character Core* education inspired me to develop my own character-based training geared toward real estate professionals within my company. Needless to say, I was a fan before I ever met Nathan personally. And, the first time I heard him teach, it became clear that Nathan is a captivating storyteller and someone who is genuinely interested in the lives of others. It is this energy and investment in people that he brings to the writing of this book.

I can speak from experience when I say: book writing is journey of discovery for the author. In my own book, *A Joy Filled Life*, I wrote a chapter titled "Follow Your Dreams." I share an observation I have made during my personal author's journey—when people lose their dream or become convinced a dream is no longer worth pursuing, the result is discouragement, depression, and a sense of resignation. They learn to settle instead of following their dreams. As a person who is an advocate for dreams, dreamers, and the action needed to make dreams come true, I admire the way that Nathan inspires people to dream again. As a result, when you spend time with him—in person or on the pages of his book—he makes you feel that YOU have what it takes to keep moving forward.

Nathan's communication style is memorable, dynamic, and encouraging. He speaks to the heart and challenges the mind through a blend of stories and current research that is convicting. With the skill of an educator, he has the ability to simplify complicated concepts without watering them down.

Over the last few years of knowing him, I have seen Nathan speak a number of times. Among the key themes of his presentations is that mental models are constantly being changed and transformed. To make his points, he offers stories from his childhood and from the lives of others. When I listen to him, I am reminded of my own upbringing. As the daughter of a tenant farmer, it has been a long journey from a dirt farm in Oklahoma to becoming vice-chairman and co-owner of Keller Williams Realty, the world's largest real estate company. Nathan has helped me take stock of my life thus far, and as a result, I am all the more grateful for the many people who have invested in my life. In addition, I am challenged to consider how I am investing in the lives of others.

If you are willing to serve, you can make a difference in the lives of others. *Sleeping Giants* reflects the heart of its author. I hope it will be a reminder to you that what you think, say, and do matters.

—Mo Anderson
Vice Chairman of Keller Williams Realty

ACKNOWLEDGMENTS

This book could not have been written without the support of my wife, Christie, and our daughters, Annalise and Arden.

Many people have helped shape my understanding of the world. I am grateful for my father, David, and my brother, Matthew, for their commitment to making the world a better place. I am also thankful for my honorary siblings: Karen Dennis, Brian Lewis, and Kristi Ravellette for the impact they have made on my life. I am also grateful for my aunt and uncle, Richard and Jana Berryhill. They have been a constant source of encouragement to me, and I am thankful for them.

I would also like to express my since appreciation to my business partner and friend, Frank Smith, and my colleagues at C3 Brands. Special thanks to Jamie O'Brien, Jeremiah Shaw, Lyn Watson, and Dr. Erin Greilick for helping me find my voice early in this project. Christina Hicks of Monocle Press has been a remarkable guide, and I am grateful for her counsel.

I am forever indebted to Dr. David and Leah Burks, Dr. Dee Carson, Dr. Steve Eckman, Tony and Kathy Kendall, Dr. Carl Mitchell, and Dr. Mike O'Neal for their gift of love and kindness. Thank you to the dream team at Hixson especially: Chuck McAlpin, Kathy Holt, Alicia Henderson, Jake and Shelly Hendrix, and Suzanne Belcher. Although they have been taken from us, I am grateful to have the voices of Eric Baird, Ralph Thompson, Pete Winemiller, and Colonel Pendleton Woods in my head.

Finally, I want to express my appreciation for a small group of friends that I affectionately call the Whistle Pigs:

Dale Bresee	James Bennett
Steven Bickley	Bruce Bockus
Steven Buck	Tom Connell
Paul Crawford	Scott Dewald
Shad Glass	Nico Gomez

Scott Griffin
Thomas Hill
David Kenyon
Scott Mueller
Trevor Nutt
Kevin Penwell
Jim Priest
Scott Schatzman
Brandon Tatum
David Whitlock

Marty Hepp
Jason Emerson
Scott McLain
Michael Newcity
Ken Parker
Myron Pope
David Ross
Frank Smith
Tim Thorne

INTRODUCTION

Throughout this book, I will be introducing you to people and concepts that I hope you will find interesting and helpful. Some of the stories are about public or historical figures, but most are friends and family. Whenever possible, I have used their real names (with permission), but there are a few times when I felt doing so would have been inappropriate. I have changed their names accordingly.

Included are several personal stories, and my purpose in sharing them is not an effort to write an autobiography. My reason for telling personal stories is to help make the underlying concepts more accessible. I have been in audiences where someone had a story to tell but did not have a point to make. I hope to have a point to make that can be explained through a story that helps make the concept more easily understood.

At the core, *Sleeping Giants* is about mental models. There are numerous definitions of mental models, but researcher and author, Peter Senge, provided one that I have found useful. In Senge's 1990 classic, *The Fifth Discipline*, he stated, "Mental models are deeply held internal images of how the world works, images that limit us to familiar ways of thinking and acting. Very often, we are not consciously aware of our mental models or the effects they have on our behavior."[1]

Mental models are continually forming, being shaped, and revised. From the time our brains were able to process information, each of us began collecting data about the world in which we live. Through each chapter, I will present a loose framework intended to challenge and inspire more profound thought about your mental model.

PART ONE

THE STORIES WE BELIEVE

CHAPTER 1

"YOU'RE NOT AS DUMB AS DANIEL"

Discovering Your Value

My father's name is David, but most people, if they call him by his first name, call him Dave. To his former students, he is "Mr. Mellor," and to the athletes who played for him, he is "Coach." Now, in his seventh decade, his shoulders are still broad, and although he carries a few extra pounds on his 5'-7" frame, he has retained the powerful physique of an athlete. His once brown hair has turned to a distinguished blend of gray and white.

When he was a child, his nickname was "Indian." The name was not meant as a racial epithet but as a description of his skin color and musculature. In the summer sun of his childhood, his toned skin became a deep brown. His appearance was reminiscent of the Shawnee, who were among the Natives that had once lived in southeastern Ohio, where he grew up.[1,2]

When I hear my father's voice in my head, it makes me smile. His voice has the raspy quality that is common among veteran coaches, but it is strong and distinct. When he is passionate about a topic, he unleashes his words, as if he were a verbal prizefighter delivering devastating combinations. A longtime coach, preacher, and teacher, he projects his voice without the aid of a microphone or sound system. He is intense, an original thinker, and he has the heart of a lion.

It was during the early years of elementary school that I recognized that he and my mother were unique. My discovery was not the result of a single experience but a series of events that eventually tipped the scales for me. Interestingly, it was not their actions that caused me

1

to take notice as much as it was the reactions of others to them that opened my eyes.

My mother's name is Susan. If for some reason our family were forced to vote on which person was the most talented, the vote would be unanimous for her. A leader, she is thoughtful, creative, funny, and a remarkable communicator. When my brother and I were young, she chose to be a stay-at-home mother. As we moved into junior and senior high school, she began working in professional roles that played to her strengths. When we left for college, she focused her efforts primarily on managing a bookstore before transitioning to business-to-business sales. Due to her blend of determination and likability, it was no surprise to any of us that she was successful.

THE TALKING TREE

The process by which we become self-aware includes a series of awakening moments. Through this process of discovery, we gain insights into how the world works and our place within it. By becoming self-aware, we also become aware of others and how our lives intersect with them. Awakening moments consist of breakthrough experiences that represent a leap forward in our understanding. They are "aha" moments in which we are able to make sense of something that had been a mystery before. When we have an awakening moment, we see the world more clearly and our perspective is changed.

One of the earliest awakening moments for me, regarding my dad, happened when I was very young. It is one of my first memories. The elementary school my brother and I were attending was hosting a fall festival. As part of the festivities, there were booths for face painting, cakewalks, ring tosses, and other attractions. To help make the event possible, parents were recruited to manage the games. Dad was asked to be the voice for a large puppet, known as the "Talking Tree."

The life-size tree was constructed from wood, cardboard, and paper. I am not sure who built it, but it was a masterpiece. Jim Henson would have been proud to have had this tree on the set of *Sesame*

Street. Hidden inside the trunk, dad became a puppeteer, and the tree magically sprang to life.

The genius of the Talking Tree was its simplicity. The Tree told knock-knock jokes that appealed to kids. The jokes were from a thick joke book that had been sitting on a shelf in our home since my birth in the summer of 1973. Dad bought the book when mom was in the hospital giving birth to me. He thought she might enjoy hearing a few jokes to help pass the time. Amazingly, my mother did not fully appreciate his comedic genius as she recovered from her cesarean section.

Even though it was the era of the *Muppet Show*, if it had not been for the fact that he was lending his voice and humor to the Talking Tree, it would not have been a draw. However, with dad telling jokes, the line for the Talking Tree began to grow. By the end of the evening, it seemed the Talking Tree had become the most popular attraction. It takes a special kind of person to make kids laugh, and he knew what he was doing.

THE STORYTELLER

Around that same time, I had a similar experience with my mother, but instead of it happening at school, it was at church. The congregation we attended was very community minded and had focused their efforts on building an active bus ministry. The busses allowed children to attend church who could not do so otherwise because of a lack of transportation. The church started with a couple of busses and whenever there was enough money saved, dad and a few of the men from the church would drive to a wholesaler and purchase additional used school buses.

One of the members at the church owned a sawmill that had a large covered area they used as a makeshift paint booth. When they were prepping a bus for paint, they would work late into the evening, taping windows, sanding and removing hardware. Sometimes my brother and I would go to the sawmill while dad painted. Because it was often late in the evening, we would explore a little, but then we would find a comfortable spot to sleep. The paint had a sweet smell, and coupled with the smell of the wood, it created a scent that I will always associate with childhood. The buses rolled in "school bus yellow," and a few days later, they rolled out freshly painted white with a blue stripe along the side. They were renamed "Joy Buses" and were added to a growing fleet. Each week, the buses rumbled through the surrounding neighborhoods, picking up children who wanted to go to church but needed a ride.

On occasion, to help build momentum and a sense of excitement, the church would host special days that were designed to make it easier to invite friends and family to visit. One of those days was "Bust the Record" day. That morning, as the buses picked up the children along their routes, the turnout was beyond what anyone could have possibly imagined. Kids kept piling on until the bus was standing room only. They sang along the way, and their voices were so loud, they could literally be heard from a block away. When the buses finished their route and arrived back at the building, they counted the number of kids on each bus to see which one had the best turnout. The winning bus had 147 very excited and happy kids on board.

There were several practical challenges in having so many children attending a church without their parents. One of those was having enough adults and teens on hand to keep the children safe and to make sure the classes were engaging. On some of the highest attendance days, the ratio between the children and teachers could easily be 30 to 40 kids to one adult.

My mother and two other teachers taught the second grade Sunday school class. When the buses were packed full, their class ballooned to 120 children. As the kids kept pouring in, she recognized the activity planned for the day was not going to work. Instead of panicking, she got creative. She looked in her purse for a prop and located a fluffy, white, powder applicator. Knowing the natural curiosity of kids, she let them see that she was looking at something extraordinary, but she kept the object of her attention concealed from their sight. With her back to the kids, she carefully cupped the applicator in her hands.

Turning to face the children, she lifted her cupped hands to eye level. They could see the white "fur," but they could not identify what it was.

Due to the sheer number of kids, she stood on top of a table to teach the class. In a matter of minutes, the entire group sat with their mouths open in disbelief. Amazingly, she was playing "make believe" with 120 7-year-olds simultaneously. The storyteller cast her spell, and the children were mesmerized. When they would get too comfortable, she would make it appear as if she was struggling to contain the tiny animal. The kids would act bravely until she twitched her hands in their direction. They jumped and laughed in delight. It takes an exceptional teacher to capture the imagination of children. Watching my mother hold her class spellbound provided undeniable proof that she was indeed remarkable.

A SAFE HOME

Around that same time, when I was old enough to understand the concept, my parents sat my brother and me down to talk about what it meant to be a foster family. They explained some of the reasons why there were children in foster care and the challenges we could expect. Even before this moment, we had opened our home to children in need, but I was too young to understand why. Consequently, throughout the bulk of my childhood, we were a foster family. Sometimes it was for just a few days, but typically it was for 2 to 3 years at a time. There are differing opinions about how best to care for children in foster care. At the time, there was very little guidance or research on the topic. Our approach was straightforward. When kids came to our home, they did not just live in our house; they became a part of our family.

KRISTI

Kristi was a little girl who came to our home as a toddler and lived with us for nearly three years while spending occasional weekends with her birth mother. From the first moment she stepped foot in our house, she became a Mellor. Many memories could be shared about Kristi, but there are a few that stand out.

Anyone who has ever eaten a meal at our house knows that among my mother's many talents is her ability to cook. Not surprisingly, the kitchen is among my mother's favorite places in the house. When she would cook, Kristi would sit on the countertop with her tiny feet resting in the sink. While mom prepared the food, they would sing or talk. Kristi would watch mom cook, and it was their way of bonding.

On many evenings, dad would brush out Kristi's long brown hair. As hard as he tried, getting her pigtails symmetrical was beyond his ability. When I became the father of daughters, I would often think of these tender moments when my father, the wrestler and football player, would gently brush Kristi's hair. It is one of my favorite mental images of both him and Kristi.

We had begun the process of adopting her, with her mother's approval, when Kristi was unexpectedly taken from us. She had gone to be with her birth mother over a weekend, but instead of bringing her back at the appointed time, she had skipped town. Although it was against the law to do so, she had taken Kristi with her. Without knowing any of this, we waited for Kristi to return, but she never showed up. After a few hours, we began a search, but there was no trace of her. The hours became days, which turned into months and then years.

At one point, someone gave us a tip about her whereabouts. We thought we had a breakthrough, but when we contacted the Department of Human Services, they said they were powerless to help because she was living across state lines. Her absence was a black hole for years and a topic we could not discuss without getting emotional. It had been nearly 30 years since she left our home when we finally found her on social media. We shared a few pictures with her from her childhood and told her that we wanted to connect if she would like to do so.

When she agreed to connect, it was as if someone who had died had been brought back to life. Reconnecting with her was one of the most powerful emotions I have ever experienced. Through our messages back and forth, we started catching up on what had happened. There were moments of joy to celebrate, but there were also moments that made my stomach turn and brought tears of anger and frustration to my eyes. My parents suggested a face-to-face meeting with Kristi, and she agreed.

At the informal reunion, no one knew what to expect. It took every ounce of my parent's strength to keep their composure when she arrived still wearing her brown hair long. My dad mentioned something about her hair, and she said, "I have always liked my long hair." Later in the conversation, my mom asked her about her hobbies. She said, "My favorite thing is cooking. I have always enjoyed cooking and would like to do it professionally someday." She may not have remembered my dad brushing her hair in the evenings before she went to bed or my mom talking to her in the kitchen, but it was evident that those moments had registered somewhere. I cannot express how grateful I am that we found her and now have a renewed relationship with her. She is a brave and strong woman, and our family will forever love her.

ADAM

Adam came to our home when he was 3. When the caseworker brought him to our house, he was frustrated, confused, and angry. When she tried to calm him, he responded violently. He made a fist and punched her in the eye with as much force as he could deliver. The blow broke her glasses and cut her face.

As my parents attended to the caseworker, he snuck into their bedroom and found my mother's fingernail polishes. He poured one bottle on the bedspread and another on the wooden bedroom furniture. He then smeared the polish around for good measure. Noticing he was gone, my mother walked into her room and saw what he had done. When she confronted him, he responded to her aggressively. He put his fists on his hips and growled, "Don't tell me what to do!"

The abuse he had endured in the first years of his life had been horrific. The chaos of his first day with us was a window into the hell he had suffered his entire life. He had only known pain and chaos. It was his normal.

The specific moment that required the state to take him from his birth family defied all logic. For reasons unknown, his mother filled their bathtub with scalding hot water and then put her child, who would have been between 1 and 2 years old, in the water. Every inch of his tender skin that touched the water was badly burned. Due to his age, he was utterly powerless to defend himself or to get out of the tub. When he came to our home, the burns had healed, but the scars, both physical and emotional, remained visible.

As might be expected, even though the abuse had been when he was so young, he remained terrified of the bathtub. When it was bath time, dad did not force him into the tub. Instead, he put on a pair of swim trunks and got in the water to show him it was safe. Slowly, Adam began to rebuild trust. In time, mom or dad would place their hands under the faucet so he could see that the water pouring over their hands was not too hot. They would invite him to do the same, and he would place his little hand under the water. Eventually, he was able to take baths on his own.

In the first few months, Adam was highly resistant to affection, and although it is a parental instinct to hug and touch, my parents were very slow to do so because of his negative responses. It was around the Christmas holidays when he came down with a particularly bad case of the flu. He was exhausted and miserable when he unexpectedly reached for my mother. She picked him up in her arms, took him to the rocking chair beside the fireplace, and quietly rocked him to sleep. We were shocked and overjoyed by the breakthrough. Based on his aversion to being touched, it would not surprise me if this had been the first time that he had ever been held and rocked to sleep in the arms of a loving parent.

After living in our home for a few years, he and his brother, from whom he had been separated while in foster care, were reunited and adopted by a family. They lived on a farm a few hours away from our home. Although it was always difficult to say goodbye to someone you would not likely see again, it was a dream come true for a little boy who wanted desperately to reunite with his brother and have a permanent home.

It takes a particular type of couple to decide to open their home to children in need. It did not take incredible insight for me to recognize the difference between my home and the previous homes of the foster kids who were sleeping in the bedroom next to mine. Once again, I understood that my parents were truly unique.

A GLOBAL PERSPECTIVE

Because of my parents' faith and love for people, it did not seem that unusual when my dad decided to go Guyana, South America, in 1982 with Benny and Kitty Mullins from our church. A former British colony, it is the only country in South America where the official language is English. A small country of fewer than 800,000 residents, it is bordered to the north by the Atlantic Ocean and to the south by Brazil. Venezuela is to the west and Suriname is to the east. Although it is not an island, it is considered a part of the Caribbean due to its distinctive culture. The vast majority of its citizens are the descendants of African slaves or indentured workers from India.

It was the first time my dad had traveled outside of the United States, and he felt an instant bond with the people he met. He had a deep respect for the determination, intellect, and perseverance of the Guyanese. Over the next several years, dad began taking volunteers with him to further the work. When we became teenagers, my brother and I started traveling with him. We would work in the capital city of Georgetown or at a church camp located on the edge of the Guyanese jungle.

While on one of these trips, dad asked me to go with him to purchase some food for the camp. Because it was so remote, some areas could only be reached on foot or by motorcycle. We traveled to a nearby village where one of the residents owned a generator and a freezer. Our goal was to buy some frozen meat. After purchasing the food, we were invited by the family who owned the freezer to stay for a meal. Declining the offer would have been considered rude, so we accepted.

Many of the homes in the area were built on piers or stilts. We climbed the stairs to the main floor and were seated at a round table in the middle of the main room of the house. The owner of the home and another man that I did not know sat at the table with us. As a teenager, there was little pressure for me to engage in conversation and doing so would have likely been considered culturally inappropriate. Consequently, I sat quietly, listening to the conversation. A few moments later, food was brought to the table. After the four of us were served, I noticed that we were the only ones who had been given food. The women and children stayed in the kitchen or lined-up against the wall of the room where we were eating.

It was a humbling moment to realize we were eating their food. I did not want to show disrespect to our hosts, but I also knew how poor the families were in this area, and I did not want them to suffer on my behalf. The Guyanese have been exploited for centuries, and our genuine desire was to serve them, not to be served. I ate as little as possible without being rude, and after the meal, we expressed our gratitude and left. If my father had encouraged us to go to Guyana to see the world from a different perspective, it had worked.

Eventually, we began taking medical supplies to the doctors and nurses at the public hospital in Georgetown. As trust was established, we asked if we could assist in the children's ward. They agreed, and we began going to the hospital with the goal of bringing joy to the kids who were confined there. The children shared one large room with multiple beds and we brought coloring books and played games with them. In addition to the children who were in the hospital due to illness or injury, some were confined to the children's ward because they had been abandoned. We were told that most of the babies left behind had HIV.

Connected to the hospital was a narrow porch with several rocking chairs. The porch provided a place to get fresh air and an occasional ocean breeze. Our task was to hold the infants and toddlers and rock them to sleep. The kids we held in our arms were small and frail. Over the course of a few days, the children would anticipate our arrival and would light up when we walked into the room. I was shaken when we came in one afternoon to rock the babies, and noticed that one of them had been wrapped carefully from head to toe in a white sheet. I looked in the crib and saw that a piece of paper had been pinned to the sheet providing the details of the child's death.

Leading trips to Guyana became a way of life for my dad. If he was effective on his own, when my mother was eventually able to join him on the trips, they became all the more impactful. Although Guyana would always have a place in their hearts, they started doing similar work in other countries as well. I estimate dad has either led or participated in well over 75 trips to different places around the world since his first trip to Guyana. It takes a special kind of people to forge friendships across the globe, and my parents, without any fanfare, have done so in Belize, Cuba, Guatemala, Guyana, Honduras, Indonesia, Jamaica, Mexico, Ukraine, and Zambia. People love my parents and it is due in large part to the fact my parents love them. It is nothing short of amazing to see what can happen when people choose to love and respect others.

Today, my parents live outside of Little Rock, Arkansas and work as a team with the faith-based, non-profit Health Talents International (HTI). Through HTI, they assist in the coordination of medical mission trips to Guatemala. Each year, there are a dozen or more weeklong programs for groups of 25 to 55 people. In addition to the short-term efforts my parents help coordinate, HTI also has two clinics that are led almost exclusively by highly qualified Guatemalans. The primary base of operations is at Clinica Ezell, located in Montellano, Guatemala. Clinica Ezell has 3 operating suites, a pharmacy, lab, diagnostic room, dental clinic, a 50-bed patient ward, and an adjacent dormitory that sleeps 60. The second location, Clinica Caris, is located in Lemoa, Guatemala. Clinica Caris has two dental operatories, two exam rooms, and a pharmacy, along with a lab and storage area.[3]

If you are looking to invest in a worthy non-profit, I would recommend HTI without reservation. Although the programs are health-related and healthcare professionals are needed, you do not have to be in healthcare to participate in a short-term effort. There is plenty of work to be done. If you would like to forge lifelong relationships and want to serve, I would encourage you to consider joining with my parents or other HTI professionals on a life-changing trip. (*More information can be found about HTI at http://www.healthtalents.org*)

A BUCKET LIST ITEM

My dad and I were talking on the phone in early 2014. At the time, my parents were living in a home they had recently built on the top of a ridge in Ringgold, Georgia. Their house was just about a mile south of the state line of Tennessee on the outskirts of Chattanooga. I was sitting in my living room in Oklahoma City. We were talking about taking a road trip, together with my brother, later in the year.

Matt Mellor is my only sibling, and he is two years older than me. He has a large frame and broad shoulders, and he stands at 5'-10". He has a full head of brown hair, inquisitive blue eyes, and an easy smile. A longtime educator and administrator, he was the principal of Daisy Bates Elementary in Little Rock, Arkansas, at the time my dad and I were planning the trip.

A cancer survivor and a devoted father, he cares deeply about the welfare of children. In addition to his work as an educator, he is a talented musician, carpenter, mechanic, IT aficionado, and lifelong learner. He holds 3 degrees from Harding University, a Bachelor of Music Education, Master of Education, and an Education Specialist degrees. He is currently pursuing his fourth degree, the doctorate in Educational Leadership.

This conversation was not the first time dad and I had talked about taking a road trip. Considering we had not yet chosen a destination nor blocked out time on our schedules, I think he sensed that another year could be lost when he interrupted and said, "Son, I've got a bucket list item." He had never used this phrase before, and it got my attention. He continued, "Fifty years ago when I was in high school, I got to go to an Ohio State football game." He paused and then said, "I would like to go back, and I would like for my boys to take me."

My dad is not the kind of person who asks for much, if anything, for himself. When we were growing up, he was the kind of dad who would buy his clothes at Goodwill so his sons could get new clothes at Sears. His "bucket list item" was not a dying wish, but it was a wish nonetheless. There was only one response available, and I said, "Yes, sir. We will make it happen." I connected with my brother, we found a weekend that would work and began making plans.

On November 1, we left from my parent's house while it was still dark to get to the famed Ohio Stadium in time for the pregame show. Although dad was a football coach, he had always had an appreciation for a good marching band, and many consider Ohio State's band to be the best. When my brother was in high school, he chose band over football, and although he would have been a good football player, there was never a single negative word spoken about it. My dad thought it was great.

With that said, one of my favorite stories about my brother was when he decided to go out for spring football at the end of his junior year. As the name suggests, spring football happens in the spring semester. The team practices together for a few weeks, and then plays an inner-squad game. Spring football provides the players an opportunity to get in shape and learn new plays, and it gives the coaches a chance to evaluate talent for the next school year.

We had a solid team, and earlier that year, the team made it to the conference championship but lost 6-0 in a tough game. Most of the starters from that talented team would be returning, and my brother had been more than capable of holding his own against several players who would eventually be named all-conference the next season when they won the conference championship in a blowout.

The coaches knew he was a leader in the band, and at the end of spring football, one of the coaches asked if he was going to play football in the fall or stay in the band. The question had been posed in a friendly way with genuine interest. Matt replied that he was, "Going to stay with the band." Considering spring football can be very physical, the coach was surprised by my brother's response. Intrigued, he asked, "Why would you go through this if you did not want to play next season?" Matt replied, "I just wanted you to know that a band kid could play if he wanted to." That fall, instead of playing on the football team, he was the drum major for the band. Although he would eventually learn to play several instruments, he played the sousaphone throughout high school and college.

Even if you have the slightest of interest in college football or in college bands, you are likely familiar with the famed Script *Ohio*. The Ohio State Marching Band has performed this formation during pregame since the fall of 1936. In single file, the band spells the word *Ohio* in cursive. Each week, one upperclassmen sousaphone player is selected to dot the "i" in the cursive *Ohio*.[4]

The three of us sat side-by-side in anticipation, and the band did not disappoint. Marching in perfect unison, the drum corps took the field. A moment later, via the famed "Ramp Entry," the band arrived. It is both impressive and surprisingly emotional to see the performance live. After the band was in position, the drum major, dressed in white and holding the Gray Baton, high stepped onto the field stopping at the 35-yard line. The drum major then did a backbend so deeply that the feather on the top of his white hat touched the ground.

The band wore dark, navy blue uniforms highlighted with white belts, gloves, and spats over their black shoes. Because it was a night game, the lights shone off of the silver instruments, especially the sousaphones. The sound generated from the 192 student musicians on the field was staggering.

As we neared the 8:00 p.m. kickoff, it was becoming apparent we were not dressed properly for the cold. Each of us wore blue jeans, long sleeve shirts, coats, and tennis shoes. When the temperature finally dropped below freezing, and the wind began to blow through the stadium, we became increasingly uncomfortable.

True to form, although each of us was shivering uncontrollably, none of us would acknowledge the cold. We did our best to remain as stoic as possible for as long as possible. When we saw someone walk past with hot chocolate, I offered to get some for the group. The drink came in a souvenir cup, and they were $9 each. It was so cold that the price did not matter. A few moments later, I was carrying three cups of overpriced hot chocolate back to our seats.

We were there to watch the game, but each of us knew the trip had little to do with football or the band. Dad's "bucket list item" was about spending a weekend with his sons. With that said, it was a nice bonus when dad's beloved Buckeyes defeated Illinois 55-14 on their way to winning the National Championship that year.

Usually, the return trip from Columbus to Chattanooga would take about 7 hours. It is a scenic drive south on Interstate 71 and then on I-75 South through Cincinnati, Lexington, Knoxville, and finally, Chattanooga. Instead, we decided to go the "long way" back so we could go through dad's hometown of Marietta, Ohio. It would add a few hours to our trip, but it would give us a chance to travel through the small town where my dad grew up. In addition to it being his hometown, it is also our family's ancestral home. Before the road trip, I had been doing some research online about our ancestors. In the process, I located a small graveyard where many of our people had been buried, but for unclear reasons, its existence had been forgotten. We thought it would be meaningful to see the place and to connect with our past.

GOING HOME

The three of us drove down narrow roads that were bordered by farms. Some of the trees still had their leaves, which were a blend of red, orange, and gold. We traveled through Beverly, Ohio and crossed the Muskingum River into Waterford. Veering right on Buchanan Road and then straight onto Wells Road for another mile and a half, it struck me that the back roads we were now traveling had very likely been the dirt paths that our family had traveled on foot or by horseback. We kept right on Township Road 141 and took another right on 142. After just a few hundred yards, we turned left onto a gravel road, which led to the small cemetery.

It felt much warmer on Sunday than it had on Saturday. The sun shone brightly, the temperature was crisp, and the deep blue sky was mostly cloudless. Dad had turned the radio off to help concentrate as we were navigating the back roads. As we approached the family plot, no one spoke, which made the crunching sound of the gravel shifting under the weight of the car seem louder than normal. The road ran parallel to the graveyard, and when we got to the end of the path, dad brought the car to a stop.

We stepped out of the car and took inventory of our surroundings. Due to the falling leaves and the proximity of the farms, the air had a pleasant and earthy quality. A century earlier there had been a wooden church on this site, but there are no longer any visible reminders of the structure. In years gone by, our family gathered here to worship and to enjoy picnics on the grounds. The location is serene and it was easy to imagine the place filled with our family enjoying warm cider, cured ham, and pumpkin pies on a pleasant fall afternoon.

It appeared there were about 100 grave markers, and the oldest was in the far northwest corner of the small cemetery. Some of the markers were made of granite, but the older ones were made of sandstone. Many of the older headstones were worn smooth by the elements, and the names were either barely legible or were already lost to history. Among the oldest ones, a few still stand, but several were either lying on the ground or had been broken into pieces. We scanned the headstones for letters and words we could decipher. There was a great feeling of joy when we found our people. Most had been laid to rest in a single row. It was interesting to note that although the majority had retained the name Mellor, some had changed the spelling to Miller or Meller. The oldest in the group was my sixth great-grandfather, Samuel. He was born on December 12, 1749, in England and had been laid to rest in this field on July 30, 1825.

The three of us stood there taking in a moment that did not require commentary. Beyond the cemetery, there are rolling hills in all directions, which are bordered by old and mature trees. There are a few ponds nearby, and north of the property, in the far distance, is the West Branch of Wolf Creek. Standing in silence, it felt that the past, present, and future had merged for a moment. While in the present, we were thinking about the past and contemplating our own futures. It was moving to connect with those who had gone before us on such a personal level. I felt at home as we stood in the same place where friends and family had gathered together to remember their loved ones, our ancestors, in days gone by.

It was while we were in this reflective mood that I asked my dad if he could show us around his hometown and let us see some of the places that were special to him. Although the detour would add even more time to our already extended trip home, he agreed. Soon, we were once again driving down curvy country roads headed toward Marietta. Our first stop would be the first house Dad remembered calling home.

DAVID RUSSELL MELLOR

David Russell Mellor, my father, was born on Sunday, April 20, 1947, in Marietta, Ohio. His parents, Glen and Helen, were both born in 1922, just a few years before the Great Depression. He was the youngest of three children.

It is unclear when or where Glen and Helen met, but by the time they were students at Marietta High School, they were a couple. Following graduation in 1940, he became a meat cutter and she worked as a telephone operator. They were both 19 when they were married at a small ceremony on July 12, 1941.

They had been married for five months and Helen was 2 months pregnant when Pearl Harbor was attacked on December 7, 1941 and America was pulled into World War II. Their firstborn, William, arrived in the summer of 1942 on July 10. Glen was drafted on October 30, 1942, but was classified as Class 3-A, which meant his service would be deferred "by reason of extreme hardship to dependents" until they had exhausted the pool of draftees in Classes 1 and 2.[5] In August of 1944, he was called up and became one of the 839,000 Ohioans who would serve their country in the Armed Forces during the war.[6]

When Glen's train departed for Camp Wolters, just outside of Mineral Wells, Texas, nearly 1,200 miles away from Marietta, Helen was 8 months pregnant with their second child. It provides a bit of insight into her approach to life when on October 3, 1944, despite having friends and family in town, she walked herself to the hospital to give birth to her daughter, Marilyn Kay.

After a few weeks of recuperation from childbirth, Helen traveled southwest to Texas to see her husband before he sailed off to the Pacific theater of war. Private First Class Mellor was an infantryman who fought courageously and was honorably discharged on February 16, 1946. A little over a year later after his return, my dad was born.

When we pulled up to 119 Sharon Street, I had no recollection of having ever seen the home before. It was the quintessential post-war, Cape-Cod style home located in a working-class neighborhood where people kept their yards nice and enjoyed sitting outdoors. Built in 1950, the single-story home consisted of three bedrooms and two baths and was nearly 900 square feet. The exterior was painted light gray with the gable a darker gray. The door and window frames were white, and the shutters were black.

Although his parents would remain married for 54 years, life in the Mellor home, especially in the early years, was a bewildering blend of emotions. Family life during my father's childhood was dysfunctional and volatile. It was a confusing time for the three Mellor children who were trying to find their way in the world. It did not dawn on me until later that there was likely a reason why I had never seen this house before as it was not likely a place he wanted to remember.

TEACHING DANIEL TO READ

Dad pulled away from his childhood home, drove to the end of the street, turned right on Vernon Street, and then right again on Victory Place. We had only gone about one third of a mile when he slowed and eventually stopped. He nodded toward a red brick school building across the street and said, "This is where my life was changed." It was the home of Fairview Heights Elementary, where he had attended the sixth grade.

My dad is not a self-congratulatory type of person, but he smiled as he pointed to a grassy field on the side of the building and said, "Do you see that field? That's where I scored six touchdowns in one game." My brother and I looked at the field but did not say anything. He translated our silence as skepticism. Without missing a beat, he said, "It was in the paper and everything."

Dad had been required to complete the sixth grade twice, although the specific reason for doing so was never shared with him. The first time was where we sat at Fairview Heights. The school, located on Harmar Hill, overlooks the Muskingum River with the city of Marietta to the east, and the Ohio River to the south. The second school, Washington Elementary, was located down the hill in the heart of Marietta, which was 1.5 miles away.

Among the influencers at this point in his life was the assistant principal and football coach, Mr. Casto. He had connected with my dad and saw potential in him. One afternoon, Mr. Casto pulled my dad aside to talk with him about a classmate who was struggling to learn how to read. After describing the situation, he said, "Daniel can't read. I would like for you to teach him how to read." Intimidated by the request, my dad's response was immediate and honest. He stuttered, "I can't do that." Mr. Casto said, "Why not?" Dad responded, "Because I am dumb." Unfazed by the answer, Mr. Casto replied, "Well, you may be dumb, but you are not as dumb as Daniel. So teach Daniel how to read."

The story had ended abruptly and my brother and I were not sure how to respond to what he had just shared. When he said his life had been changed, we had assumed it was for the positive. Considering his principal and coach had seemingly agreed with him when he said he was dumb, we wondered if we had misread the situation. I said, "So when you said your life was changed, was that a positive thing?" He laughed, put the car in drive and began to pull away. He said, "Yes, it was positive. I realized at that moment that I did not have to be the smartest person in the world to make a difference. I just needed to be a little farther down the road than someone else, and I could help them."

IDENTITY

In many ways, the most significant challenge of life is about identity. At the beginning of our lives, we depend on our senses and the insights of others to help us form a mental model of our world. Through trial and error, we learn not to touch hot things, to dress appropriately, and how to engage others. Interactions with friends and family give meaning to words and help create a framework for understanding. Through these experiences, we learn what is socially acceptable and what is not, and we gain insights into the more profound things of life. At first, the world is small, but in time, for most, the world begins to expand. An afternoon at a friend's house provides helpful clues into how other families interact. We watch reality shows, follow people on social media, and read about people we will never meet because we are deeply curious about how others experience life. We want to know if our mental model is an accurate and valid assessment of the world.

When contemplating one's identity, it is essential to recognize that mental models are not rigid or fixed. It is worth noting that a small change in the way one perceives themselves, good or bad, can have a disproportionately significant impact on their lives. Self-perception is being shaped and reshaped throughout a lifetime. Consequently, who you are is not set in stone at the age of 20, 40, 60, 80, or 100. At every stage, new things are learned that have the potential for enhancing our ability to anticipate needs and navigate life. For example, if you had a time machine, the 40-year-old version of yourself could give the 20-year-old version of yourself good counsel.

It is also worth noting that our brains prefer predictability and routine, and we tend to become increasingly resistant to ideas that require a significant change of course, especially when the end result is unclear. Consequently, even if our mental model is inaccurate or damaging, we are likely to stick with it versus enduring the discomfort required to consider a new perspective. Change is a choice, and you can choose a new path if you are willing to endure discomfort. If you do not like where life is headed, you can choose a new way of thinking.

A CHANGED MENTAL MODEL

In my dad's situation, an influential educator provided my dad with a new perspective because he saw my dad differently than my father saw himself. Whether my dad recognized it or not, both of the stories he told intersected with Mr. Casto. As the football coach, I am assuming Coach Casto would have known my dad had ability on the football field. He witnessed my dad in an environment in which he felt competent, if not exceptional. Also, as the assistant principal, he would have noticed my dad was a friendly, street-smart, and helpful kid who was able to connect with others.

Clearly, Mr. Casto saw something in my father and believed he was capable of more. This ability, to see things both as they are and as they could be simultaneously, is the gift and burden of leaders. Thankfully, at a pivotal time in his life, my father intersected with a leader who cared deeply and sought to push him towards his capacity. The ability to visualize someone as a success before their success is a foregone conclusion is the hallmark of master educators and life-changing coaches.

Through their conversation, Mr. Casto let my father know there was a need to help a classmate and that he believed my dad could fill the need. The offer was rejected because my dad believed he lacked the intellectual ability to be effective. In short, he was focused on what he did not have. Mr. Casto responded by challenging this belief, and by having my father focus on what he did have versus what he lacked. With some guidance, my dad was forced to consider a new perspective, and the result was a modified or transformed mental model. Mr. Casto had awakened a future giant.

If I had access to your thoughts and memories and could read the story of your life, what beliefs would we have to address before you could fully pursue your potential? Do any of the following sound familiar?

I am not smart enough.
I am too critical.
I don't have the presence of a leader.
I don't look the part.
I don't have the right education.
I am too young.
I am too old.
I am not inspiring.
I am too afraid.
I don't have access.

I can't change.

People wouldn't follow me.

NEUROPLASTICITY

Over the past couple of decades, there have been remarkable advances in understanding how the brain works. One of the most significant breakthroughs is the concept of neuroplasticity. Neuroplasticity is an umbrella term that describes the process by which the brain is organized, both functionally and physically. The key discovery is that the brain is "plastic" or malleable throughout life and is not fixed or rigid. The implications of neuroplasticity are far-reaching, as it suggests that, "you are not stuck with the brain you have." Through focused effort, physical activity, and rest, you can change the way your brain functions.

There are many reasons why changing how we think and act is difficult. In 1949, Donald Hebb provided an explanation in his book, *The Organization of Behavior*. In what would become known as the Hebbian Theory, he explained how the brain works during the learning process.[7] His postulate is summarized in the phrase, "Cells that fire together wire together." The core idea is that during the learning process, when an activity is successfully repeated several times, a pattern emerges that becomes the preferred pathway.

One can disrupt and change their mental model, but it takes considerably more effort to do so at the age of 60 versus the age of 6. However, the way you think is not fixed and can be changed. If your rationale for not pursuing your goals is rooted in the belief that your brain is incapable of learning something new, this is not true. If you want to learn to be a better communicator, you can learn to do so through intentional and purposeful practice. As you practice and learn new ways of doing things, over the course of a few months, new neural pathways will emerge.

If you want to change, it is possible, but not without a fight. This fight is not a battle with a nameless competitor; this fight is between the "current you" and the "future you." To see the "future you" winning over the "current you" will require the type of personal reflection and honesty that most brains prefer to avoid. To move forward will require the conscious decision to be uncomfortable and to choose a new path.

THE CHALLENGE

A few months prior to this book being completed, a friend of mine, Eric Baird, passed away from cancer. Eric was one of those people who could seemingly connect with anyone. We forged a friendship, and when I put together a small group of executives for a four-day leadership development experience, I invited him. The program was held in Jackson Hole, Wyoming. In addition to our class time, we also spent time each day hiking or sightseeing in Grand Teton National Park.

Although Eric attended the program, he was not feeling well. Accordingly, he was trying to adjust his diet and lose some weight. After returning from the trip, he was diagnosed with pancreatic cancer, and the prognosis was not favorable. Through prayer, surgery, chemotherapy, and sheer determination, he waged war against his illness.

The toll cancer took on his body was astonishing. As his body grew weaker, however, it seemed his resolve was growing stronger. It said a great deal about him that while he was fighting for his life, he would text friends and family to see if there was anything they needed. Following his final round of chemo, there was a glimmer of hope that the cancer might have gone into remission. This hope was short lived, however, when tests soon thereafter indicated the cancer had invaded his liver.

After being diagnosed with liver cancer, I received a text from Eric to give him a call. When I called him back, he told me he had bad news. He said that he had been having some seizures and that when he went to the hospital, he learned that the cancer was now in his brain. After speaking with the doctors, he had been told there was nothing else he could do to prolong his life. The physicians had indicated that he likely had as little as two weeks to possibly two months to live. He told me he was calling because he did not know how much longer he would have clarity of thought and the capacity to express himself. He wanted to share a few things with me before losing the ability to do so.

He then said something that I consider to be among the most courageous things I have ever heard in my entire life. A man of deep faith, he said in a determined tone, "I do not intend to waste this." He continued, "When we lived in Portland, we had a neighbor who was a good person but did not believe in God." He excitedly said, "He did not want to talk about his faith at that time, but I think he might listen to me now." Tears instantly filled my eyes, I opened my mouth to respond, but I could not speak due to the lump that was forming in my throat. I did not want to break down in front of him. He said, "I want to use what is happening to me for good." He then repeated himself, "I do not want to waste this."

Whether you share Eric's perspective about faith or not, some moments in life are unquestionably holy. I was sitting in my office with the door closed, talking to a friend on the phone, and we both knew it was likely our last conversation. He was aware that he no longer had months and years but was limited to days and weeks. I was thankful that he could not see my face, and I did my best to control my emotions. My forehead was resting on the desk as I listened to his voice on speakerphone. If you had been sitting with me, you would have sat in silence too. My friend was teaching me a valuable lesson about life. He had not called for his well-being. He had called for mine.

Although he had waged a tremendous and fierce battle against cancer the entire time he was sick, he was not blind to the seriousness of his illness. A strong and solid man, he lost half of his body weight through the ordeal. In the months leading to his passing, he did everything possible to make the transition easier for his wife, friends, and family. He considered what he was going through as an opportunity to build bridges, mend fences, and strengthen relationships with others.

When he passed, almost everyone who had gone on the trip to the Tetons a year earlier attended the funeral. The service was supposed to last about an hour, but it ended up lasting three. Friends and family spoke about different segments of his life, but there was a common thread that emerged through the words of each speaker. Eric was someone who found his purpose in serving others. He was the happiest when he was helping. He had chosen to reframe his illness as a teaching opportunity and a way to bring people together.

As I was writing this book, I was struck by the themes that emerged organically. Perhaps the most frequent theme was the link between serving others and living a life that matters. Over the years, I have had the privilege to provide leadership services to hundreds of companies and to spend thousands of hours engaged with individual leaders. The most successful people I know are those who find the highest sense of satisfaction in investing in the lives of others. If you are willing to serve, you will always have a purpose.

My hope in writing this book is to help awaken those who need to be awakened and to help those awakened to recognize their ability to activate others. If you feel you are already fully motivated and engaged, my plea is for you to use your perspective to awaken others. There are few things more tragic than watching people shuffle through life aimlessly. I believe people want to lead lives that matter, but for a host of reasons, they have concluded that what they want is beyond their reach. This is not true. At any point in life, in an instant, people can choose a new course.

CHAPTER 2

"SECOND LAST NAMES"

Identity Ownership

I was born at the Good Samaritan hospital in the historic town of Vincennes, Indiana, on Tuesday, July 31, 1973. It was the same hospital where my brother was born on May 17, 1971. Founded in 1732, Vincennes was Indiana's first city. Built by the French to protect its fur trade from the British, the town was constructed along the banks of the Wabash River, which delineates it from the neighboring state of Illinois.[1] In 1970, nearly 20,000 people called it home.[2]

My parents moved to Vincennes in 1970, a few months after getting married, so dad could become the Assistant Director at the YMCA. Before Vincennes, the two were living in Searcy, Arkansas, where they were attending Harding College, which would later be renamed Harding University. When they arrived in town, they joined a local church and when it was discovered that dad had attended a Christian University, he was asked to teach the teen class. Unexpectedly, after teaching a few times, dad felt drawn to ministry. Soon, he was offered a position with a church in the nearby town of Princeton, which was 25 miles south of Vincennes.

The young family moved into a picturesque one-story home at 404 West Spruce Street in Princeton, which was the first house I would call home. The house had been built in 1900, but due to the quality of materials used in construction, the house looked as if it were new. The exterior was made of natural autumn gold sandstone, which had been cut and expertly placed by stonemasons. Dad worked with the church, and mom worked with The Arc of Gibson County. The Arc provided training and development opportunities for people with intellectual and developmental disabilities.

Although my parents enjoyed the work in Princeton, dad felt he would benefit from additional training to be able to preach and teach with greater effectiveness. When a growing church in Williamstown, West Virginia, which was located just across the Ohio River from his hometown, opened a small Bible College in 1974, he decided to attend. We moved east to Marietta in 1975 and lived in a two-story wooden duplex, painted white, at 109 Wooster Street. Our house was located directly across a narrow alley from my grandparent's home.

After taking the courses he felt he needed, we moved back to Indiana, and dad began working with the church where he had volunteered when they had first moved to Vincennes. From the first moment they entered the church building in 1970, he and my mother had felt welcome and accepted. When they returned in 1977, it felt like a homecoming. The church, which began meeting together in August of 1922, was a hardy group. In 1927, the congregation purchased the property at the corner of Ninth and Hart. They constructed a basement in the hope of adding the top floor when they had the resources to do so. Resources would prove difficult in the coming years as the nation struggled its way through the Great Depression and World War II. It was not until 1951 that they were able to complete their facility. They worshiped there for a generation until they built on a new and larger site in 1977. Although I have faint memories of the old building, I have many good memories of the new one. It was opened the week before Christmas, and it felt like it was a gift to the community.[3] The church was not immune to the ups and downs of life, but it was a great place to be a kid in the 1970s. It was the type of place that cared deeply for families and kids, especially those from underprivileged backgrounds.

HEADED SOUTH

In 1981, the summer before my third-grade year, dad accepted an opportunity to work with a church in Spanish Fort, Alabama, and we moved south from Vincennes, Indiana to the eastern shore of Mobile

Bay. The church held a goodbye party, and we loaded up our possessions for the trip. The moving van was white with a blue stripe around the middle of the cab. Painted on each door were the words "Dixie Leasing, Inc." and the contact information. With dad at the wheel, we made our way south through Kentucky, Tennessee, and finally across the state line of Alabama. We detoured slightly to see the U.S. Space and Rocket Center in Huntsville. Although the tour did not inspire me to pursue a career in aerospace, it did convince me there were few things better in the world than freeze-dried, astronaut ice cream. The next day, we made the final push toward our rental home at 30630 Bay Road on Pineda Island, located just outside of Spanish Fort.

On occasion, I travel back to Mobile for work. I am always excited to get back to the place where I grew up. Whenever possible, I add a few hours to my trip to have the time to travel across the Causeway. I roll the windows of my rental car down and breathe in the air. The smell of Mobile Bay always makes me feel like I am home.

DEFINING MOMENTS

After living in the cinder block rental house for a few months, we then moved six miles south to nearby Daphne. In the early 1980s, it was a town of fewer than 5,000 people. Considered an excellent place to live for both young families and retirees, it has grown considerably since the time we lived there and is now home to nearly 25,000.

My parents bought a home at 107 Belrose Avenue. It was a comfortable 1,400-square-foot home that had been built in 1935. The home still had its original hardwood floors and plenty of windows. On the side of the house was an enormous fig tree, and along the back property line, a large kumquat tree. What made the house truly special was its proximity to the beach. From the front porch, it was about 500 feet to a set of stairs that led down a steep incline to the sandy shores of Mobile Bay.

Our lives are a composite of moments. Some of those moments are more impactful than others because they provide a context for future events. Because of the significance of these moments, we categorize these types of events as "Defining Moments." One of my defining moments was when I was a student at Daphne Elementary School.

Daphne Elementary is a red brick school building with a classic and timeless appearance. Built around the same time as our home, the facility faces Main Street. It is a long building with a prominent main entrance that is flanked by white columns. Constructed long before air-conditioning was available, the classrooms were large and the ceilings high. The windows were often left open, and the ceiling fans were left on high to help create a breeze in the hot and humid afternoons.

I was in the fourth grade when a teacher suggested that I participate in the Optimist Club Oratorical Contest. She never explained why she thought I would be good a candidate, but it was an honor to have been asked and I agreed to give it a try. In the weeks leading up to the speech, I worked hard preparing and memorizing each line of my presentation. Although I lost the contest, it was a formative experience, and the bronze runner-up medallion sits behind a glass bookshelf in my office to this day.

I am grateful for the teacher who went out of her way to encourage me, as well as the Optimist Club for hosting such an event. For me, the moment was life altering because it changed how I perceived myself and how others perceived me. She was among a group of influencers who would begin shaping my mental model. She saw something in me that I did not yet see in myself. Because I trusted her vision and participated in the speech contest I became, "Nathan Mellor…the speaker."

SECOND LAST NAMES

I was in my late 20s or early 30s when my dad and I were talking about how our perceptions of ourselves and of others impact life. In that conversation, dad said, "You have to be careful with second last names." I had never heard the phrase "second last names," before, and I assumed it was a David Mellor original. I asked him what he meant by it, and although we talked about it more, I did not fully grasp the concept at the time.

One of the things that I love about learning is that you can carry an idea or concept around in your brain for years before it fully matures. My dad's phrase, "second last names," had been in my mind for a long time before it crystallized. On the day the concept clicked, I was speaking at a community event that brought together a broad cross-section of people interested in ethical leadership. It was a large gathering with several hundred in attendance.

On the morning I was to give the speech, I was nervous. To help collect my thoughts, I had gotten up early to rehearse my presentation a few times. When this did not work, I decided to go ahead and drive to the venue. It is often beneficial for me to see the place where I will be speaking and to meet some of the people that will be at the program before the event. I parked my car near the back of the lot and reviewed my notes a few more times until I felt I had done all the preparation I could do. I got out of the car and made my way toward the complex of buildings to what I assumed was the entrance. As I approached, I could see through the glass doors that the place was already buzzing with activity. Once I got inside, I introduced myself to a few people, and they directed me to the individuals leading the event. After a quick greeting and a review of the schedule, they shared they had a logistical problem they were trying to solve, and they wanted to get my thoughts.

They said that following my presentation they were planning to serve a buffet lunch in an adjoining building. To get everyone through the line in the time allotted, the organizers were looking for ways to streamline the process. They wanted to make sure nothing was happening in the main hall after my speech that would keep people in the room any longer than needed. It was suggested that after speaking, I go directly from the stage to the banquet hall, while the emcee concluded the session. If we did this, I could greet people in the banquet hall, and it would help them stay on schedule. I told them I would be happy to do whatever was needed.

A few minutes later, one of the coordinators I had just met approached with someone new in tow. She was smiling proudly when she said, "I want you to meet your host." As I was shaking the hand of the new person, the coordinator said, "She has volunteered to assist you when you are greeting people at lunch. You are going to love her. She has been part of this organization forever. She knows everybody."

I got the distinct impression when talking with my newly deputized host that she had been drafted for the job. She was visibly nervous, and it was obvious she was taking one for the team. I have always appreciated people like her, and I thought it said a lot about the organization and her that she was willing to work out of her comfort zone for the sake of the group.

Following the presentation, as the emcee took the platform, I made my way to the banquet hall. My host was already standing at our assigned spot, and nearly immediately after, the crowd began to form a line. As people filed down the buffet lines, my host, standing directly behind me, said, "When people are coming up, I will tell you who they are." I nodded in agreement.

As the first person approached, she leaned forward and said, "This is Timothy Kidwell...he is a local banker." She paused for a moment and then said, "...and he drinks a lot." As she finished the sentence, Timothy was reaching out his hand. We shook hands and talked for a few seconds. As he turned to find a place to sit, her words came back to mind. I thought, *did she say, "He drinks a lot?"*

There was no time for a follow-up question. I had just turned back to the oncoming group when she leaned forward again and said, "This is John Finch...he sells insurance..." The pause was shorter this time. She continued, "He has been married four times."

She was giving me their second last names, and it was not pretty. I hesitated and wondered if I should say something. I then turned back to my well-intentioned host and said, "I appreciate your help, but I do not need to know their second last names."

Second last names are powerful because they shape how we perceive others. The impact of second last names is typically determined by the influence of the person sharing the moniker. Compact thumbnail sketches of complex mental models, they can be positive or negative, true or false. They are valuable because they provide insight into both the person being described as well as the person giving the description.

TRAINED TO SEE THE PROBLEM

One afternoon, I was talking with a friend of mine that I do not see often, and we were enjoying catching up. Chris and I talked about his family for a few minutes. He then said, "Can I ask you a question about my work?" I replied, "Absolutely. What is on your mind?" He explained that he had opened a retail store a few years earlier, but he was struggling to get traction. He said they had a great selection of products, a visible location, and a good online presence. He concluded, "I think I know why we can't seem to turn the corner. It is because of customer service. I just don't know what to do about it."

I asked him to describe the situation, and he gave one example after another that proved his point. I was listening in the hope of gaining insight into his mental model about himself and about his team. He was focused on the problem and not on the solution. The problem was clear, but the solution was not. His issue was not just customer service; it appeared he was dealing with something deeper.

After hearing his initial thoughts, I asked if he had talked with his team about his expectations. A common challenge for leaders is communicating what they want in such a way that others can understand what is needed and take the appropriate action steps. Instead of answering my question, he sidestepped it. I circled back to the question for the second time, and he ducked it again. On my third try, he finally opened up. He explained his relationship with the team was at the breaking point, and he no longer had the patience to deal with them. He did not know what to do next. He then blurted, "I hate my team."

Chris is a good man who was in a tough situation. He did not truly hate his employees, or he would have just walked away. If things did not change, however, his feelings would crystalize and would become a reality. His mental model was working against him. He was no longer looking for answers; he was now looking for somewhere to place blame. He had a form of tunnel vision, and he was searching for proof that the way he was seeing the world was accurate. I said, "I don't think you hate your team." After talking it through, he backed off. He smiled and with a frustrated laugh said, "The problem is they are idiots." He had just given me the second last name for his team.

It is a scary thing when you have invested yourself in something that is not working. It can be terrifying when you cannot simply work harder to make things better. When this is the case, there is often something lurking deeper. In those moments, when a leader needs to see the larger picture, to see the system, it is critical to take a step back. With that said, without some help, it is challenging to see things from a different perspective when leaders are locked-in on problem identification versus problem solving.

As long as Chris thinks of the people on his team as idiots, they will prove him right. As long as Chris thinks of himself as an idiot, he will prove himself right. He is adopting a second last name that will set the course of his life. If he does not change course, not only will his team underperform, when they have moments when life is going well, they will dismiss the wins as anomalies. He is training himself and his team to see what is wrong. In time, he will only be able to see what is wrong. Unintentionally, he is creating a habit loop of negativity. He can break free but not until he claims personal responsibility for his identity and the identity of his team.

INTENTIONAL THINKING

The drift toward negativity is understandable and predictable. Our brains tend to focus on perceived threats, and when we receive negative feedback, it is commonly perceived as a threat. We are constantly scanning for emotional and physical threats, and our brains do not regard positive interactions as threats. Because of this tendency, over the course of a lifetime, we develop a great sensitivity for negativity, as it is part of an elaborate defense system that is intended to promote safety and wellbeing. Constant negativity undermines leadership effectiveness, however, as it robs people of courage versus instilling it within them. If you have ever worked in a climate of stress and fear, you already know that increased anxiety does not translate into better performance.

I am not suggesting that we only focus on the positive, but I am suggesting that focusing on the positive is more likely to lead to the results you are seeking. We tend to see what we look for in others, and if we are not actively looking for the good, we are unlikely to see it. This is one of the reasons why so many leaders are keenly aware of their faults, but they remain largely unaware of their strengths.

MY NAME IS MO

A few years ago, I was invited to speak at a leadership retreat being hosted for a group of approximately 30 senior level leaders from Oklahoma City. The program was being held at the Holland Blue River Ranch, near the small town of Tishomingo in south-central Oklahoma. The 1,750-acre ranch is notable due to its numerous granite outcrops and cliffs and the presence of the Blue River, which meanders through the property for nearly two miles. The Blue River is a 141-mile long tributary of the Red River. A free-flowing stream, it is unencumbered by dams or man-made structures that could limit its flow. Pristine, clear spring water pushes across the property at a rate of approximately 30,000 gallons per minute.[4] The river is known for its bass fishing in the summer, and in the colder months, it is host to anglers throughout the region that are in pursuit of rainbow and brown trout.[5]

Prior to the start of the program, several people were sitting in rocking chairs on the front porch, while others were standing nearby in the shade. The porch ran the length of the home and provided shade; the weather was pleasant, but warm. There was a welcome breeze drifting across the fields of Bermuda grass.

The ranch is large, but it is not easy to find. Consequently, when hosting events there, it is not uncommon for people to have to backtrack after taking a wrong turn or two. Because of this, we were not surprised when we got a call from one of the participants that she had made a wrong turn, but would be arriving shortly.

The final mile or so is a well-maintained dirt road, and a few moments after the phone call, we saw her car coming down the last mile. She was moving fast, and behind her, a cloud of dust rose into the sky. Based upon the speed of the car, the person driving was evidently comfortable on dirt roads. She pulled up to the main house, and the cloud that had been following her drifted over the car, and blanketed it with a coating of fine dust.

I did not know the driver, but it seemed that nearly everyone else did. She smiled warmly as people began to greet her. As she walked toward the house, I looked at the car once more. At a distance, I thought it was a Mercedes, but as the car got closer to the house, it seemed a little longer than most Mercedes. As I looked again, the badging gave its identity away. The car was an ultra-rare Maybach, which is the Mercedes luxury brand. I smiled as I thought about the fact that this was likely the only one that had ever been off-roading.

The group of leaders assembled in the living room for introductions. Seated in chairs around the room, people stood and shared something about themselves. When it came time for the Maybach driver, she stood and said, "My name is Mo." She paused, smiled, and continued, "I am 79 years old. I turn 80 in three months, and I cannot wait!" She paused again and said, "My 70s have been my best decade, and I cannot imagine what is going to happen in my 80s."

Sometimes you meet someone with whom you feel an instant bond. I liked Mo, and I loved her approach to life. I scanned the room and noticed almost everyone was smiling as she spoke. She seemed to have the same impact on people as my parents. People responded to her because of the way she made them feel about themselves. She said, "I am the vice-chair of Keller Williams, where we have 140,000 employees." Since that time, the number of associates at Keller Williams has grown by tens of thousands, and it continues to increase due to their unique culture.

I do not think I was the only one inspired by Mo. This woman, who has helped build one of the world's most exciting companies and was just months away from her 80th birthday, had chosen to invest her time in a program designed to help her become a more effective leader. Whether she knew it or not, she had set the tone for the group with her choice to be enthusiastic and positive.

Over the next year, the group would get together monthly for an all-day program. The more I learned about Mo, the more I appreciated her approach to life. She had been raised on a tenant farm; she then married her high school sweetheart, went to college, and became a teacher. At her husband's urging, she left the classroom and decided to start selling real estate. She quickly found her stride. After building and selling her real estate business, she was hired by Keller Williams to serve as president. In that role, she earned the second last name, the "velvet hammer." The Keller Williams website provides insight into Mo's perspective. It states, "Mo's mission has been to help people experience the higher purpose of business–caring, sharing, and giving. Led by this mantra, Mo has single-handedly cultivated KW's value system and culture."[6]

During the monthly sessions that followed, tables were pushed together to form one long row of tables where everyone could have lunch together as if we were one large family. I was sitting beside Mo. I decided to tell her how much I appreciated her. I am sometimes reluctant to express my gratitude to someone like Mo because I do not want people to get the wrong impression. When people become successful, they can become targets for those who will flatter them for ulterior purposes. I checked my motives and thought, *I do not want anything from her and I want her to know she has been a source of inspiration to me.*

I said, "When you introduced yourself at the first gathering of our group, I knew then you were a person of character." She said, "What makes you say that?" I responded, "You said you were 79 and would be turning 80 in 3 months." She nodded in recognition of what she had said. I continued, "You then said that you could not wait until you were in your 80s because your 70s had been your best decade." She smiled, still waiting for my point. I said, "I could tell you were a person of character because you are not looking for the path of least resistance. You made it clear to me that you intend to speed up versus slowing down. That takes courage and character." I concluded, "Most people don't say they can't wait until their 80s. Not only did you say it, but you are also living it."

By defining the future before she has lived it, Mo created a "pre-memory" of what is to come. When she imagines her preferred future, she is able to visualize what that life will be like and make adjustments accordingly. By visualizing what life will be like in the future, she is better poised to anticipate what she will need when she gets there. Each time she tells someone how great her 80s will be, the more she believes it, which in turn makes it more likely to happen.

CHOOSING YOUR PATH

When dad said, "You've got to be careful with those second last names," he could have just as easily said, "You've got to be careful with those mental models." The way we perceive the larger world and ourselves, is complex, nuanced, and flexible. As we experience life and gain new insights into how the world works, we are continually comparing and testing new ideas against old ones. Through the process, we make decisions about which concepts should be adopted, ignored, or discarded. When my teacher at Daphne Elementary School suggested that I participate in the Oratorical Contest, she was shaping my mental model. When I became known as Nathan Mellor...the speaker, I had been given a second last name.

It is your right and responsibility to take ownership of your mental model. I am not as interested in the "second last names" others have given you as much as I am interested in the "second last names" you have given yourself. For a number of reasons, it is important to be able to answer the questions "Whom do you want to be?" and "Are you on the right path to becoming whom you want to be?"

When my grandfather Alden Gilliam died in 2009 at the age of 97, I received a few of his books and a handful of his papers. One of his traditions was to make annual goals for himself. It was interesting reading through some of his thoughts. He would ask, "What should the goals be for an 85-year-old?"

You are responsible for owning your identity. Consequently, I want you to imagine how you would answer the questions asked earlier. "Whom do you want to be?" and "Are you on the right path to becoming whom you want to be?"

CHAPTER 3

"HOW TALL ARE YOU ANYWAY?"

Dealing with Doubts

Early in my dad's career, he was grappling with what he wanted to do for the long-term and was weighing his options. This type of thing, considering a career change, is not uncommon for people who are challenging their mental models. It is a way of testing the validity of their experiences. Among the possibilities he found intriguing was the idea of becoming a ranger with the National Park Service or the U.S. Forest Service.

Before I get too far into the story, it is only fair to admit that when I first heard the story about his interest in becoming a ranger, it had already become a part of family lore. There are a handful of versions that are told by various family members. Some suggest the tale is a legend, while others recount it with the highest confidence and offer the promise that their version is the "most accurate." In my experience, you should be wary of people who make such assurances. Fortunately for you, I happen to be a student of such things, and have been able to piece together the actual story with the greatest attention to detail. Therefore, between you and me, my version happens to be the "most accurate" telling of the tale.

To help set the stage for the story about my dad's career options, I want to provide a bit of context by telling another related story. Knowing more of his back-story is among the many reasons why I admire him. The man he is today cannot be fully appreciated without understanding his motivators. The following is just one of many stories that I could have chosen from my dad's life that captures his blend of intensity, humor, and perspective.

THE WRESTLER

I was in high school when my dad and I were talking one afternoon about his wrestling career. I am not sure how we got on the topic, but he did not talk about his athletic career often. I always enjoyed hearing stories about his life. It was a casual conversation, and we were discussing some of the lessons learned through adversity and loss.

He was sharing about his first wrestling match when he was a freshman at Marietta High School. Because of his high expectations of himself, he was shaken when he took to the mat and was summarily pinned. The loss was devastating, and he replayed the moment over and over again in his mind. He had been outmaneuvered, and although he strained against his opponent with every ounce of strength available, he could not break free.

Everyone has a voice inside his or her head that provides guidance. What that voice says is crucial to success in life. After a defeat, the voice will urge someone to dig deeper or to give up. Whether he knew it at the time or not, it was on that night that my father started down the path to becoming a coach. Instead of relying on someone else to be the source of his motivation, using his inner voice, he began coaching himself. He threw himself into training, improving his technique, growing stronger, and learning to cut weight to wrestle in his preferred weight class. Whenever he had a spare moment, he was doing push-ups, sit-ups, or some exercise intended to make him stronger or faster.

He then said, almost as an afterthought, "That was when I stopped sleeping on my back." The tone of the sentence implied that I already knew what he meant, but this was not the case. I said, "I am not following you. Why did you stop sleeping on your back?" He replied, "It was part of the mindset that I needed. I made the decision to not sleep on my back to help me remember my goal." He continued, "I did not want to get used to the feeling of being on my back."

I processed his response for a moment. I thought of the determination of a freshman that consciously chose not to sleep on his back as a form of self-punishment for being pinned and as motivation to not be pinned again. Not knowing his high school record, I asked, "Did it work?"

He replied, "I was never pinned again." He paused briefly and said, "The problem was I had the wrong goal. I made my goal to never be pinned again. My goal should have been never to lose again. You can still lose without being pinned."

THE RANGER

Dad was not too many years removed from his wrestling days when he walked into the office where he could get an application to become a ranger. Both his father and grandfather had worked for the federal government for the bulk of their careers. They had both served in the U.S. Army, and they both had been letter carriers for the United States Postal Service. He was familiar with a life that required a uniform.

Life as a park ranger, especially in the early years of the National Parks and U.S. Forest Service, was difficult. The role was demanding, lonely, and often unappreciated. Consequently, the job description for the role was intentionally blunt. The *Use Book*, written in 1905, provided a sketch of what life was like as a ranger in the U.S. Forest Service. It stated that applicants must be:

> thoroughly sound and able-bodied, capable of enduring hardships and of performing severe labor under trying conditions. He must be able to take care of himself and his horse in regions remote from settlement and supplies. He must be able to build trails and cabins, ride, pack, and deal tactfully with all classes of people. He must know something of land surveying, estimating and scaling timber, logging, land laws, mining, and the live-stock business.[1]

Just in case it was not clear, the *Use Book* continued, "Invalids seeking light out-of-doors employment need not apply. Experience, not book education, is sought, although the ability to make simple maps and write intelligent reports upon ordinary forest business is essential."[2]

Although the role of a ranger for the U.S. Forest Service is a different life from the role as a ranger for the National Park Service, they both appealed to people seeking a challenge. Horace Albright, who was the superintendent of Yellowstone National Park, made it a practice to send the following cover letter to ranger applicants in 1926:

> Applicants for a ranger's position must be 21 years of age or must attain that age by June 15th. If you are not 21 or will not be by June 15th, don't apply. If you have a reputation of appearing unusually youthful or immature for a man of 21, don't apply. We want men who are mature in appearance. We prefer men of 25 to 30 years of age.
>
> The ranger is primarily a policeman; therefore, he should be big in frame, tall, and of average weight for his age and height. We always prefer big men to small men, other conditions being equal. If you are small of statue, better not apply.[3]

Based on the fact that my dad's family did not do much hunting or fishing, the idea that he could actually become a ranger was faint. He was interested nonetheless. Upon opening the front door to the office of the National Park Service, he walked inside and approached the desk of the person positioned nearest the entrance. He stood in front of her for a moment waiting for her to acknowledge his presence. Without making eye contact, she said, "Can I help you?"

He replied, "I am here to get an application for the park ranger position." Instead of responding or reaching for an application, she sat motionless. With the least amount of exertion possible, she eventually tilted her head in his direction and looked him over. Exhaling, she asked with a skeptical tone, "How tall are you anyway?"

His eyes narrowed and his jaw involuntarily clinched as he attempted to ignore the self-important tone in which she had asked her question. He replied, "I'm 5'-7"." She could not disguise her satisfaction in being the bearer of bad news. With a matter-of-fact tone, she said, "Well, you can't even apply for this job unless you are 5'-10"."

THE RESPONSE

The trigger was not what she said, but how she said it. She had enjoyed shutting him down a little too much. It was when one side of her mouth formed a smug half-smile that he began calculating the cost of responding. He cleared his throat to speak. She looked up at him, surprised that he was going to respond.

Just in case you wondered if a man who is 5'-7" can command a room, it might be helpful to point out that leaders including Dr. Martin Luther King Jr. and Winston Churchill; entertainers and actors like Robin Williams, Tom Cruise, and Al Pacino; as well as icons including Bruce Lee, Henry "The Fonz" Winkler, and storytellers like George Lucas and Steven Spielberg are all under 5'-7".[4] As the quote most commonly attributed to Mark Twain says, "It's not the size of the dog in the fight. It's the size of the fight in the dog."

His words were measured and direct. Starting slowly and quietly and growing in volume and intensity, he said, "Are you telling me that I can serve my country in the Vietnam War and win the Congressional Medal of Honor...represent this nation in the Olympics, and win the silver medal, but I can't even apply for your job?"

Her mouth opened, involuntarily, in shock. Her eyebrows raised, and she stared at him with wide-eyed amazement. He did not interrupt the silence; he was waiting for a response. In a thin and penitent voice, she said, "I am sorry...I did not realize who you were."

Her answer suggested that perhaps his status might have made a difference. He turned to leave. When he got to the front door, he looked back and said, "Well...I didn't do any of those things..." He

paused for a moment to let the statement register and continued, "…
but it really shouldn't matter."

There were many reasons why it could be argued that a ranger should
be of a certain height, weight, age, and demeanor. In consideration
of the lawlessness historically associated with the areas in which the
rangers would be serving and the emotional response that is common
when dealing with land use, it likely made all the more sense in the
minds of the policymakers that they needed people who had the best
odds of protecting themselves in the face of danger. By choosing tall,
athletic, young men, they were sending a message to those who were
breaking the law that they meant business. They were attempting to
show force. Over time, the image of the strong, uniformed ranger
conveyed safety and security.

There are limitations to this approach, however, as the rationale
was assumed but not necessarily accurate. As a result, others who could
have served who did not fit the profile because of their height were not
given an opportunity to prove their ability. Because they could not
prove their ability, they could not disprove the rationale. Consequently,
the mental model remained unchanged.

As much as we would like to think of ourselves as having the
wherewithal not to have our futures shaped by the opinions of others,
the reality is that we are unlikely to recognize it when something is
being said that is not true due to a lack of knowledge about how the
system works. When dealing with the woman who told him that he
could not be a ranger because he was not 5'-10", he was agitated by
her tone, but he believed her message. He responded to a disrespectful
tone, but he assumed what she said about his height was true.

YOU ARE THE CEO OF YOUR LIFE

What the woman said to my dad about the height requirement was not
accurate. There had been a minimum height requirement for rangers
in the National Park Service for decades, but it was not 5'-10". A
1940 description of rangers, written by Hugh Miller, superintendent
of the Southwestern National Monuments, stated, "Applicants must

measure at least 5 feet 7 inches in height without boots or shoes and weigh at least 145 pounds in ordinary clothing without overcoat or hat."[5] Furthermore, all height restrictions of this kind were lifted in 1971 due to legal action that argued the practice was discriminatory to many men and most women.[6]

Due to her position of authority, my dad believed her and left the office never knowing if being a park ranger would have been something he would have enjoyed. It underscores a critical truth, which is that just because we believe something does not make it true. In this situation, the woman to whom he was speaking was wrong.

There will always be people in your life, some well-intentioned and others not, who will tell you who you can or cannot be. Sometimes they are right, but sometimes they are not. Regardless of their opinions, however, you are the CEO of your life, and it is your responsibility to chart your course.

In my experience, the greatest challenge for people seeking to build a life that matters is not the opinion of others. The most significant obstacle is the mental model they have chosen for themselves. Although there is a risk of people thinking too highly of themselves, the more common problem is that people do not think highly enough of themselves.

ACCESS GRANTED

In many situations, there are people who have the ability to succeed, but they lack access to opportunities. Whether it is the consequence of intentional or unintentional discrimination, unfortunate timing, or just bad luck, there are times when people, due to reasons beyond their control, are denied the chance to pursue their dream. When this dynamic exists, when hard work and character are not enough to break through, access to opportunity must emerge from another source.

The most impactful and transformational leaders are those who use their influence to provide opportunities for others. Instead of investing themselves in the lives of those who were likely to succeed anyway, they invest themselves in those who would not be able to pursue their goals otherwise. In the course of my lifetime, I have only met a few of these types of leaders. One of those leaders is my friend, Mike O'Neal.

My friendship with Mike began when I joined the faculty at Oklahoma Christian University (OC) in Oklahoma City in the summer of 2006. I had been on the campus for a few weeks when I asked to meet with him to talk about a few ideas I hoped he might find interesting. Within a matter of minutes, I recognized that I had stumbled upon someone distinctive.

A native Oklahoman, Mike was born to Foy and Margie O'Neal on Wednesday, February 6, 1946. He was raised in Antlers, Oklahoma, which is located in the southeastern part of the state. Founded in 1887 within the Choctaw Nation, the town derived its name from a set of antlers that were fastened to a tree that marked a nearby spring.[7]

When Mike was a teenager, Antlers was home to nearly 2,200 residents.[8] Although the abundance of whitetail deer made the area famous—it is known as the "Deer Capital of the World"— the town owes its existence primarily to the construction of the St. Louis and San Francisco train lines, which prompted the establishment of a post office in Antlers.[9]

Although Mike is not a tall man, the first time I walked with him across the campus at OC, I had to keep increasing my pace to keep up with him. Athletic and trim, he has worn glasses most of his life and what remains of his hair is close-cropped. Mike laughs easily, is deeply patriotic, and is in constant learning mode. Although his hearing is impaired due to a weapon discharging too close to his ear while serving in the Vietnam War, he is an attentive listener.

His graduating class at Antlers High School consisted of 47 students. After graduation in 1964, he left the familiarity of Antlers and moved 170 miles northwest to attend Oklahoma Christian College (OCC). OCC was located on the outskirts of Oklahoma City, along the boundary of Oklahoma City and the city of Edmond. At that time, the campus was one of the newest in the United States. The school had been founded in 1950 in the town of Bartlesville but had relocated to this 200-acre site in the fall of 1958. When he pulled onto the sparse property, the clean lines of seven modern buildings greeted him, which included four academic buildings, two dormitories, and a cafeteria.

The first two years of his college experience were at OCC, and he then transferred to sister school Harding College for the final two. Harding was 270 miles to the northeast of Antlers. At the time, it was not uncommon for OCC students to transfer to Harding to complete their degrees. The schools had a unique and supportive relationship with one another. In the fall of 1966, Mike left Oklahoma and moved to Arkansas to complete his degree.

It did not take long for the transfer student to make his mark. In the two years he was at Harding, it is difficult to imagine him doing more academically or socially. In 1967, he won the Ganus Award as the male student making the highest grade point average. When he graduated in 1968, he had maintained a perfect 4.0 and tied another student with the highest overall GPA.[10] He was inducted into Alpha Chi for his academic achievements, and was twice named among the "Who's Who Among Students in American Universities and Colleges."[11] In addition to being an exceptional student, he was also proving his ability as an emerging leader. He was elected Student Association president his senior year while simultaneously serving as the captain of the business team, which took first place in Michigan State's International Intercollegiate Marketing Competition in 1968. [12]

Upon graduation, he began an 18-month tour of duty with the U.S. Navy along the shores of the South China Sea. Utilizing his organizational skills, he was named Director of Outdoor Storage Unit Activity in Da Nang, Vietnam. In this role, he was responsible for directing the storage operations of more than 100 acres of construction and petroleum products. He threw himself into his assignment with the same energy he had used throughout his collegiate experience. With characteristic focus, he arrived at the Outdoor Storage Unit each morning at 7:00 a.m. and worked until 10:00 p.m. each night. His superior officers recognized his commitment, and in recognition of his exemplary service, Lieutenant O'Neal was awarded the Bronze Star.

In addition to his work with the U.S. Navy, O'Neal also sought to serve the people of Vietnam. As an Officer, he had access to a vehicle and would repeatedly travel into a restricted zone to provide supplies and encouragement to an orphanage. He spent his Sundays working with a Vietnamese church in Da Nang, providing preaching and teaching through an interpreter for the three families in attendance.

While stateside, in May of 1969, he sat for the CPA exam. Among the 17,954 people who took the test that spring, he earned the highest score in Oklahoma and the 17th highest in the United States. Due to his resume, he received a scholarship to Stanford University in 1971, where he was awarded a Juris Doctorate degree with a concentration in business and tax law in 1974. Upon completion of his degree, he was invited to join the faculty at Harding College as an assistant professor of business administration and a development officer.[13] On December 21, 1974, he married Nancy Louise Lavender in Reynoldsburg, Ohio.[14]

In 1976, Mike joined the administration of Pepperdine University in Malibu, California. The school, which was founded in 1937 and originally located in South Los Angeles, had relocated to Malibu in the fall of 1972. With its expansive views of the Pacific Ocean, the new campus instantly made Pepperdine among the most picturesque universities in the United States. Mike would serve as General Counsel and Vice President of Finance and Administration until 1991 when he transitioned to the Vice Chancellor role. During this time, the O'Neal family grew with the addition of a son, Michael, and a daughter, Mandy. In 2002, Mike was named the president of his alma mater, Oklahoma Christian University.

COMING HOME

There were several reasons for returning to Oklahoma, but among the most significant was the potential he saw in OC. The school had experienced a series of financial setbacks in the late 1990s, but otherwise, it was an institution with a solid academic reputation and a remarkable history of service. Once on the job, he began working with campus leaders to identify and adopt sustainable business practices. In addition, he sought a path to expand academic offerings, restore broken relationships, and forge new ones with alumni, donors, and community leaders.[15]

In 2004, Richard and Pat Lawson gave OC two gifts that would permanently alter the trajectory of the institution. The first consisted of a $30 million donation to the school. Richard, a 1966 OC graduate and member of the OC board, had launched Lawson Software with his brother and a third partner in his garage in 1975. When the company later sold for $2 billion, the Lawson family gave generously from their proceeds to help stabilize OC.[16] The second gift was an invitation for Mike to join them on a trip to Rwanda, which included a personal introduction to the president of Rwanda, Paul Kagame.

Although Mike considered a trip to Rwanda compelling, he was concerned that it would be a distraction from the work at hand. OC was beginning to turn the corner financially, but even with the considerable gift from the Lawson family, it was not yet out of the woods. He was reluctant to travel at such an important time, but the Lawson's had already met President Kagame, when they hosted him on a business trip to Minneapolis, and based upon their passion, he made plans to join them.

The story of Rwanda will forever be connected to the Rwandan genocide that began on April 7, 1994. Over the course of 100 days, Hutu extremists killed an estimated 800,000 Tutsi men, women, and children.[17] The Clinton administration was slow to grasp the nature and scale of what was happening in Rwanda and was reluctant to label it a genocide.[18] The United Nations Security Council, following the loss of American lives in Somalia, was reluctant to get involved. Instead of stepping in to stabilize the situation, they escalated the conflict dramatically when in the early stages of the genocide they reduced the number of U.N. peacekeepers by nearly 90%.[19] Although news outlets were sharing the story of what was happening in Rwanda, the headlines that summer were dominated by the drama surrounding O.J. Simpson. For many, the significance of what happened in Rwanda would not be recognized until the movie, *Hotel Rwanda*, brought the genocide back into the public eye in 2004.

After landing in the capital city of Kigali and interacting with the people of Rwanda, Mike soon understood why the Lawsons felt the trip was necessary. As Mike and Nancy were waiting for their luggage at the airport in Kigali, Mike said to his wife, "I don't know why we are here, but perhaps God has something in mind." The nation, which is known as the "land of a thousand hills" is undeniably beautiful. In addition, it was clear there were leaders in key positions that had been first-hand witnesses to the destructive power of hate, and they wanted to redeem their loss by building something better. As he listened to their stories, it became apparent that the history of Rwanda and OC would become intertwined. He had met people with amazing abilities and drive who wanted a new way of life but lacked access to the opportunities needed to pursue it.

One of the key reasons why Mike was drawn to the people of Rwanda was because of the historic efforts of Rwandan President Paul Kagame. General Kagame commanded the force that ended the Rwandan genocide in 1994. From 1994 through 2000, he served as vice president and minister of defense. Considered by many to be the de facto leader of Rwanda following the genocide, he was named president in 2000.

When Mike met President Kagame met in 2004, it set in motion a series of events that would lead to the Rwandan president speaking at OC's graduation in the spring of 2006, where he was awarded an honorary doctorate. At that time, it was announced that OC would launch the Presidential Scholars Program, which would begin with 10 high-potential Rwandan students enrolling at OC in the fall. Through the program, which has now educated hundreds of Rwanda's emerging leaders, students would receive full scholarships (half from OC and half from the Republic of Rwanda) to attend school, which would allow them to pursue an undergraduate degree in a scientific field.

President O'Neal had a deep love and respect for each of the presidential scholars. He would often remark in amazement, "Do you realize that the Rwandans are taking these courses in their third language? They also speak Kinyarwanda and French!" OC is highly regarded for their School of Engineering and has an exceptionally high acceptance rate into medical schools and other graduate schools. He could not have been prouder of the work ethic and success of the Rwandan students. He believed their hard work was enhancing the experience of the students from the United States. He felt they were setting the pace, and he loved the idea that a young person from an unlikely place could thrive if just given the opportunity. In short, the way he felt about their success was much like how the people from his small hometown felt about his.

In 2007, he asked me to join him for lunch one day with a local leader who had recently launched a program called, Peace Through Business Afghanistan. Dr. O'Neal had read about it in the paper and had requested a lunch meeting to discuss the concept more. By the end of the meal, there was an agreement to host Peace Through Business Rwanda the next summer at OC.[20]

In the spring of 2008, Mike and I traveled to the United Nations Headquarters where he presented at the VII Infopoverty World Conference: "Low Cost-Smart Technologies to Fight Poverty and Save the Planet." On our way to New York City, we stopped in Washington, D.C. to meet with the senators from Oklahoma and the Rwandan ambassador to provide updates about the work that was being done and to strengthen relationships. Everywhere we went, his mission remained the same; he wanted to open doors of opportunity for others.

Working behind the scenes, he would look for student leaders who were passionate about service, and then look for ways to encourage and support them. An example of this approach was his efforts to support Ryan Groves. Ryan and his older brother had a dream of helping provide clean water to people throughout Africa. To accomplish this, the two created a student-led non-profit called Wishing Well. They hosted concerts and art shows, produced a documentary, and captured the beauty of Rwanda and the need for clean water through photography. Students in schools and churches across the United States began raising money to help fund Wishing Well's efforts to increase awareness and sponsor wells. Ryan would be among the first to tell you that Mike O'Neal changed the course of his life and that his encouragement made Wishing Well possible.

When Mike learned of a group of Rwandan students at OC who wanted to launch a similar effort called Rwandans4Water, he did the same for them. He also used his influence to convene the leaders needed to launch the Kigali International Community School. In short, whenever possible, he was quietly using his platform to provide access to opportunities for others, and the vast majority of the people he has served will never know his name.

In 2010, the OC community hosted President and First Lady Kagame for the graduation of the first class of Presidential Scholars. In the four years they had called OC home, the Rwandans had earned the respect and admiration of their classmates and established high expectations for future Presidential Scholars. When the final grades were tallied, the group had a combined GPA of 3.79.[21] They could do the work; they just needed access to the opportunity.

As part of the festivities surrounding the presidential visit, there were numerous events. One of those was a breakfast that was held primarily for community leaders from Oklahoma City to meet leaders from Kigali. I was seated next to the mayor of Kigali, Aisa Kirabo Kacyira. We talked about the future of Rwanda. She felt that the future of Rwanda was tied to its commitment to character. She said, "Before the genocide, some people planned to do evil. Today, we must have people who are planning to do good."

Mike stepped down from his role as president in 2012 and was named president emeritus. In 2013, he was named the first chancellor of the University of Rwanda.[22] The position is largely ceremonial, but it provides an opportunity to positively impact the 30,000 students and 2,150 members of the faculty and staff. [23] He considered it one of his greatest privileges to serve for several years as one of approximately 25 people from around the world (including Rick Warren, Dale Dawson, Prime Minister Tony Blair, et al.) on President Kagame's Presidential Advisory Council. It is a long way from Antlers, Oklahoma, to Kigali, Rwanda. It is awe-inspiring to see what can happen when someone chooses to use their abilities to activate and unleash the potential of others.

CONCLUSION

The woman my father spoke with about the job at the National Park Service was not interested in opening the door of opportunity for others. If she had been, she would have engaged him differently. She would have expressed empathy and then suggested other options that might have been a better fit. Instead of using her position of influence to add value to the lives of others, she had become disengaged and territorial.

Her approach to life is all too common and, I am assuming, was taught to her by others. Unfortunately, unless she eventually selected a different path, each day that she sat behind her desk, she was becoming increasingly comfortable with her way of doing things. If something did not change, I can only assume her mental model would continue to perceive life as something to be endured versus something to be experienced.

What makes Mike's approach to life unusual is his mental model. From an early age, he considered it his responsibility to serve others. Consequently, the accolades and opportunities that he earned were viewed as tools to help him pursue his purpose with greater effectiveness. If he had chosen to apply his skill as an accountant, lawyer, and executive for personal gain, he would have been very successful, but his success would not have opened as many doors of opportunity for others. Instead, he sought to apply himself where he was needed on behalf of others. As a result, when his life intersected with the people of Rwanda, there was little, if any, hesitation in his response. He had been preparing for the moment his entire life.

HOW ARE YOU OPENING DOORS OF OPPORTUNITY FOR OTHERS?

The following is an excerpt from a speech given by President Paul Kagame on February 10, 2017. It was given 5 days after Chancellor

Mike O'Neal's 71st birthday, and it is a fitting tribute to his work. President Kagame stated:

> I would also like to take this opportunity to pay tribute to Mike O'Neal, the former president of OC, a friend, and more or less a citizen of Rwanda.
>
> He played the key role in initiating and driving our partnership more than a decade ago, as he has just been explaining.
>
> So we thank you, Mike and Nancy, for the years of dedicated service to our nation.
>
> They first visited Rwanda in 2004 with OC trustee Richard Lawson and his wife Pat, and that's where the relationship started. By the way, I want to ask right from the outset that you pass our best wishes and greetings to the Lawsons.
>
> They saw what we were trying to accomplish in Rwanda and also how Oklahoma Christian could make a real difference.
>
> Most importantly, they understood that our approach was fundamentally values-based, much like OC's educational philosophy.
>
> It was, therefore, a meeting of both minds and hearts, and under Mike's leadership, the Oklahoma Christian community took immediate action.
>
> In 2006, the Presidential Scholars Program was born, and the first 10 Rwandans arrived on campus in Oklahoma.
>
> Today, OC offers an MBA right here in Kigali, as you have heard from the speakers, and hundreds of young Rwandans have benefitted from an Oklahoma Christian education.
>
> Many are now working here at home, contributing to our country's development.
>
> In addition, an incredibly diverse range of beneficial initiatives have blossomed over the years, undertaken

together with the many new friends who have gotten to know Rwanda because of their connection to OC.

The relationship with Oklahoma Christian is, without doubt, among the most productive and meaningful that we enjoy with institutions of higher learning around the world.

In our view, that strength comes back to the shared character traits and positive mindsets that we recognized in each other from the outset, and which we seek to instill in our young people.

Let me remind you of just one example. The first Rwandans who came to Oklahoma Christian didn't just live in dormitories. They stayed with host families and became part of a home.

Over time, we saw that these families had come to love our children as their own; and thank you, all of you, in the Oklahoma family. They helped our students to be the best they could be.

I would like to commend the OC alumni for two things in particular.

First, for working hard to get good results, even where it might have been a struggle to catch up academically and linguistically.

It is important to understand how important this is in our country's context. Success is never just about the individual who achieves it.

When each of us performs at our best, we create new possibilities for others that may not otherwise exist.

By showing that Rwandans could not only compete, but excel, you played an important part in ensuring that the opportunities you enjoyed would multiply and continue to be available in the future.

Secondly, it is admirable to see the alumni coming together to give back to our country. The Alumni

Association and the Scholarship Fund are very important steps in this direction.

I wish to, of course, as we have been informed earlier, mention that Jeannette and I are very proud alumni of OC. So we will contribute.

I can only say to all of you: keep it up and continue to build on these efforts in various ways going forward.

The story of Rwanda and Oklahoma Christian University is a valuable lesson to all of us about the power of human relationships and shared values to drive change and sustain ambition.

One of the traits we share, again, is tenacity in the face of adversity. Our respective experiences have shown us that you can come from Rwanda or Oklahoma, or anyplace else, and strive to be among the best.

That is why it is also important for us to continue on this journey together for many more years to come.

I wish to once again thank you, the leaders of Oklahoma Christian University, and the members of that family, which has become our own. We will do our best, within our means, to ensure that this relationship continues to be a very productive one.

Thank you, God bless you, and enjoy the remainder of the evening."[24]

CHAPTER 4

"I THINK YOU ARE GIFTED"

Leaders Challenge Beliefs

In 1974, researchers Chris Argyris (1923-2013)[1] and Donald Schön (1930-1997)[2] introduced the concepts of single and double loop learning to the emerging field of organizational development.[3] At the heart of their work is the theory that the actions people take have meaning and purpose to the person acting. Consequently, as someone goes through life, his or her actions are connected to their mental model or, what Argyris and Schön called, our governing variables. When people take action, the effectiveness of the action is judged against the feedback received. If an action is effective, it is considered consistent with our governing variables. Through this process of taking actions and evaluating their effectiveness, we each create a library of causal theories about what to do or how to act or think in a broad variety of situations. Argyris and Schön labeled these causal theories as Theories of Action.

Through their research, they identified two kinds of theories of action: 1) espoused theories and 2) theories in use. Espoused theories are the governing variables that "an individual claims to follow."[4] Theories-in-use are the governing variables "that can be inferred from action."[5]

> The discrepancy between what people say and what they do is an old story. It is sometimes expressed in the saying, "Do as I say, not as I do." However, the distinction between espoused theory and theory-in-

use goes beyond this common conception. It is true that what people do often differs from the theories they espouse. We are saying, however, that there is a theory that is consistent with what they do; and this we call their theory-in-use. Our distinction is not between theory and action but between two different theories of action: those that people espouse, and those that they use. One reason for insisting that what people do is consistent with the theory (in-use) that they hold, even though it may be inconsistent with their espoused theories, is to emphasize that what people do is not accidental. They do not "just happen" to act in a particular way. Rather, their action is designed; and, as agents, they are responsible for the design.[6]

Based upon Argyris and Schön's theory, our actions are connected directly to our governing variables or mental model, whether we are aware of it (espoused theory) or not (theory in action). When observing how people learn, they found there were two types of approaches: single loop and double loop learning. The difference between the two can make a profound impact on how we understand the world.

In the single loop learning model, the governing variable or variables are assumed and the focus is on the effectiveness of the actions taken in maintaining the governing variable. An analogy that is often used to describe this model is a thermostat and a heating or cooling system. Imagine a thermostat has been set at 72 degrees. The setting on the thermostat represents the governing variable. Once the variable of 72 degrees has been established, the effectiveness of the heating and cooling system is measured against whether the temperature is maintained at 72 degrees. When a sensor provides feedback to the thermostat that the temperature has fallen below 72 degrees or has risen above 72 degrees, an action is taken. If it is too cold, the heater will be turned on with the goal of maintaining a temperature of 72 degrees. If it is too hot, the air conditioner will be turned on with the same goal. In this situation, the governing variable is assumed and is not questioned. As a result, the feedback loop is focused on one primary objective, the effectiveness of the heating or cooling system in keeping the temperature at 72 degrees. This is a single loop learning model.

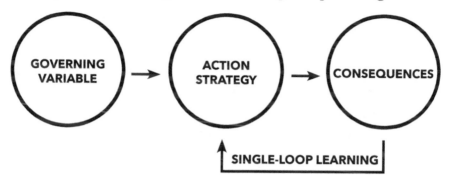

In the double loop model, both the effectiveness of the actions taken is considered as well as the validity of the governing variable. Using the example of the thermostat, in a double loop, the person setting the thermostat would ask, "Why are we setting the temperature at 72 degrees?" They would additionally test the effectiveness of the heating and cooling system to maintain the temperature.

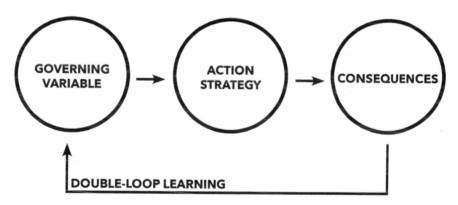

Depending on our approach to life, the lessons we learn will either strengthen our existing mental model, or they will transform it. Among the key reasons that the double loop approach to life is challenging is that it creates tension. This tension is a warning system designed to protect the brain from too quickly or too easily abandoning our existing perspective, which would result in internal chaos. Our mental models can be changed, but the process often takes considerable time and effort. Sometimes we are forced to exchange one perspective for another, and at other times, we maintain a belief but it is given additional depth.

For example, a 20-year-old may understand the importance of saving for retirement, but they will likely have a deeper understanding of the importance at the age of 60. The value we place on health may change once we have endured a prolonged illness. Our appreciation for forgiveness may grow when we have made decisions we regret and long for a clean slate.

If we are willing to endure the discomfort of having our assumptions challenged, our mental model can be transformed throughout our lifetime. Although every phase of life is important, it is during the formative years of childhood and adolescence that our initial mental model emerges. Because of this, it can be helpful to go back to this time in life to gain a better understanding of the factors that led us to where we are today. When we consider the past, I would ask that you not review it from a single loop perspective, which is limited to judging the effectiveness of your actions, but that you consider the double loop perspective.

Over the next few pages, I will use my life story to illustrate how a mental model is formed and transformed. Writing my own story was surprisingly emotional. My hope is that my experiences will prompt you to consider your mental model from a new perspective.

LEAVES ON THE TREES

My academic career began in 1978 at the Washington Elementary School in Vincennes, Indiana. The building was an impressive, three-story, red brick, and limestone structure. Constructed in 1925, it is a physical reminder of an era when public buildings were intended to stand the test of time.

I have long ago lost any connection with my classmates, but according to the official class picture, the 1978 kindergarten class consisted of 18 children and 2 teachers. In the photograph, 16 of my classmates are seated in rows on a large carpet that has been placed over what was likely the original checkerboard tile floor. The teachers are sitting behind the children. Mrs. Blice is seated in a wooden student desk, and Mrs. Minderman is sitting on a light-oak library chair. I am one of two children who are not seated. I am standing in the back of the room beside Mrs. Minderman.

It is an odd thing to look at a picture of oneself from a time that cannot be recalled. In the class photo, my hands are shoved deep into my pockets, and I am one of the few children not smiling. My head is turned to the right, and I am looking at the camera with my left eye. On the back of my individual photo, which was taken the same day as the group photo, my mother had written, "Came home with temperature and acute tonsillitis after picture!" The fact that I did not feel well would explain why I was standing beside the teacher. There was another reason, however, why my head was turned to the side. I had never noticed it before, but it was a critical clue to how my mental model would be shaped, but, at the time, it would have little, if any, meaning.

In the fall of 1979, I walked across the street from our home at the corner of McDowell and McKinley roads to start life as a first grader at Franklin Elementary. I loved school, and I felt cared for by the teachers there. Although I came from a stable and supportive home, was never bullied by my classmates, and had dedicated teachers, I was not progressing in my classes. I was 6 years old and had only been in "all-day" school for a few months when I was categorized as one of the "slow" learners.

It was during a routine vision screening at school that a local ophthalmologist noticed something was wrong with my eyes. Based on the findings, I was sent to his office for a full work-up. The doctor was a family friend and had recently upgraded his equipment to have the most advanced instruments in town. Disbelieving the initial prognosis using the new tools, he examined me again using his older and more familiar equipment, but the prognosis remained the same.

There were two primary concerns, and both related to my right eye. The first was that as a result of astigmatism (blurry vision), I had developed amblyopia (lazy eye). The second issue was the loss of peripheral vision (tunnel vision). Although my left eye was functioning well, the vision in my right was 20/300. This meant what my left eye could see clearly at 300 feet, my right could only see at 20 feet.

Due to the massive differential between the two images, my brain began selecting the clearer image from my left eye and rejecting the blurry image being sent from the right. As a result, the weak eye was becoming weaker due to lack of use. When I was tilting my head to one side in my class photo, it was an unconscious effort to align my "good eye" with the camera. Not only was the blurriness and lack of depth perception making it difficult to trace letters or catch a ball, but the loss of peripheral vision also made learning to read more challenging. Because my right eye was not functioning well, when I would read from left to right, I could only see a few words at a time, which made reading a more laborious and slow process.

Using the best practices available at the time, the doctor took an aggressive approach to my case, for which I am grateful. Although much has been learned since that time about my type of vision problems, it appears the treatment he prescribed was very effective. Working with him for well over a year, he designed a regimen that included "patching" my stronger eye to help force the weaker one to respond. In addition, there were numerous exercises designed to force my brain to recognize the images being sent from both eyes instead of just one.

As my brain began to remap, the images from my right eye started to register with greater intensity. Eventually, I was fitted with glasses, which would continue to force my brain and eyes to work in greater coordination. On the day I received my glasses, it was immediate sensory overload. I could see things that I had never seen before. Filled with amazement as we drove home, I excitedly said to my mother, "There are leaves on the trees!"

Learning to wear glasses took time. Because the change in my vision impacted the way my brain processed information, one of the side effects was a headache. To help me stick with it, my parents said that if I would wear my glasses for two weeks in a row, they would buy me a basketball. The bribe was effective, and although wearing glasses has always made me uncomfortable, I began to wear them consistently.

Over the next few years, the progress made in improving my vision began to slow and eventually plateaued. At that time, we were told I was unlikely to see any additional progress regarding the astigmatism. I was encouraged to wear glasses for eyestrain but was told it was optional and that even with corrective lenses, my vision could not be improved any further. The progress from 20/300 to 20/60 (or better) had been a fantastic improvement.

During those years, my vision had improved, but my mental model concerning my academic ability had not. It was in these early years, that my original mental model emerged. Although I liked school, I did not think of myself as a good student.

A NEW START

In the summer before I started the third grade in 1981, we moved from Indiana to Alabama, and I enrolled at Daphne Elementary. When we got there, I was pleasantly surprised to find that the curriculum in my new school was a review of much of the curriculum I had just completed. As a result, I was considered a strong student. I thought it odd that in my new school, wearing my new glasses, the teachers and my classmates assumed I was smart.

The performance gap between my classmates and I began closing as the year progressed. The curriculum in Indiana may have been different from the curriculum in Alabama, but the intellectual ability of the kids was not. By the fourth grade, when we began learning new material, any advantage I had was gone.

It was in the fifth grade that I concluded I was not going to be an academic all-star. At the beginning of the school year, we were assigned to our classes, some of which were based on academic ability. There was one cohort that appeared to be for the highest performing students. I do not know how they chose which students would be in the lead group, but I was surprised to learn that I had been placed in it.

It only took a few weeks for my teachers to recognize their mistake. One afternoon, I was asked to stay behind to talk with the teacher. After the other students left the classroom, she explained that she thought it would be better for me if I were in the other class. Although I was embarrassed to have to go back to the regular class, it reinforced my earlier mental model. I was not supposed to be in the "smart kids" class because I was not smart.

ACROSS THE BAY

When I was about to enter the seventh grade, dad was offered an opportunity to coach and teach fulltime at Mobile Christian School. To be closer to the school, we moved "across the Bay" from Daphne to Mobile. Our new home at 5408 Timberlane Drive was a ranch-style home built in 1974. Located less than 2 miles from the school, the house was brick and had three bedrooms and two baths.

The decision to move to Mobile would prove to be a pivotal one in the life of our family. Although Mobile dwarfed Daphne in population, the school where my dad was teaching was considerably smaller than the one I was leaving. As a result, I felt more confident in trying my hand in sports and other activities that I am not sure I would have pursued otherwise.

I was able to adjust to the new school socially, but I felt I was always in "catch-up" mode academically. It was a common sight to see me walking from one class to the next while frantically cramming for a quiz or test that I had forgotten. It was around this time that I began noticing that I forgot to bring home my books much more regularly than my classmates. In addition, although I would take notes in class, I was seemingly unable to keep them organized. In the classes where the teachers required that we turn in our notes, I was continually asking friends if I could use their notes as a template for writing my own. It was frustrating to stay up late copying notes that I had taken the first time but had lost or misplaced.

On a positive note, even when school was challenging, I enjoyed learning. Also, I had a good short-term memory, and even when I forgot to study for a quiz or test, I could usually flip through the pages of the textbook while walking to class and recall enough to pass. The problem was that I was passing the tests, but I was not grasping the deeper concepts. Furthermore, I was falling into a routine of using one class to complete the homework that I had forgotten to do in another class. On those days, although I may have appeared to be listening to the lecture, I was completely distracted.

When I started the eighth grade, I felt the pace, which had been too fast for me in the seventh grade, had only increased. With considerable effort, I passed all of my classes in the first semester with grades of C or better. The second semester was tougher, and as the school year was coming to an end, I knew it was going to be tight. My primary concern was my English class. Even though I was trying, the concepts seemed beyond my reach. In addition to not being able to follow along during the actual class, I did not possess the study skills needed to catch up on my own. Every time I went to class, I felt I was falling further behind, and I did not know what to do.

I was more hopeful about pre-algebra. Although my grades did not necessarily reflect it, I genuinely liked math. The class started out reasonably well, and I earned a C for the third quarter. During the fourth quarter, however, my lack of mastery began to show. As the problems became more complicated, my grades faltered. Although it had been a tough quarter and I knew my grade would be poor, I thought I would still pass the class.

In the last week of the semester, the teacher met individually with each student to review his or her grades before the final exam. When my name was called to come to the teacher's desk, I knew it was not going to be pretty. After some quick calculations, I was told that I was going to get a solid D for the fourth quarter. I had earned a C in the third quarter, which meant if I got a high A on the final exam, I could earn a C- for the semester. Conversely, if I got an F on the final, I would get a D for the course.

I had never made an A on any test in the class, and I did not think it remotely possible to get an A, much less a high A, on the final exam. As a result, I did not study much for my pre-algebra final and used the time to focus on my other classes, especially English. I took my pre-algebra exam, and it was not good. After the exams had been graded, most of the teachers posted the final grades to their doorframes or a bulletin board. Although I was confident I got an F for my final exam in pre-algebra, I was curious to see the actual score.

When I saw the grade, I was confused. The failing grade for the final exam did not surprise me, but I was shocked to see that my grade for the semester was an F as well. I thought there must have been a mistake. Based on the conversation with the teacher, I thought I had a D for the fourth quarter, but according to the grade that was posted, I had earned an F. This grade, coupled with the F on the final exam, meant I had automatically failed the course. I asked the teacher about the grade and reminded her of our conversation a few days earlier. Based on her response, it was apparent that either she did not remember our discussion, had remembered it differently, or I had just misunderstood her. The grade would stand.

I was afraid of what was to come next. Although part of my fear was related to my parents' response and the embarrassment I would have to endure from my friends, these were not my primary concerns. My greatest fear was that I had been running as fast as I thought I could, and I had not been able to keep up. I assumed things would only speed up in the future, and if this were the case, what hope did I have? After failing two classes, my mental model was becoming crystallized. I was good at athletics, music, and leadership, but I was not a good student.

CS ARE BETTER THAN DS

There may have been numerous conversations about grades over the years, but I can only recall the one that happened that night. It was not that grades did not matter in our home, but my parents had made it clear that grades were not the only thing that mattered. My brother and I were in our respective bedrooms when dad called out from the living room, "Boys, come in here."

I do not know if my brother knew why dad was calling for us, but I did. My stomach dropped, and my legs felt weak. Once in the living room, he motioned for us to sit on the couch. The couch was full-sized and had been upholstered in a dark navy windowpane style. Draped across the back of the couch was a white afghan comprised of colorful "granny squares" that had, in fact, been knitted by my great-grandmother Hankins. My brother took his place at one end of the couch, and I sat at the other.

To this day, I am not sure why my brother, who was two years ahead of me in school, was there. Perhaps it was for moral support, or maybe Dad thought it would be helpful for him to see how things would be handled if he ever failed a class. One way or the other, I was glad he was sitting there, even if he had done nothing to deserve it.

My dad's body language was hard to read. He was not angry, but it was clear he was concerned. It was also evident that he did not know how to start the conversation. He closed his eyes for a moment and leaned his head back as if he were looking heavenward for guidance.

When he started, he sounded tired. He said, "Boys, let me tell you something about grades…" He paused, looking for the right words, and then said, "…Cs are better than Ds…." He paused for another moment and concluded, "Try to make Cs." He looked at me to see if I had understood his message. Wide-eyed, I nodded in agreement. Without saying another word, he stepped forward and gave me a high five. I do not recall ever having another conversation about grades.

He recognized that my poor grades were not due to a lack of motivation, so he did not try to motivate. He sensed that adding more pressure would only make the situation worse. He knew I wanted to succeed but lacked the ability to do so. From my perspective, his recognition of this was one of the reasons why he was a great coach.

An unintended outcome of the conversation, however, was how it shaped my understanding of grades. My translation was simple: C = good, D = not as good, and F = not good. On the other end of the spectrum, a B = a pleasant surprise, and an A = astonishment.

From that point forward, I do not recall getting another D or F in high school, but I resigned myself to the idea that I was not "book smart." I began looking for the path of least resistance in school. I did not attempt to take any classes that were not required if at all possible.

AN UNPREPARED GRADUATE

My junior year, we moved from Mobile to St. Louis, Missouri, where I enrolled at the Christian Academy of Greater St. Louis. Dad taught a few classes and coached at the same school while also working with a nearby church. The school was very small, and because of limited class options, they had to get creative for me to complete all the courses needed for graduation. Because I was behind my classmates in math, I took my class as an "independent study" with some guidance from the math teacher. My senior year, I moved back to Mobile for the first quarter of the year to play football and then returned to St. Louis until graduation. Due to some of the scheduling issues, I had been able to avoid the more challenging math and English courses while still being able to graduate from high school.

An exchange that I feel sums up my final years of high school happened on the day that I graduated. Following commencement, the principal was circulating among the families and graduates. He was a good man who I believed was sincerely interested in the lives of the students, but he had spent the bulk of his adult life in the military, and was not in his natural environment. When he came to me, after offering his congratulations, he asked, "So, what are you planning to do after graduation?" I responded, "I am planning on going to college." I then told him I was considering studying psychology.

His raised his eyebrows, frowned, and tilted his head slightly to one side and said, "Really?" He looked down as if processing something important and said, "Wow." He concluded, "Do you think you are smart enough to do that?"

I am not sure what his motivation was for the comment, but I was not offended by it. It stung because it hit too close to home. In truth, I had been wondering the same thing.

Looking back at that time in life, I could not be more grateful for the opportunity to attend Mobile Christian School and the Christian Academy of Greater St. Louis. The academic challenges I faced while in these schools had nothing to do with the quality of the instruction. I do not doubt that if I had not attended those schools, it would have been much worse. I was only able to attend private school because my dad either taught or coached there. Even as a teenager, I felt it was an honor to attend those schools, and my feeling has not changed over time.

OFF TO COLLEGE

I looked at a handful of schools, but I always thought Harding University would likely be the best fit for me. It was where my parents had attended, and we had visited the campus several times over the years. Besides, my brother was already there, and having both of us at the same school was convenient for our family. On the day it was time to go, I packed up my car and headed south from St. Louis to Searcy, Arkansas. Before I left, I grabbed a bottle of Pepto-Bismol for the road. I was doing my best to act as if leaving for college was no big deal, but my body knew the truth. I was unsure if I had what it took to make it.

Among the reasons I wanted to go to Harding was that they provided me an opportunity to play football. I was not a good enough football player to be offered a scholarship, but I had been invited to be a walk-on. For the next two years, I played special teams and cornerback. It was a positive experience, but the longer I was in school, the clearer it became to me that the game that had meant so much to me in high school did not have the same appeal in college. It was not my greatest passion, and I was an average collegiate athlete at best. After earning my letter my sophomore year, I hung up my cleats.

Although my GPA was not impressive, I was passing my classes and had adjusted to college life. Academically, the real test would begin in my junior year. My undergraduate major required that I pass three semesters of Greek to be able to graduate. I had been told the classes were very challenging. One person said that Greek was a "sifting class," and it was designed to force some people out of the program.

When I started the first semester of Greek, I was relieved to find the professor was a caring person and an experienced educator. It was clear he was not trying to push people out of the program. He was trying to help them. With that said, it was also clear that the class was going to be very tough.

I found that one of the key challenges of learning another language is that it requires a good grasp of English grammar. Lacking this, I was quickly overwhelmed. In the first few weeks of class, when I raised my hand to ask for an explanation, the professor, Dr. Duane Warden, responded with an answer that gave additional insight into something pertaining to English grammar. Not only did I not understand Greek, but I also did not understand the terminology he was using to explain Greek. I found it all the more disconcerting when I noticed my classmates nodding their heads in agreement with his explanation. I felt a sense of panic. I knew how much was riding on the class, and I was lost.

The class met five times a week. My section met in the morning, but there was another section that met in the afternoon. Both sections were covering the same material. Dr. Warden said that everyone was welcome to attend both sessions of the course if that would help them gain a better understanding of the material. I would often attend the class both in the morning and in the afternoon in the hope of picking up the concepts through sheer repetition.

I passed the first semester with a D, but much like pre-algebra back in middle school, as the content became more complicated in the second semester, I was failing. I am not sure what prompted Dr. Warden to make the announcement, but one day in class, he said, "If you are willing to put in the work, if you will attend class, and turn in your assignments on time, you will not fail this course." I appreciated his confidence, but thought to myself, *I am about to disprove that theory.*

On the day of the final exam, I took my time making sure I answered the questions as thoroughly as possible. I was among the last students to complete the final, and when I turned it in, Dr. Warden invited me and another student to his office so he could grade the papers for us. He knew we were anxious. I stood near him as he went through each page and marked the incorrect responses. When he finished grading, he looked at me and said, "I told you if you would put the work in, you would not fail this course."

I earned an F. He gave me a D. It was an act of compassion that I would never forget.

The lesson I took from the experience was that I was not smart enough to learn Greek. At that time, it did not even cross my mind there were other factors that may have contributed to my academic challenges. I was just thankful to have completed 2 of the 3 required classes.

LEADERSHIP

Although I was struggling academically, I was growing as a leader. Faculty and students began inviting me to speak at campus events, and I was being asked to take on additional leadership responsibilities. I found that after quitting football, my college experience was very different. Namely, I had more time for other activities. My brother played in the pep band for home basketball games, and they needed an extra trumpet player. He invited me to join them, and I agreed. It was fun to share that experience with him, even if it was for just a couple of games. The next semester, he suggested that I join one of the campus choruses, the University Singers; he was the student director. When I got there, I felt a bit self-conscious about being a former football player joining the choir, but it ended up being one of my favorite memories of college.

Furthermore, if I attended the practices and performances, I could earn an A every semester I took University Singers as a class. My junior year, they asked me to be the president of the University Singers, and I was also asked to be the president of my social club. My senior year, I was elected as the president of the Student Association.

Serving as the student body president changed the course of my life. Much of the work was public, like leading committees, speaking at events, and planning projects. Other aspects of the role happened behind the scenes. One of those was a weekly meeting with the university president, Dr. David Burks.

DR. BURKS

David Basil Burks was born on Thursday, May 13, 1943, to Marie and Basil Burks in the Ozark Mountain community of Ava, Missouri. Although he was born in Missouri, he was raised in the southeast New Mexico town of Truth or Consequences. In 1950, 4,700 people lived in the town where his father was the superintendent of schools.

Following graduation from Hot Springs High School in 1961, David loaded up his car, a green 1949 Ford, and traveled northeast.[7] He exchanged the arid desert climate of New Mexico for the humid, sub-tropical weather of central Arkansas. Due to his mother's poor health, David and his sister, Karen, had learned to live independently earlier in life than most. When he got to Harding College, the idea of things like curfew seemed unnecessary for someone who had already learned how to live on his own. Initially, the adjustment was uncomfortable, and he decided he would transfer to the University of New Mexico at the first opportunity. While waiting for the right opportunity, he began building friendships with faculty and classmates that would cause the dream of returning home to fade away.[8]

Not only did he stay at Harding, he threw himself into the experience. One of the reasons he had chosen Harding was because of his involvement with the award-winning yearbook, *The Petit Jean*. A photographer, he had been granted a scholarship at Harding to take photos for the yearbook.[9] Through the experience, he had been given unique access to campus life. In addition, he was learning to be a leader by serving as a Resident Assistant his junior year[10], the same year he served as president of his social club, Beta Phi Kappa. It was through his social club that he met his future wife, Leah Gentry, who had grown up on a farm in Alhambra, Illinois, before heading south to attend Harding.[11]

His senior year, David was elected Student Association President. He began dating Leah that fall, and the two were engaged in November. They graduated together in June of 1965 and were married in August. The newlyweds moved to Austin to pursue his MBA in accounting from the University of Texas. David had been offered a fellowship at the university and was also offered the additional opportunity to teach two Principles of Accounting undergraduate courses. He completed the degree in August of 1966 and then accepted an offer to work with Exxon on an assignment in Baton Rouge, Louisiana.

He felt his career path was set when he and Leah welcomed their first-born son, Bryan, into the world. A call from Harding disrupted their plans. Dr. James Hedrick, a beloved professor, was calling to ask him to return as a member of the faculty. The family packed up their home and made their way back to Arkansas.

Prior to the call inviting him back, he had not considered following in his father's footsteps as an educator, but when the offer came, it felt like the right thing to do. In August of 1967, a tall, thin, and very young professor with thick glasses stood behind the lectern and began teaching. After teaching for four years, in 1971, the Burks family moved to Tallahassee, Florida, so David could pursue his Ph.D. in higher education administration from Florida State University. Ten days prior to moving to Florida, the family grew by one with the addition of their second son, Stephen. After the coursework was completed in 1974, he graduated, passed the CPA exam, and they returned to Searcy. He was named the dean of the school of business from 1974-1987 and became the president of the university in May of 1987.

When I began meeting with Dr. Burks in August of 1994, I had no idea how my time with him would shape my future. I had been told that he was a "businessman." The label was meant to imply that he was more about numbers than he was about people. When I met with him, I anticipated he would be focused on the business aspects of the institution. I found he had either changed from what he had been earlier in life, or he had been mislabeled. It was true that he was comfortable with numbers, blueprints, and strategic plans, but this was only part of the story.

What I soon discovered was that he was someone who cared deeply about people and ideas. He had the heart of an educator and wanted to see people grow. He had a growth mindset in every aspect of life. As a result, he wanted to see the school grow numerically, he wanted the campus to grow with new buildings, and he wanted to see the academic offerings grow too. All of this was an outgrowth of his genuine desire to see people grow personally and professionally. His passion for growth at Harding was simple. He wanted to provide as many people as much possible access to what he considered to be a life-changing learning experience.

Once I understood his motivation, I regarded him as a trusted mentor and guide. Through the process, he wanted to help me grow as a person and leader. Significantly, he applied the same standard to himself. He was always seeking new experiences and new challenges that would help him grow. My friendship with him was the most unexpected benefit of having served as Student Association President.

My year as president was an incredible learning experience. It was a year of constant activity, which often meant early mornings and late nights. Every week there was something new. One week we were planning a flood relief effort to Georgia. The next we were promoting a school activity. The next we were trying to raise funds for the people of war-torn Croatia. It was challenging, fun, and transformational.

As the school year was coming to a close, my focus began to turn toward a trip that summer to Dubna, Russia. Starting in 1992, I had gone to Russia each summer to teach English. For the summer of 1995, I had recruited two teams of students. On the trip, there were several veteran teachers, and it was something of an all-star team. The first group taught during the first half of the summer, and the second group relieved them for the last half. Even though I loved the team, the people we were serving, and the work, it had been a long year, and I felt tired as we boarded the plane heading to Moscow. By the time I returned, I had lost a lot of weight and was emotionally and physically exhausted.

When I returned to campus for my final semester, (I was on the four and a half year plan) I had not anticipated how different life would be when I was no longer in a position of leadership. Furthermore, I had decided to wait to take my last semester of Greek during my final semester of school. I knew the decision to take a year off of that class was risky, but I was afraid of failing and did not want to do so while I was Student Body President.

A few weeks into the fall semester, I called home and told my parents that I felt as if everything was unraveling. I said that I did not feel like I had anything left in the tank. After hearing me out, dad said, "Stick with it for a couple more weeks and let's see how you are doing. If things don't get better and you need to come home, we will make it happen."

GRADUATE SCHOOL

He has never admitted it, but I assume my dad called Dr. Burks to let him know that I was struggling. That week, I received a call from the university president's office. Claudette Bratcher, Executive Assistant to the President, was calling to see if she could arrange a lunch for Dr. Burks and me. The invite was an instant morale boost as I had missed our conversations. When I got to the office, I was directed to the conference room, which was likely the most formal meeting space on campus. When I entered the room, it was clear that our lunch was meant to be something special. One end of the long table had been draped in black tablecloths, and the table had been set for two.

We took our seats, and he said he wanted to talk about my future. Due to the relationship we had built the previous year, I felt comfortable being transparent with him. I told him that I wanted to develop people and organizations. As I sorted through my thoughts, he listened patiently and thoughtfully. After a few clarifying questions, he said, "I think you are going to need a master's degree to do some of those things." He said, "I want to help you do that." He then listed a handful of schools he would recommend, one of which was Harding. He said that if I would choose from the list, he had relationships with their leadership and thought they would be willing to grant me a scholarship through a graduate assistant role.

Although the conversation occurred in 1995, when I think about the moment, it still makes me emotional today. I said, "Thank you. I want to go to Harding and learn from you." I felt he had awakened a sleeping giant within me and opened a door to a future that had been shut. I finished my undergraduate degree a few months later and walked across the stage on December 16, 1995.

I KNOW WHO YOU ARE

There are hundreds of experiences that I could point to as being significant in helping shape my perspective while at Harding. If I were asked to choose from among the top 10, one of those was the day I met Dr. Dee Carson. I had just started the graduate program, and Dr. Carson taught one of my first courses, "The Art & Science of Teaching." She was an experienced teacher and administrator who was passionate about her field and had high expectations of her students.

It was the first day of class, and while I was looking for a place to sit when Dr. Carson recognized me and said, "Nathan Mellor." I had spoken at several events where faculty were present, and I could only assume she knew me from one of these programs I walked toward the front of the classroom to see what she wanted. She was standing behind a table, and I sensed she had something she wanted to share. She pointed her index finger at me and said, "Nathan Mellor. I know who you are." I was trying to read her eyes to get a sense of where she was going with the conversation, but I was not having much luck.

As my classmates continued to file into the classroom, she said, "I think you are gifted…but do not know it." She paused to let me take in what she had just said. She continued, "I expect you to make an A in this class." I responded, "Yes, ma'am." She motioned toward a desk near the front of the classroom and said, "Sit there."

I sat down and Dr. Carson began the class. I leaned over to a classmate and asked, "Do you have a pen?" They nodded and handed me one. I asked another if they had any paper. From that moment onward, I took notes on everything Dr. Carson said. I was determined to prove her right.

Although there have been many people who have helped shape my life, my intersection with Dr. Carson was a watershed moment. Her conversation with me was one of the reasons why I believe that someone's entire life can be changed in a single conversation at just the right time in their life. I could not recall ever having someone tell me that I was gifted academically.

The decision to chart a new course may be made in an instant, but our brains tend to be resistant to change, even when a new mental model may be helpful. My journey to becoming a better student required adopting new habits. I had to learn to take better notes, to give myself more time to study, and to try different approaches to learning. The path forward was not easy, but when I walked across the stage to receive my graduate degree in 1997, I felt a great sense of relief and gratitude.

THE NEXT STAGE

Christie Bishop and I became friends while on a Student Association flood relief trip to Albany, Georgia. She was one of 130 students who had traveled there from Harding to assist in the cleanup following historic floods in the summer of 1994. One constant throughout high school and college was that I was not good at dating. As much as I wish I could claim the reason was because of the people I dated, the reality was that I was the only common denominator in a series of well-intentioned relationships that did not end well.

When I met Christie, there was no pressure to date. Instead, we became friends. I enjoyed talking with her and found that she and I had many shared interests. In some ways, it was a surprise to both of us when we recognized that our friendship had grown into something more profound. On May 17, 1997, Christie and I were married in a small ceremony in the Burks' backyard.

Although Harding had been a good place for us, I felt called to ministry. I began looking for opportunities, and in the summer of 1999 was hired to work with a church in scenic Chattanooga, Tennessee. It was here that our daughters Annalise and Arden were born and we made friendships with families that will last a lifetime.

The church had been through some tough times in the 2 to 3 years prior to my arrival, and they were looking to get back on track. They had a strong core of dedicated people and a ministry staff that cared deeply. As the team formed and found its stride, the church began to grow. Over the next four years, the attendance nearly doubled. During that time, I placed more pressure on myself to prepare new and relevant material for 5 to 7 presentations each week. This was in addition to other ministerial duties like visiting the sick, meeting with members, performing weddings and funerals and being active in the community. The church met in a relatively new building, but we were quickly running out of space. After contemplating their options, the congregation purchased a little over 100 acres of land for a new campus and a few years later, built a new facility.

While working full-time with the church, I was also teaching online college courses for a school based in Michigan. I had begun teaching occasional 6-week courses following the completion of my master's degree in 1997. As the demand for online degree programs grew, I was invited to teach additional courses. When we moved to Chattanooga, to help make ends meet, especially after our children were born, I was teaching every class offered. When I was at my busiest, I was teaching 20 to 24 classes per year, which would have been considered a heavy load for a full-time professor.

Following a familiar pattern, when the workload increased, I increased my pace accordingly and was consistently working 12 to 15 hour days. Adding fuel to the fire, I thought I was doing the right thing in 2003, when I talked my wife into building a new home. We hired a friend to assist as the General Contractor, but whenever possible, to keep our costs down, we would do any of the work that we thought we could do ourselves. Sensing I was running too fast, people would occasionally tell me that I needed to slow down or I was going to burn out. I agreed, but I also believed it would be wrong to slow down. I considered the stress that I placed on myself, on my marriage, and on my family to be part of the sacrifice required.

Instead of questioning why I was running so fast, I was locked in a single loop approach when a double loop was what was needed. My focus was solely on running faster. Due to a constant feeling of restlessness and a growing sense of tension at home I shared my concerns with a few close friends. They suggested that I talk to a professional counselor. I followed their advice and made an appointment. The counselor listened as I described my situation and then gave me an informal screening for Attention Deficit Disorder (ADD). I answered her questions and was told that I was a strong candidate for ADD. Until that moment, I had questioned whether ADD was even a real thing. Based on the results, she recommended a local psychiatrist.

I made the appointment with the doctor. In addition to talking with me about my life, he administered two tests—the first to determine if I had ADD and the second an IQ test. When I shared the challenges I felt I was facing, specifically about the challenges Christie and I were having, he listened and then said "relationships could be challenging." Instead of offering hope, he asked if I had considered divorce. I told him that I had not and he proceeded to try to convince me to consider it. While it was true that my wife and I had challenges to address, the majority of the issues we were facing were mine and had nothing to do with her. With the benefit of retrospect, if I had followed his advice, I am confident it would have been the single worst decision I would have made in my life.

Based on the interview and tests, he confirmed I had ADD. I filled the prescription given to me, but the initial dosage was wrong. When I began taking the pills, I was unable to sleep; I lost 20 pounds in a matter of weeks, had occasional hallucinations, and felt like a different person. My judgment was off and I felt increasingly impulsive.

If I had been running too fast before, on the wrong medication, I was running even faster. Eventually, when I recognized I was unable to slow down the speeding train on my own, I blew up the tracks instead. I decided that the best plan forward was to just walk away from my commitments. I wanted out of my marriage and my job and I began down a path that was inconsistent with the values I had held my entire life. When the dust settled, I found myself alone in the midst of a self-made disaster zone. My actions during that time had negatively impacted my life and the lives of my friends and family. I am not sure if it was due to exhaustion, the medication, guilt, pride, or a blend of all of the above, but even now when I try to recall that time, my brain recoils. In an effort to make things better by seeking help, I felt I had made things much worse.

When I came to my senses, I knew that I had violated the trust of those closest to me. Although the church was gracious, supportive, and forgiving, I was broken by the experience and did not feel I could continue in my role. Christie and I wanted to rebuild our lives and marriage. We concluded the best way to do so was a change of context.

Eventually, we found the prescription and dosage that worked. The difference was like night and day. I felt like myself again. When taking the correct amount, I could not even tell that I was taking medication, and there were no noticeable side effects. I still take the medication today and I am incredibly grateful to live in a time and place where access to this type of medication is possible. It is estimated that about 70% of adults with ADD, and 70-80% of children with the disorder, find medication to be helpful.[12] To help ensure my care is managed well, I meet with my family doctor on a regular basis to safeguard against any immediate or long-term side effects.

Hitting the wall is a common problem for those with ADD. In 2012, Rachel Klein, Ph.D., published the results of a study that compared the lives of 135 Caucasian males who had been diagnosed with ADHD, free of conduct disorder, at the age of 8 with a group of 136 males without ADHD in childhood, 33 years after their initial diagnosis. The objective of the study was to gain insight into how the lives of those diagnosed with ADHD compared to their counterparts by examining their employment, financial, and educational attainments along with marital history and other key factors.

The results were sobering. As a group, those who had been diagnosed with ADHD had 2 and a half fewer years of formal education, and only 3.7% of the men had earned higher degrees, which was significantly less than the 30% in the control group. They were more likely to have antisocial personality disorders, substance abuse, and dependence, and divorce. In addition, 36.3% of those diagnosed with ADHD had been incarcerated versus 11.8% of the sample group. Concerning marriage, 9.6% of the ADHD group were currently divorced versus 2.9% from the comparison group. The ADHD group divorce rate was 31.1% versus 11.8% among those without the disorder.[13]

GOING BACK TO SCHOOL

When I was diagnosed with ADD, the psychiatrist had me take an Intelligence Quotient (IQ) test. I had taken an IQ test once before in a college class and was told I could come by the next day to get my score, but I never went back. I concluded that getting confirmation that I was not smart was not going to help anything.

During this I.Q. test, the doctor went through a series of questions and exercises to gauge my memory and knowledge. He tallied the score and then said, "If 100 is average, what do you think you scored?" I thought about it for a moment and answered honestly, "105." He asked why I chose that number, and I told him that I had always gotten average grades. He responded, "That is not uncommon with people who have ADD." He said, "You just scored a 145."

After being diagnosed, I began working on my life from a new perspective. Through the process, I also was able to work through how to align my actions and beliefs better. Just as glasses had helped me see better, taking medication for ADD was helping me think more clearly. Although I was thankful for the greater clarity, I also wondered what life would have been like if I had been able to address the disorder earlier. With the ability to maintain focus on one subject, would I have been able to pass English and pre-algebra?

Christie and I began to consider our options, and I felt going back to school would help me transition to a new career. A program that had captured my imagination was the Straus Institute for Dispute Resolution at the Pepperdine University School of Law. Located in Malibu, the program is one of just a few of its kind in the nation, and *U.S. News and World Report* perennially ranks it as the #1 program of its kind in the world.

I connected with the director of the Straus Institute, and after a series of conversations, he encouraged me to apply to the Master of Dispute Resolution program. I filled out the application, which included references and my transcript from Harding, and sent the materials directly to him. Based upon my conversations, I was hopeful, but not confident that I would be accepted.

Due to the popularity of the program, the application process was highly selective, and I knew being chosen was a long shot. I was told that half of the applicants (many of whom were already practicing lawyers and judges) were not accepted. When I did not hear anything after a few weeks, I connected with them again and was told there must have been a mistake because they did not have some of the information they needed. I filled out the application again and sent it once more.

When I did not hear anything for a few more weeks, I contacted the school. The semester would begin soon, and I needed to know one way or the other. To make the program work, I would be moving my family from eastern Tennessee to southern California, and there were several things I would need to finalize to make it happen. A few more days passed before I received official notification that I had been accepted.

I was speechless. I had just been accepted into the top program in the world. My emotions were all over the place, but more than anything, I felt grateful. I was intimidated by the idea, but my wife and I were looking forward to a new start. I hoped with my new approach to life, I would have a chance.

THE FUTURE

Our house was sold, and we began boxing up everything we owned. Friends helped us pack, and my dad and I drove two U-Hauls with two cars in tow to a new life in California. After getting things into our rental house in Westlake Village, I went to the campus the next day to sign a few documents pertaining to my student loans.

When I got to campus, the person working with me on my student loans greeted me, but seemed off. I sat down, and he said, "I am so sorry, but I have some bad news. I made a mistake in processing your student loan. I do not know what to say, but I am very sorry and it is my fault." He walked me through the specifics, and the result was that the amount available was about half of what we expected. I told him I understood, gathered my things, and then drove down the Pacific Coast Highway for a few miles to find a place to pull over and collect my thoughts.

Although Pepperdine is expensive, tuition is only part of the challenge. For me, the real issue was the cost of living. Through the traditional student loans, I could get the money needed to pay for my classes, but the amount available for living expenses was being reduced drastically. The plan had been to begin the Master of Dispute Resolution (MDR) degree at the School of Law, and then if I were accepted into the program, I would start on my Doctorate in Organizational Leadership the next year.

As I sat on the beach watching the waves crash against the shore at Paradise Cove, I had an epiphany. I thought, *I could save an entire year's worth of living expenses if I did both programs concurrently.* Considering the minimum GPA for either program was higher than what I had been able to maintain for most of my academic career, and I would have to work two jobs at the same time, it was a risky move. Equipped with a new mental model and a highly supportive family, I felt that I had the ability to do the work.

As soon as possible, I met with the director of the Organizational Leadership program and explained the situation. Due to a reciprocal relationship with the School of Law, they said I could be accepted into the doctoral program, but I would need to provide a writing sample. That afternoon, I completed the writing sample and, after a quick review, was told that classes would begin the next week.

To help keep me motivated, I purchased two wooden frames in which the degrees I was pursuing would eventually be placed. I hung the empty frames on the wall and tried to visualize what it would be like to complete the program. There were a few times when I felt I had bitten off more than I could chew. However, I was learning to think differently, and I used these moments of panic as a reminder to stay focused.

I graduated with the Master of Dispute Resolution degree in 2005 and was then invited to join the staff as an assistant director and adjunct professor. A year later, I finished my coursework for the doctorate. Knowing I could work on writing my dissertation anywhere, we contemplated whether we would stay in southern California. Although we enjoyed life there, we decided against it. I applied for an opportunity to teach in the School of Business at one of Pepperdine's sister schools, Oklahoma Christian University.

There were a few bumps along the way with completing my comprehensive exams, which consisted of a 50-page thesis. My first thesis was rejected, so I had to write another and was relieved to have successfully defended it. To show that the stumble I had with my initial thesis was not a sign of things to come, I wrote and defended my dissertation in one semester. I received my doctorate in a beautiful commencement in the spring of 2007 and was chosen by the faculty to represent the program at the graduation celebrations.

KEEP FIGHTING

On one of my trips back to Pepperdine, I stopped by to see my colleagues at the School of Law. It was a relaxed conversation between friends, and it was good to see them. In the course of the discussion, one of them said, "Did we ever tell you how you got into the program?" I shook my head "no," and then they shared the story.

Evidently, sending an application directly to the director was not the normal protocol. When it arrived, it was placed in one of several stacks of papers and got lost in the shuffle. When I sent a follow-up regarding the status of my original application, it could not be found. A second application was requested, and it was sent directly to the director again. When I sent a follow-up regarding the second application, they were horrified to realize the second application had also been misplaced. Instead of asking me to apply a third time, they made their decision about my acceptance in the program based upon my interview and recommendations. I was accepted prior to receiving my official transcripts or test scores. It was an incredibly rare exception.

If the applications had not been lost, it would have been unlikely that I would have been accepted into either program. They would have looked at the academic achievement of my past and would have concluded I was not a good candidate. Thankfully, they did not. When I look at the degrees on my wall now, I feel a sense of gratitude.

As I look back, I consider how my mental model was formed and how it slowly changed. Growing up, our family once had a motto that we looked to for inspiration when life got tough. We had been in a challenging situation, and dad said, "Let me tell you what it means to be a Mellor." He would continue, "We may not be smart, but we are tough." Over time, I would just say, "Tough, not smart." Every time I said it or thought it, I was unknowingly strengthening a negative mental model that was not true. It was not true for my father, and it was not true for me. Unfortunately, it is easy to believe things that are not true, especially when it fits the story we have believed about ourselves. Thankfully, I had been taught not to give up and had been given the freedom to challenge the status quo.

For the record, I am not trying to imply that I think I am the smartest person in the world. Truthfully, I do not even think I am the smartest person in my house. What has changed is that I have learned to fight the impulse to think I lack the intelligence needed to learn. Among the key reasons I experienced a breakthrough was that I was raised in an environment in which we were taught to "stick with it." By refusing to give up, you give yourself a chance. You never know when you might catch the break that leads to your breakthrough.

WHO ARE THEY?

One of the exercises that we often use in our executive education programs is having leaders take the time to identify some of the people who have had the most significant influence on their lives. We then ask them to share about these people in a small group setting or in front of the entire group. It is a genuine honor to hear people speak openly about the people who invested in their lives. Often the person identified is a parent, grandparent, coach, or teacher. It can be surprisingly emotional for people to share their stories. In nearly every story told, there was someone who challenged their beliefs, believed in them, and sacrificed on their behalf.

Who are the people in your life that helped expand your mental model? Take a moment to literally write down the names of three people who have positively influenced your life. Beside each name, write a couple of sentences about how they helped shape your mental model. If they are still alive, make the commitment that you will let them know what they have meant to you. If they have passed, honor their memory by telling someone about them. In either case, find a way to express your gratitude.

Who are the people in whom you are currently investing? Identify three people that you can intentionally encourage and challenge. Consider how you can use your influence and experiences for the sake of others. How can you use your words, actions, and access to help them discover, form, and transform their mental model and approach to life?

PART TWO

A NEW VISION

CHAPTER 5

"SIX WEEKS UNTIL I FELT FULL"

Learning Patience

I met Pendleton "Pen" Woods when he was in his mid-80s, and I was in my mid-30s. We were working at the same university, and I had been invited to lead a newly formed outreach program. In addition to the new initiatives we would be launching, I would also be responsible for a few existing programs that would be consolidated into a new department. As part of the new organizational structure, Pen and I would be working together, and I was to be his boss. When the university president told me about the assignment, he said, "I hope you will enjoy working with Pen. He is an American hero."

Born in Fort Smith, Arkansas, on December 18, 1923, he loved his hometown and would talk about it often. Positioned at the confluence of the Arkansas and Poteau rivers, on the border of Arkansas and Oklahoma, the town began as a frontier military post in 1817. The region was home to numerous homesteaders that were a part of the western migration in the mid-1800s. For many Native Americans, northwest Arkansas and the Oklahoma Territory had become home due to forced relocation. For European settlers looking for a new life in the Wild West, Fort Smith was a staging ground for those preparing to take their chances on the Frontier.

Due to the transient nature of the city, it became known for its bars, brothels, and criminals. In response to the need for stronger law enforcement, the city successfully pursued and hired Judge Isaac Parker, who became known as the "Hanging Judge." Judge Parker famously sent 160 people to the gallows throughout his career.[1]

Today, the location where Judge Parker presided is a National Historic Site. Considering Pen's father, John Powell Woods, and both of his grandfathers were lawyers, they would have known the place well. In a rare boast, Pen shared, "The building that housed Judge Parker's Courtroom was built later and was not part of the original fort. My grandmother and her sisters were responsible for saving that building from being torn down."[2]

When speaking of his family, he said, "I have ancestors from both sides who were in the Civil War. My great-grandfather Gaines was a prisoner of war. He was on the south. He was on a prison ship on the Mississippi and didn't know how to swim. He and some other prisoners jumped overboard and swam to shore. That was the first time he swam."[3] In time, the fact that Pen's great-grandfather was a prisoner of war would become an astonishing historical footnote for the family.

Fort Smith has become known for its law enforcement heritage, its natural beauty, and its industry. The frontier town has grown to become the second largest city in Arkansas. If Fort Smith is a city built on the legacy of survivors and explorers, Pen Woods should be considered among its favorite sons.

SCOUT TO SOLDIER

The summer of 1937 was an important time for Pen. He was barely a teenager when he traveled to Washington, D.C. to participate in the first Boy Scout jamboree hosted in the nation's capital. The jamboree began on June 30th and concluded on July 9th. Even though times were tough and the Great Depression persisted, there were 27,732 Scouts and Scout leaders in attendance. While there, he participated in hikes to governmental buildings, including the White House and the Bureau of Printing and Engraving. Highlights of the trip included participating in a grand review for President Franklin Delano Roosevelt on Pennsylvania Avenue and climbing the steps of the Washington Monument.[4] Throughout the event, he met other Scouts from across the nation who understood his commitment to values. Based on his experiences, it would not have been a surprise to anyone that by the time he graduated in May of 1941 from Fort Smith High School, he was an Eagle Scout. He possessed a quick mind, a talent for writing, and a willingness to work. In the fall of 1941, he enrolled as a student at the University of Arkansas.

Pen was in his dormitory in Fayetteville, Arkansas, on Sunday afternoon, December 7th, when someone yelled to turn on the radio. They gathered around to listen to the news about the attack on Pearl Harbor by the Japanese. School officials met with the students who planned to enlist, and encouraged them to consider the Enlisted Reserve Corps. He did so, and in May of 1943, he and a group of approximately 100 fellow Razorbacks were called up. He was among a group of student-soldiers who were noted for their intellectual ability and joined the Army Service Forces Training Center (AFRC) to study Engineering. When the program was shuttered in the spring of 1944, these soldiers were sent back to infantry basic[5] and Pen was then assigned to the 99th Infantry Division.[6]

The 99th had two nicknames. The first was the "Checkerboard Division," due to the distinct, three-lined checkerboard design of their shoulder insignia. Positioned on a black shield, the checkerboard was made of blue and white squares. The 99th was originally conceived as a unit from Pennsylvania; the black background was intended to represent the iron district. The horizontal band of blue and white squares was inspired by William Pitt's coat of arms and was designed to be a respectful nod to Pittsburgh's namesake.[7]

The second nickname was "Battle Babies," due to the fact they were inexperienced in battle. In time, this moniker, Battle Babies, would become a source of pride. In the winter of 1944, they were untested and unproven. In a matter of weeks, they would have the opportunity to prove themselves in some of the toughest fighting to be endured in the entirety of World War II.

PATROLS

Throughout November and December of 1944, American forces made daily patrols behind the famed Siegfried Line. The entire area was heavily mined and reinforced by heavily defended cement installations and strongholds. Although the work was dangerous, it was considered crucial to gaining real-time intelligence about the intentions of the Germans. According to Major General Walter Lauer, the patrols were typically four to 50 soldiers, and the primary goal of the patrols was to "reconnoiter and to capture prisoners for identification purposes so that my own and higher headquarters would have definite knowledge of any changes in the German tactical units which we faced."[8]

On December 10, 1944, Private First Class Pen Woods and a group of 12 to 13 soldiers from the 99th were on patrol behind the Siegfried Line when they encountered the Germans. Instantly, they were surrounded and cut off.[9] Although two soldiers in the rear were able to escape, their squad leader was killed and another soldier was wounded.[10] Pen stated, "It happened very suddenly. I tried to fire, but the Browning Automatic Weapon (BAR) was frozen up. I had fallen into a snow-covered ravine, and snow got inside of the weapon."[11] Pen and seven other soldiers from the 99th, specifically the 99th's 394th Infantry, Company B, had become prisoners of war.

The group was marched to an empty, snow-covered field where they assumed they would be shot. Instead of being led to their deaths, however, two large doors opened that led to an underground bunker. A German officer, who was alarmingly well informed about life in America and about the 99th specifically, interrogated them. In addition to identifying their company and battalion, the officer correctly identified where they had trained in the United States (Camp Maxey) and where they had been stationed in England before coming to the Ardennes Forest. One of the American soldiers, Clarence "Red" Deal, was from Oklahoma City, and their captor, who had traveled in Oklahoma, asked if Bishop's Restaurant was still a good place to eat.[12]

The Americans were loaded onto trucks to be taken to a nearby prison compound. Because of the snow, the road conditions were poor, and as they made their way to the prison, the truck overturned. Before the soldiers could escape, however, German guards were able to cover them at gunpoint.[13] The next day, the group was taken to the nearby city of Düren.

Prior to the war, Düren had been an enclave for affluent Germans. By the time Pen and the other prisoners arrived, the city would have been unrecognizable to most of its residents. A few weeks earlier, on November 16th, the Allied Air Force had unleashed one of the most concentrated bombings in the European Theater on the town. The bombing destroyed 80% of the city's buildings and knocked out a German division.[14] When the air raids stopped, over 3,000 civilians and soldiers were dead.[15]

On December 11th, the American POWs, along with a British flyer, spent the night in a simple, second-story jail cell. The cell had window openings, but the glass was gone, and all that remained were iron bars. There was no relief from the freezing air blowing unhindered into the cell. The soldiers had been given a single blanket, and they decided to share it among the group. To stay alive, the group laid on the floor in a wagon wheel formation with the blanket draped over their feet and legs.[16]

For most soldiers stationed in the region during the winter of 1944, the weather was among their chief concerns. Even with the soldiers' vigilant efforts to stay warm and to keep their feet dry, there was only so much that could be done when the temperature would drop to -10 F° in the evenings.[17] Amazingly, frostbite caused as many evacuations as war wounds during the campaign

It is not clear when Pen's feet were initially frostbitten, but in captivity, there was little that could be done to help. In an interview given decades later, he said, "I had frostbite on my feet, and it took almost a year after I got back to the states before I recovered. During that year, layer after layer of skin peeled off my feet. That whole year I had a numbness in my feet, and I thought it would be permanent. Some people still have problems with their feet, but I recovered completely."[18]

On December 13th, the prisoners were loaded in boxcars headed to Frankfurt. The boxcars were called "a forty and eight." The term originated in WWI because they were originally designed to hold 40 men or eight horses. The Germans filled each with approximately 100 captives. As they traveled, the POW train was given the lowest priority and was continually being pulled aside to allow other trains to pass.

Due to the delays, the trip of approximately 150 miles, which would normally take a few hours, took days. It was unknown to them at the time, but the reason Pen's train took so long to get to Frankfurt was because of the sheer number of soldiers and equipment being sent by rail to the front lines in preparation for the attack. When they finally arrived in Frankfurt, there was nowhere to go. The POWs remained housed in their boxcars until they were redirected to a new location, 8 days later.

THE BATTLE OF THE BULGE

Recycling a strategy that had proven successful in May 1940, Hitler sought to split the Allied armies in northwest Europe by attacking in the heavily forested Ardennes region. To be successful, the offensive, known as Operation Mist, demanded the element of surprise, overwhelming force, and speed. Later known by the Allies as the Ardennes Offensive or the Battle of the Bulge, the offensive was Hitler's bold, yet desperate, effort to regain the upper hand in the war.

On Saturday morning, December 16th, 2 days before Pen would turn 21, the Germans began their last stand. The Allied soldiers along the Siegfried Line had no warning that they would soon be in the direct path of 200,000 German soldiers and 1,000 tanks. The Battle of the Bulge began at 5:30 a.m. with nearly two hours of shelling along the front lines. Following the deafening barrage, the Germans started their surge forward. Among the first obstacles to Nazi victory were Pen's brothers in arms, the Checkerboard Division, specifically the 394th Infantry. If the Germans could take the area occupied by the 394th, they would have a clear path north. Companies A, B, and C were positioned along the crossroads, but the German onslaught desperately outnumbered them.

Major General Walter Lauer described the scene:

> Down south on the front of the 394th Infantry, the
> 1st Battalion 394th, which sat astride the Losheim-

Bullingen Road, was hit simultaneously by a two-pronged attack of infantry and tanks. The tanks attempted to drive straight down the road. It was a relentless attack, consistently reinforced, which during that day of fighting practically wiped out all of Company B. Time and time again these doughboys fought off the hordes of fanatical S.S. men. These so-called supermen followed behind their Volksgrenadier soldiers whom they drove ahead as so many cattle to slaughter, to force the disclosure of our doughboy positions and machine gun locations before they came on the scene in their super glory! They miscalculated—not only were these first waves of Volksgrenadiers mowed down but so were these supermen. They then became fanatical; they used every trick in the book and many not in the book—all to no avail. When things looked blackest for our side, our staunch defenders would counterattack to drive the enemy back.[19]

According to Rifleman Jerome Nelson, when the battle began, Pen's comrades in Company B felt the full force of the Blitzkrieg. "I was in Company E, and our company was bypassed. But Company B on our right flank, they were hit head-on, and in about 20 minutes of combat, they had eight survivors. The rest were either killed in action, wounded, or taken prisoner. They really, you know, caught the full strength of that onslaught."[20]

In the days following the launch of the offensive, Allied prisoners of war began to arrive from the front lines at the makeshift Stalag in Frankfurt. Once there, they began sharing with one another about what had happened. The 99th had fought bravely, and although they were unlikely aware of the significance of their efforts, their sacrifice had been crucial to slowing the German attack, which would ultimately lead to Allied victory. After a few days in Frankfurt, Pen was on the move again as his train strained toward the city of Limburg.[21]

Pen arrived at Stalag XII A on December 20th. The building to which he was assigned was similar in size to a high school gymnasium and consisted of one large room and a latrine in an adjacent room. He recalled the prison being so crowded there was nowhere to lie down "without being crisscrossed over one another." He said, "There was only one latrine in the corner of the room, and in order to use it, they would have to crawl over the bodies of fellow prisoners." The situation was made worse as the sewer lines to the latrine froze, and their waste would "flow back into the room."[22]

Pen's story is recorded in Robert Humphrey's book, *Once Upon a Time in War: The 99th Division in World War II.*

> Woods and Deal were locked in a large building, so crowded that not all the POWs could recline simultaneously on the concrete floor. Woods, suffering from dysentery, began crawling over his recumbent fellow prisoners toward the latrine at the end of the building, but couldn't move fast enough and soiled his boxer shorts and long underwear. All he could do was remove the underwear and try to wipe the mess off his body and then throw away the fetid clothing. From then on he lived and worked without underwear.[23]

On December 23rd, their camp was targeted by friendly fire. Humphreys recounted,

> During this time, the Americans were bombing during the daytime and the British were bombing at night, hoping to hit an air base neighboring the prison. Somehow, the British misjudged their target the night before Christmas Eve and showered the prison camp with bombs. The windows of Woods' building were blown out, and the building next to his took a direct hit, killing 40 American prisoners.[24]

The soldiers spent Christmas Eve pulling the dead and injured from the rubble. When asked about the experience nearly six decades later, Pen retained the pain of the memory. "'You could imagine what a miserable Christmas it was,' he said. The prisoners tried their best to maintain a Christmas spirit. One decorated a dead branch with a few pieces of paper and cloth to 'represent decorations,' Woods said. Some of the men sang Christmas hymns on Christmas Eve. 'Pretty soon, all over the prison the prisoners were singing 'Silent Night,' Woods added. 'There was no Christmas feast—hardly any food at all. That's the way we celebrated Christmas in 1944.'"[25]

A week after Christmas, Pen was moved again. His new home was Stalag III-A in Luckenwalde. Although he would have to share a narrow mattress and blanket with a bunkmate, he had an actual bed for the first time since his capture. Each morning, prisoners were served coffee that Pen suspected was simply boiled wood. There was food each day, but there was not much to go around. Lunch consisted of a third of kohlrabi, and dinner included a loaf of German bread, which was divided by ten men.[26]

According to Pen,

> The hunger at Luckenwalde was bad. The basic urge in life is food. All other urges disappear except for food. We would sit around all day and talk about food. I didn't enjoy that talk because I was so hungry and did not want to think about food. We had a few paperback books and I read them, trying not to think of food. It was interesting that everyone talked about fancy food, not the basic steak and potatoes, but fancy desserts and exotic dishes. One man kept a notebook and wrote down every type of food the men talked about and said when he returned to the states he was going to try every one of them. Another man added peanut butter to all of his dishes. He would describe how to prepare a dish, then add peanut butter to it. Hunger is not in the stomach. Hunger is all over the body. It is in the blood. You are hungry in your fingertips, your ears, your nose, even in the tips of your toes. You are hungry everywhere.[27]

At this point, four of the original group who had been captured on December 10th were still together. While in Stalag III-A, it was common for lower-ranking prisoners to be selected for labor camps. Prisoners were chosen to work in the field for 12-hour shifts, digging foxholes for German soldiers.[28] Pen said, "The four of us decided that whatever happens to one of us happened to all of us. Anytime they would come in to move anybody anywhere, we'd lock arms. If you get one, we're all going, whatever it is. They got one of us one time, and so the four of us went to a labor camp in Jüterbog, Germany, which is near Berlin."[29]

On April 20th, his opportunity to escape presented itself. Pen shared, "The Russians were shelling the entire Berlin area and had blown up a portion of one of the stockade fences which enclosed us. We took off and spent 5 days on a cross-country trip back to our lines. We bypassed another Russian shelling at Torgow, Germany, before getting back to the American side."[30]

In an article titled, *We Captured a Town*, Pen shared more about the escape from the labor camp. He wrote:

> Avoiding roads and sleeping in barns, we had no difficulty as far as German troops were concerned, because they had virtually all moved to the Eastern Front and Americans were stopped at the Elbe River as a result of the Yalta agreement with Russia.
>
> Reaching the Second Division, we spent the night with one of the Infantry companies. The men in the company were taking it easy because there was no enemy across the river and they had orders not to advance.
>
> The next morning, celebrating our first freedom in months, we roamed the area and found an abandoned German fire engine, which a fellow former prisoner knew how to hot-wire. A dozen of us jumped on the fire engine, ready for a joy ride. One of our group had an M-1, which he had picked up.
>
> Without realizing it, we crossed our own front line and entered a village, which had not yet been occupied.

Immediately, we began hearing German townspeople, who obviously had been waiting for troops to arrive, hollering, "Americans! Americans!" Almost immediately, white flags began to pour out of nearly every building in town.

So on April 26, 1945, 12 former POWs, riding atop a German fire engine, and armed with a single M-1, captured a town.[31]

Unlike many of his generation, Pen was willing to talk about his experiences in World War II. A student of history, he understood that his story was unusual and captivating. In addition, it seemed that he considered telling his story to be a public service. Consequently, he told it often. He wrote about it, participated in numerous interviews about his experiences, and would often speak to groups about it.

On occasion, Pen would come into my office to talk about life. On some of those occasions, we would talk about his experiences in Germany. It was interesting to me to note that when he talked about what he had endured, he would inevitably talk about hunger. After his passing, when I began researching more about his life, I noticed the topic also came up frequently in his interviews and writings.

One day, we were talking about hunger and he said something very similar to what I found in a 2002 article in the *Journal Record*.

The prisoners often talked and dreamt about food, "fancy things their mothers or wives made at home. Food imaginations really ran wild," Woods explained. Woods said hunger was more than just in the stomach. It was "all over the body. The stomach actually shrunk itself, but the blood had tremendous malnutrition," he said. "When you reach this point, it makes no difference how much you eat. You could eat to the point of regurgitation and you'd be just as hungry as when you finished because the blood could not absorb it." Woods said it took six weeks after coming home before he quit being hungry.[32]

If there were any lingering effects of his time as a prisoner of war, I felt it was likely connected to the hunger he experienced during that time. He became more animated when the conversation would drift toward this topic. In addition, he was the only person with whom I have ever worked who would leave open cans of food in the office refrigerator. It may have been more of a generational thing than anything else, but he did not waste food.

When Pen and the fellow prisoners escaped and made their way back to the Allied front lines, there was an understandable desire to eat as much as possible as quickly as possible, but they were warned that giving in to this impulse could prove lethal. To keep the men from eating too much, they were monitored until their bodies were able to adjust and begin absorbing the life-giving nutrients again. I was struck by the idea that it took six weeks after escaping from the work camp before Pen felt full again.

I am not sure why Pen's story about not feeling full for 6 weeks after escaping resonated with me so strongly, but I felt it provided a unique insight into the man. If you have ever been hungry, really hungry, it is not a feeling that is easily ignored. The patience and discipline needed to stay on a prescribed diet while the feeling of hunger persisted is astonishing. Although he was eating the right foods and following sound advice from doctors, there was no relief. During that time, he stayed focused and trusted that he was on the right path. I cannot imagine how it must have felt when the gnawing feeling of hunger finally went away. It must have been like a dream.

There are numerous life lessons from what Pen endured. One of the most important for me was the value of perseverance. Pen learned persistence as a teenager when he worked toward becoming an Eagle Scout. He demonstrated persistence when he was told he would have to go through boot camp a second time, and did not complain. He did not give up when he was trapped in the boxcar for 8 days. He stayed focused when he moderated what he was eating although he was racked by hunger.

Sometimes there is a lag time between doing what you know to be right and seeing the desired results. The lag time can be a matter of minutes or hours. At other times, the lag time can be 6 weeks, 6 months, 6 years, or 60. Pen's secret to success was persistence. He was a lifelong learner, and he found purpose in serving others. When Pen and I began working together, he was already at an advanced age but he refused to slow down or plateau. Some of the members of the team referred to him as "The Energizer Bunny." He amazed us with his work ethic and his involvement in numerous projects.

The office area our team shared had been built in the early 1980s. The carpet had become threadbare, and the color combinations were dated. However, the complex had been constructed well and the offices were spacious and quiet. When we decided to update the offices, we changed out the carpet and painted the walls. To help make the painting process easier, a few of us helped Pen move things away from the walls. As we did, we found stacks and stacks of framed recognitions, plaques, and other mementos celebrating his life. One of the stacks was a couple of feet high, and as I moved it, I was dumbfounded by what I found. Although our little team knew Pen was special, we had no idea how many others felt the same.

The first framed certificate I picked up was Pen's recognition as a Daily Point of Light honoree on September 14, 2006. The next was an honorary doctorate that had been bestowed upon him in 2005. Another recognized him as Oklahoma's representative for the Older Worker of the Year in 2007. It was clear that Pen was someone who had made an impact on many lives, but I was only scratching the surface. His entire office was filled with recognitions that he had kept but not displayed.

When Pen returned to the states following the war, he worked as sports editor for a newspaper for 8 months and then resumed his studies at the University of Arkansas.[33] In 1948, he graduated with a degree in journalism and an ROTC military commission as a second lieutenant. On April 3, 1948, he married Fort Smith native Lois Robin Freeman. The couple moved to Oklahoma City, where Pen began working for Oklahoma Gas & Electric (OG&E) as the editor of their in-house publication. It was also during this time that he joined the

Oklahoma National Guard as the Public Information Officer for the 45th Infantry Division.[34]

The famed 45th Infantry was the first National Guard Division to be called up to serve in Korea, and Pen went to war once more. The youngest member of the division staff, he hosted war correspondents and was responsible for the 45th division's newspaper. The newspaper was "the only newspaper produced and printed entirely on the Korean peninsula."[35] Through his efforts, Oklahomans could hear about their loved ones on a weekly radio program, the "Voices of the 45th." Also, as televisions became increasingly popular, an Oklahoma-based television station sent over a camera, which allowed the 45th to provide a weekly television show. It was a point of pride to Pen that the 45th was the first division to have both a radio and television show.[36]

Pen was passionate about history and preserving it. In 1969, after 21 years at OG&E, he joined the staff of Oklahoma Christian College. Among his goals was interviewing Oklahomans who could tell the story of the young state. Considering Oklahoma was founded in 1907, many of the people he interviewed could provide first-hand knowledge of its history. In time, he would record the voices and memories of nearly 3,000 people.[37]

When he retired from the Oklahoma Army National Guard on December 23, 1983, a plaque, which included pictures of him in 1942 as a private and in 1983 as a colonel was hung in the dining room of the Oklahoma Military Academy. He was also presented with the Oklahoma Distinguished Service Award, the state's highest military honor. Six years earlier, he had completed the 30 allowable years of commissioned service. Instead of stepping aside, he chose to vacate his Colonel's commission and become a Sergeant to be able to continue serving. On his final day of service, he was made a Colonel again upon his retirement.[38]

Colonel Pendleton Woods died at 8:30 a.m. on Monday, December 1, 2014. His wife, Robin, preceded him by a little over a year when she passed on August 5, 2013. Before his passing, Pen had his computer and printer brought to his room at the Veterans' Center.[39] Although he had already either authored or co-authored 16 books, Pen was still attempting to share with others.[40]

Although there are many examples of Pen's service, one that I find most fitting was his commitment to the veterans' hospital in Oklahoma City. Beginning in 1983 and continuing through 2012, he served as a volunteer on Sundays. Every Sunday for nearly 30 years, he would help set-up equipment for chapel service and deliver the newspaper to patients. When his health deteriorated to the point that he had to use a walker to maintain his balance, he did not stop serving. Instead of stopping, he attached a basket to the walker and continued his route.[41]

KARAVAI

When I think of Pen's approach to life, I am reminded of a ceremony that I attended while working in Russia during the summer of 1995. The event, which included a large, round loaf of bread called a Karavai, was called a "Friendship Ceremony." The bread was served on a large platter, and in the middle of the loaf was a small porcelain bowl filled with salt.

Everyone was invited to tear off a piece of the bread and then dip it into the salt. The salt was the key to the ceremony. It was said that to truly be friends, you had to share a kilo of salt together. Considering a kilo is 2.2 pounds, it meant you would have to share many meals together. The message was simple, building a deep and meaningful friendship takes time, but it is an investment worth the effort.

Pen was able to accomplish amazing things because of the clarity of his life goals and his willingness to endure hardships in pursuit of his goals. In 2011, at the age of 87, he was being interviewed about an award that he was receiving. There was a sentence in the interview that stood out to me. He said, "Public service is fun. It's not just work; it's enjoyable."[42]

I loved Pen and did my best to gather together a list of the recognitions and honors bestowed upon him throughout his lifetime. Below is an incomplete list of what I was able to find. With the understanding that Pen considered service to be fun, take a moment to read through the listing. For someone who viewed serving other as the key to fulfillment, Pen had a full and meaningful life.

45th Infantry Division Association—President

45th Infantry Division Museum—Among the Founders of the 45th Infantry Division Museum

45th Infantry Division News—Editor

99th Infantry Division Association Founder—Member

American Advertising Federation—Board Member

American Advertising Federation—Silver Medal Award, 1987

American Association of Industrial Editors—Vice President

American Cancer Society, Oklahoma County Chapter—Director

American Ex-Prisoners of War—State Commander, Outstanding Ex-POW, 2007

American Institute for Public Service—Jefferson Award, 1994

American Legion

American Red Cross, Oklahoma County Chapter—Public Relations Chairman

Boy Scouts of America—Eagle Scout (Awarded at the First National Jamboree in Washington, D.C., 1937)

Boy Scouts of America—Silver Beaver Award

Boy Scouts of America, Last Frontier Council—Lifetime Board Member, Scoutmaster, Explorer Post Leader and other leadership posts.

Campfire Girls Council—Board Member, Vice President

Central Oklahoma Business Communicators—President, Honorary Lifetime Membership

Central Park Neighborhood Association—Co-founder and Board Member

Disabled American Veterans (DAV)—Volunteer

Daughters of the American Revolution—Medal of Honor, 2005

DECA, Oklahoma—Volunteer

Employer Support of the Guard and Reserve (ESGR), Oklahoma—Public Affairs Committee

Executive Service Corps—Consultant

Ex-Prisoners of War in Oklahoma, Commander (Local and State)

Freedoms Foundation at Valley Forge—National Spirit of '76 Award for Patriotic Service

Freedoms Foundation at Valley Forge, Oklahoma City Chapter—Board Member and Vice President

Junior Achievement—Volunteer

Jaycees, Oklahoma Junior Chamber of Commerce—Outstanding Young Man Award in 1953, Received the First Ever Lifetime Membership Award in 1959, International Director

Kappa Sigma Fraternity, University of Arkansas—Commissioner of Chapter Publications, Editor of *The Caduceus* from 1979 to 1985

Keep Oklahoma Beautiful—President

Keep Oklahoma Beautiful—Named their Lifetime Achievement Award the Pendleton Woods Lifetime Achievement Award

KOCO-TV—"Five Who Care" Award, 1994

Korean War Veterans Association

Military Academy at West Point—Oklahoma Liaison Officer

Military Order of the World Wars, Colonel Pendleton Woods Chapter—National Staff, Oklahoma State Commander, Regional Commander and Oklahoma City Commander (The Oklahoma City Chapter of MOWW was named the Colonel Pendleton Woods Chapter in his honor. It was the only chapter in the nation that was named after someone while they were living.)

Military Order World Wars—Silver and Gold Patrick Henry Patriotism Medals

Museum of Unassigned Lands—Chairman

National Association of Area Agencies on Aging—Community Champion Award, 2012

National Cowboy Hall of Fame—Chairman of the Western Heritage Award, Volunteered in the efforts to bring the National Cowboy Hall of Fame to Oklahoma City

National Eagle Scout Association—Chairman, Outstanding Eagle Award

MetLife Foundation—Older Volunteers Enrich America Award
Oklahoma—Older Worker of the Year, 2007
Oklahoma Centennial Celebration, 2007—Volunteer
Oklahoma Centennial Celebration (Semi), 1957—Volunteer
Oklahoma Christian University—The Pendleton Woods Tree Grove
Oklahoma Christian University—Honorary Doctorate, 2005
Oklahoma City Advertising Club—President, Honorary Lifetime Member
Oklahoma City Mental Health Association—Board Member
Oklahoma City Beautiful—Founder
Oklahoma City Bicentennial Commission (1974-1976)—Executive Director
Oklahoma City Clean and Green Coalition
Oklahoma City History Preservation Commission
Oklahoma City Independence Day Parade—Chairman
Oklahoma City Mental Health Clinic—President
Oklahoma City Zoo Amphitheater—Board Member
Oklahoma County Historical Society—Founding Member
Oklahoma County Senior Nutrition Foundation—Board Member, Secretary
Oklahoma Distinguished Service Medal—The State's Highest Military Honor
State of Oklahoma Directional Signage Task Force—Chairman
Oklahoma Epilepsy Association—Founder and President
Oklahoma Genealogical Society
Oklahoma Historians Hall of Fame—2007
Oklahoma Historical Society—Editor of the Oklahoma Historical Society Newsletter, Mistletoe Leaves
Oklahoma Junior Symphony—Board Member, President
Oklahoma Journalism Hall of Fame—2001
Oklahoma Library for the Blind—Volunteer Reader
Oklahoma Lung Association—Public Relations Committee
Oklahoma Military Hall of Fame—2002
Oklahoma National Guard—State Historian
Oklahoma Safety Council

Oklahoma Travel Industries Association

Oklahoma Veterans Council—Chairman

Oklahoma Veterans Medical Research Foundation—Charter Director

Oklahoma Zoological Society—President

Oklahomans for Resource Preservation—Board Member

Points of Light Foundation—Daily Award for September 14, 2006

Senior Nutrition Program—Board Member

Sigma Delta Chi (now the Society for Professional Journalists)

Sons of the American Revolution—Member

State of Oklahoma—Recognized December 18 as Pendleton Woods Day

Tree Bank Foundation—Founding Board Member

Tree Bank Foundation and The Oklahoma Prairies Chapter of OSDAR—Planted a tree and dedicated a plaque in memory of Pen Woods at the 45th Infantry Museum, 2015

University of Arkansas Alumni Association, Oklahoma City Chapter—President

Variety Health Center—Honorary Lifetime Director

Veterans Administration Hospital (Oklahoma City)—Volunteered in excess of 7,000 hours. Set-up equipment and handed out newspapers every Sunday from 1983-2012

Veterans of Foreign Wars

Will Rogers Centennial Commission—Board Member

Words of Jesus Foundation - President

The Edmond Outlook, POW Makes The Great Escape

There is an African proverb that states, "If you want to go fast, go alone. If you want to go far, go together." Pen went far because he understood there are no shortcuts when building a life that matters. A life that matters is built upon meaningful relationships, which take time to build and grow. Pen found his purpose in serving others. Because his actions and values were in alignment, he was constantly learning and being transformed. As a result, he never stopped and never plateaued.

Even at the age of 90, when his life was coming to a close, he was still advancing.

What are your goals?

Who are you serving?

How are you growing?

CHAPTER 6

"CATCHING CATERPILLARS"

Setting Goals

Although significant changes were happening within the Soviet Union throughout the 1980s, there were few who would have predicted the entire system would collapse. When the politburo elected Mikhail Gorbachev as general secretary on Sunday, March 10, 1985, there was a mixed response. Some felt the conservative nature of the U.S.S.R. would not allow change to happen quickly, while others saw his appointment as the opportunity for sweeping reforms.[1] When he was elected at the age of 54, he was the youngest member of the politburo.[2]

As General Secretary Gorbachev took the reins of power, the political and economic systems of the Soviet Union were in crisis. Although the U.S.S.R. was a superpower, their status was based largely on the strength of their military and not on the strength of their overall economy. To preserve the Soviet Union, Gorbachev would need to change it from within, while simultaneously managing the pressures being placed on the system by the West, especially the United States.

Upon his appointment, Gorbachev began to make immediate changes in reshaping the politburo and establishing new expectations. By taking a more hands-on approach to leadership, he sought to provide a clear path forward.[3] In a nationally televised speech given on Friday, May 17, 1985, Gorbachev used a very different approach than his predecessors. Instead of force, he used charm and directness. He acknowledged both the slowed economic development and inadequate living standards throughout the Soviet Union. After stating that the strategies adopted in the past were no longer effective, he launched dual programs intended to provide greater freedom and stimulate economic growth. In the speech, he pledged a new path forward that would correct the mistakes of the past. He said, "We have to travel a long road now but in a short span of time." With this speech, the era of *glasnost* (openness) and *perestroika* (restructuring) had begun.[4]

Among the challenges facing the leader of the Communist Party in the Soviet Union were the efforts of the United States to modernize its military, expand its nuclear arsenal, and explore space-based technologies capable of eliminating the threat of nuclear attack by ballistic missiles. To keep up with a renewed arms race required a stronger economy, and there were numerous reasons why this was unlikely to happen. To retain its position as a global leader, the Soviet Union was in a race against time, and it was losing.

It took an incredible amount of resources and effort to maintain unity among the 15 republics that comprised the U.S.S.R. As the Soviet system shuttered and the fissures began to grow the republics demanded freedom. The first to declare its independence was Estonia on Wednesday, November 16, 1988.

I was in high school when the Berlin Wall fell on Thursday, November 9, 1989, and I was fascinated by its implications. Our family did not get the daily paper, but I stopped off at a gas station and purchased one because I wanted to be able to read what happened. I also wanted to keep it for history. Looking back on it, it may have been the only newspaper I obtained solely for its historic value. I was amazed by the idea that the world could change so dramatically and so quickly.

It was on Wednesday, March 12, 1947, that the Truman Doctrine, which made the Cold War official, was enacted. Consequently, the Cold War had been a constant throughout both my parents' and my lifetime. None of us had ever lived in a time when the Soviet Union was not considered a threat to democracy. I was relieved by the idea that the Cold War was seemingly coming to a close.

As the existence of the Soviet Union hung in the balance, I was sitting in the Benson Auditorium on the campus of Harding University. It was the fall semester of 1991, and Harding's President Dr.

David Burks was making announcements to the student body about campus events that week. He then highlighted a few international opportunities that were being planned for the summer of 1992. He said, "There is an opportunity for students to go to Russia this summer to teach English." He continued, "There is someone sitting here this morning who needs to go to Russia, and if you would like to go, I would encourage you to go to the informational meeting."

I am not sure why, but I thought, *He is talking to me.* I had never met anyone from Russia, and I could not speak or read Russian. Based on the challenges I had in the past with English grammar, I was not sure if I was even qualified. Nonetheless, I went back to my dorm room, called my parents, told them what happened, and said, "I think I am supposed to go to Russia." In retrospect, they handled it much better than I think I would have if one of my children called me to share they felt they were supposed to travel 6,000 miles to spend a month teaching English in a country that had been our official enemy for the past 44 years.

On December 26, 1991, not long after signing up for the trip, the Soviet Union was formally dissolved. The day before the dissolution, on Christmas day, Gorbachev resigned, and Boris Yeltsin was named the president of Russia. When I heard the news about the changes happening, it did not dawn on me that perhaps this was not the best time to be planning a trip there.

Our group would be teaching in the city of Rostov-on-Don. As the name suggests, Rostov is a port city built on the Don River, about 600 miles southeast from Moscow. A city of over one million inhabitants, it is at the northern tip of the Black Sea. At the time, there had been travel advisories issued warning against travel to Russia in general and Rostov-on-Don specifically. In addition to the relative political instability, there were concerns about the growing role of organized crime in the area. When I connected with the other people going on the trip, who were much more experienced travelers than I, they did not seem too concerned about the warnings, and I followed their lead.

I had not been in Russia long when I began to question the wisdom of my decision to travel there as an 18-year-old. One afternoon, I was walking back to the hotel from the school where we taught. Normally, we walked in groups, but on this day I was alone. As I neared the hotel, three men in their early 30s stepped toward me. Based on the fact that they were all wearing black leather coats on a warm day, I assumed they were a part of the Russian mafia. In an instant, I was surrounded. They motioned for me to go into the nightclub, which was next to the hotel. I knew I was in trouble, but I did not feel I had many options. I scanned the sidewalk for anyone who might be from our group and did not see anyone I recognized. I walked through the front door; the restaurant was dimly lit and empty. It is surprising what goes through someone's mind in a moment like this. My actual thought was, "I cannot believe I am going to die like this. My mother won't even know what happened to me."

They took me to a corner booth, and I sat down with one of my new "friends" on either side. Although we could not communicate in Russian, it was clear we were waiting on someone else to arrive. I tried to act relaxed and not show fear. A few minutes after sitting down, someone walked out from the kitchen with strawberries in a bowl, a small steak, and some potatoes. They placed the food in front of me and motioned for me to eat. It was the first time since we had been in Russia that I had seen a steak.

It was clear that food had been given as an act of hospitality. I had not been robbed or harmed, but I could not make any sense of the situation. Although I was not hungry nor in the mood to eat, I felt it was expected. They motioned for me to eat. When given a fork and knife, I took it as a sign that they did not mean me harm. I picked up the utensils and forced myself to eat.

It was 20 to 30 minutes later that the front door opened again and a young man entered. He was not dressed in the style of the other men. Although he was young, when he arrived, the other men, who were at least ten years older than him, seemed to relax. He smiled when he got to the table and introduced himself in English. He explained that he had been learning English, but had no one with whom he could converse. We talked for a few minutes, and I learned that his father was a local judge and that although our team of teachers was small, everyone in the city knew a group of Americans was there teaching English. Over the next few weeks, we would meet a few times to converse and would end up becoming friends.

One of the great benefits of travel, especially international travel, is the realization that people, regardless of their country of origin, tend to have similar needs and goals. Although there were exceptions, I felt the typical Russian was doing the best they could, in a tough situation, to make life as good for themselves and their families as possible. I felt a kindred spirit with my Russian friends.

When the program ended, even while on the return flight, I knew that I wanted to go back. It was the first time I had been in a teaching role, and I felt it was a good fit. The conditions were not too bad, and although I had lost about 15 pounds while there, due to drinking some bad water, I could avoid this in the future by using a water filter. When I got back to campus, I began researching options to return.

The next summer, in 1993, instead of going back to Rostov, I connected with a group that was seeking English teachers in the town of Dubna, which is about 80 miles north of Moscow. Dubna is a small city that is divided in half by the Volga River. Surrounded by woods, the site where the city stands today was chosen as the location of a proton accelerator to be built for nuclear research. Following three years of construction, the accelerator was commissioned on December 13, 1949. The town of Dubna was officially recognized along with the Joint Institute for Nuclear Research (JINR) in 1956. Designated a "City of Science," Dubna could not be found on most maps until after the fall of the Soviet Union.

Today, the city has slightly less than 70,000 inhabitants, and due to its relationship with JINR, it holds a place of honor within the scientific community. It is estimated that JINR employs approximately 4,500 scientists, engineers, and technicians from throughout the world. Of this remarkable group, over 1,300 hold their terminal degrees. The city of Dubna also has the distinction of having an element named in its honor. The element, Dubnium (Db) is a synthetic chemical with the atomic number 105.

Our typical Russian students included people who had a relatively good grasp of the language but wanted to enhance their conversational capacity. The age of the students ranged from older teenagers to senior citizens. On occasion, we would work with younger students, if they were unusually advanced. One of those advanced students was barely a teenager and was one of two people I have ever known who had a photographic memory. In addition to being younger than most of our students, he was small for his age and seemed to have trouble with one of his legs.

When working with people in a one-on-one setting, deep friendships often emerge. During the first few sessions, we would try to get to know the students by asking questions about their interests and hobbies. When this young student was asked, "What do you like to do for fun?" he responded that he liked butterflies and collected them. When asked about which kind he liked most, he demonstrated an amazing grasp on the topic and began listing the different types he found most interesting. His passion for his hobby was contagious, and he lit up talking about the beauty of the butterflies. He said, "They can be found in the forest. But they are too fast, and I am too slow to catch them." He smiled to himself as if he had a secret and said, "Because the butterflies are too fast for me to catch, I catch caterpillars...and then I wait."

I do not have a background in entomology. Consequently, I am not sure if catching caterpillars is the normal way of growing a butterfly collection, but his explanation moved me. The patience required was compelling, and his level of commitment was unexpected from such a young person. As I thought about it more, I found what he said to be profound. There are times in life to chase butterflies, and then there are times to catch caterpillars.

The reason the student *had* a butterfly collection versus *wishing* he had a butterfly collection was due to his willingness to innovate. He knew what he wanted, but also knew that he could not realize his goal without a different way of thinking. He was honest about his situation; he did not have the ability to catch butterflies. If he followed the obvious path, he would have used a large net designed specifically for the task, but he knew this approach would not work for his situation. He could have hired someone who was faster to catch the butterflies on his behalf, but money was tight. This option was not viable. Instead of giving up, he learned to innovate. This discovery, that new paths can be created, is both a life-changing and a life-giving discovery.

In the world of psychology, this concept is known as locus of control. Someone with an external locus of control often feels they are along for the ride but cannot change the course of their lives. If they are in a bad situation, this is due to external factors that are beyond their control. Someone with an internal locus of control feels they are captain of their ship. When they see a storm forming, they will chart a new course. They believe their actions can change the situation and will respond accordingly.

If he accepted his situation as hopeless (external locus of control), he would have concluded, "I cannot catch butterflies." If he did not accept his situation, he would begin looking for options that would allow him to realize his goal (internal locus of control). The first step in the process of claiming control of one's life is often found in establishing goals. He knew his goal—a butterfly collection—but because he was flexible about how to reach his goals, he was not trapped. In the end, he could reach his goal, but it would take perseverance and patience.

REFRAMING

When we choose to change our perspective about a situation, in which the facts remain the same, we are choosing to reframe the situation. When used positively, cognitive reframing offers a way to purposefully assign new meaning to an experience in order to consider it from a more beneficial viewpoint. The ability to consider alternate interpretations of a situation, in turn, can provide a deeper understanding.

A foundational academic description of the concept of reframing comes from the 1974 book, *Change: Principles of Problem Formation and Problem Resolution* in which the authors, Watzlawick, Weakland and Fisch provide the following, "To reframe, then, means to change the conceptual and/or emotional setting or viewpoint in relation to which a situation is experienced and to place it in another frame which fits the 'facts' of the same concrete situation equally well or even better, and thereby changing its entire meaning."

The ability to reframe is also helpful when placed in a situation that is beyond one's ability to control. For example, one summer, our family took a road trip of epic proportions. We loaded up the car in the heat of the Oklahoma summer and headed west with the goal of seeing the Pacific Ocean. In total, the trip would take us over 5,000 miles through several states in the Northwest. Our primary destination was a beach house located in the tiny town of Copalis Beach, Washington. We had chosen the location, 2,050 miles from our home, without knowing much about the area, but it was affordable and was not too far from Olympic National Park. We were looking forward to having a few days exploring the beach and the natural beauty of the region.

As we neared the house, our level of anticipation grew. The area is awe-inspiring with massive trees around every bend. The final mile or two of the trip was along a gravel and dirt road with a maximum speed limit of 15 miles per hour. We made the final turn, pulled into the driveway, and stopped. Before getting out, I scanned the property and noticed two things immediately.

The first was the condition of the rental home. When choosing a house using a website, one hopes that the actual home looks something like the photographs online. To our surprise, the photographs did not do the house justice. It looked better in real life.

The second thing that caught my eye was the active construction site next to our rental home. Less than 15 feet from the front door, which was located on the side of the home, a new house was being constructed. It looked as if the crew had just completed the first exterior wall, and based upon the amount of lumber that was sitting in the yard, they would be framing for the next week or two. I looked at my wife and said, "You've got to be kidding me."

On Monday morning about 9:00 a.m., a small construction crew arrived and began their work. To their credit, they were very good at what they did and worked steadily for the next 12 hours. We had hoped to be able to sit out on the deck of the house with a view of the beach, but with the music blaring from their boom box and the sound of hammers swinging, it was counterproductive. When we went inside the house, we had to turn the television up loud enough to drown out the sounds of construction. Although we consider ourselves low maintenance, by the end of the day, I was frustrated.

That afternoon, I looked through the contract to see if we had any options. I found "construction" had been listed under the "Acts of God" section. The paragraph stated there was no refund available. What bothered me was that we could have chosen another home if we had known there was construction. When we moved our things into the house, I noticed a Ring™ Video Doorbell on the front door. This meant there was a motion-activated video camera aimed directly at the construction site. Consequently, the owners had likely known, before we arrived, that the construction had begun. Although it was not their fault that someone was building next to them, I felt the fact that it was happening had been purposefully concealed.

I decided to write an email to the homeowner to express my frustration at driving such a long distance to stay somewhere peaceful, only to have the peace disrupted by construction they likely knew was underway. If we had been notified prior to arrival, we would have been able to make a better choice about whether their home was the best fit for our family. I was not expecting them to do anything, but I wanted them to consider the perspective of those who would be staying there for the remainder of the summer.

A few hours after sending my email, I got a response. The homeowners expressed how sorry they were about the construction. They shared they knew the foundation had been poured, but after it had been poured, there had not been any activity. They then stated, "If you can find another place to stay, we would be willing to provide a complete refund. If you choose to stay, we would like to offer 50% off of what you have paid."

I was surprised by their offer. It had not been requested or expected, but I was grateful for it. After getting their email, we looked for options that would work for our family, and the family dog, but there was nothing available. I let them know we appreciated and accepted their offer of a 50% refund.

From that point forward, I decided to hear the hammer differently. I chose to give the sound of the hammers new meaning. Every time I heard the hammer strike its target, I imagined I was earning a quarter. Four hammer strikes was a dollar bill. By reframing the situation, what had once been a source of irritation had been given new meaning.

There are times in life when we are confronted by situations that we cannot change. Although we cannot change what is happening, we can change our perspective about what is happening. By reframing the situation, we force ourselves to consider alternative ways of processing our situation, which allows us to refocus and regain an internal locus of control. Instead of being a victim of our circumstances, we are able to add meaning to it.

DAVID NATANOVICH BELL

One of the people I met while working in Dubna was David Natanovich Bell. Over the course of three summers (1993-1995), I would have the opportunity to spend time with him in a handful of contexts. Although he was already 52 years old when I was born, he was the kind of person who could seemingly connect with anyone, regardless of age. Thin and a little taller than average, he was highly expressive and direct when he spoke.

During those three summers, we shared meals together, and it was an honor to have been a guest in his apartment. In many ways, he embodied Dubna for American guests. For most, he was the first person they would meet when they arrived in town. Also, he liked to take the visiting groups on a tour of the city to help them acclimate. Although he would give the same tour dozens, if not hundreds of times, it never felt routine. It was while on this tour that he and I bonded over the fact that his name was David and his father's name was Nathan (David Natanovich), and my name is Nathan and my father's name is David (Nathan Davidovich).

He was born on Saturday, May 14, 1921, in Houston, Texas, to Nathan and Anna Belkovsky. The Belkovsky family fled to the United States in 1910 following the death of David's grandfather in anti-Jewish violence near Kiev. To make the transition to their new home easier, they abbreviated their last name to Bell. During the time the family lived in Houston, Nathan and Anna had three children (Bertha, Leon, and David),[5] bought a modest house, and joined the American middle class.

David was 10 years old in May of 1931 when his father returned to Russia to help guide a tour. While back in the motherland, an old friend who was an official in the agriculture ministry convinced him to stay. In December, the Bell family left the uncertainty of the Great Depression and the mild weather of Houston to join Nathan in the midst of the Russian winter.[6]

The Bell's moved from their single-family home into a large house in Moscow that had been converted into small apartments. Their new home had two rooms for the five to share. It was a harbinger of what was to come when one of their neighbors, a communist bureaucrat, asked Nathan to give him one of his family's two rooms. According to David, "Daddy refused." The bureaucrat responded, "We'll see."[7]

It was on a Monday morning, March 14, 1938, that Nathan was arrested by Stalin's police while sitting at his kitchen table. Accused of spying, an accusation he denied, he was sent to the Kazakhstan desert, and the family was turned out on the street. In the freezing cold of Moscow in March, Anna and her children slept in a park. David, who was now a teenager, would eventually find a place to live in a dormitory at his school. Anna, devastated and destitute, became a caregiver for the elderly in exchange for a bed.

Anna remained in Moscow until 1940, when she was able to join her husband in Kazakhstan. Nathan would live only another three years. David described his father's 1943 death in a 2003 *New York Times* article. He said, "The diagnosis was heart failure. But he had no job, no income. There was hunger, absolute weakness. The word I use is that life just seeped out of him."[8]

When Russia entered World War II—or the Great Patriotic War as they called it—in June of 1941, David was not immediately called up to serve in the Soviet military. At the time, he was a student in Moscow at the D.I. Mendeleev Chemical-Technological Institute. He and his classmates were tasked with logistical support and night shift patrols on the roof of their school, but he was not called up until April 1943. After completing an accelerated officer training, he earned the rank of junior lieutenant and fought on the 3rd Belorussian Front, which was formed in April of 1944.[9] The losses among his comrades were heavy. In combat for 381 days, there were 166,838 Russians killed, 9,292 missing, and 667,297 wounded, ill, or frostbitten.[10] In addition to serving as Commander of the Sappers, David was also tasked with the extremely dangerous job of removing rusted landmines. His most serious brush with death was when he stepped on a mine in a field that was so thick with explosives that if he had fallen, it would have tripped two or three more. Fortunately, he stepped on the smallest type of mine and when he did so, he had placed his full weight on the heel of his boot. The subsequent explosion launched him straight into the air, and when he landed, he was in the exact same spot. If he had landed in any other way, it would have cost him his life. He was injured three times during the war, but considering the plight of so many of his friends, he considered himself lucky to have survived.[11]

I can only remember talking with David about his time in the military on one occasion. Although we worked in Dubna, we would take occasional excursions to Moscow to see the sights, and when possible, David joined us. On this afternoon, we were walking through Red Square, and our little team was excited to be in such a recognizable and historic location. It felt surreal to be walking in the shadow of the Kremlin and Lenin's tomb.

It was a pleasant and warm day, and our team was relaxed and having fun. At one point, someone said something funny and everyone laughed. Sensing that our mood was making David uncomfortable, I asked him if he was ok. At that time, we knew very little about his story. In the conversation that ensued, he said, "I think it is hard for Americans to understand what it is like to live in fear." As an example, he shared, "During the war, there were informants in every unit. You were required to report anything that anyone said that might be in opposition to the government. To make sure they were getting the truth, the government would plant people in the unit to say things just to make sure they were reported. If you did not report what was said, it could cost you your life. As a result, you learned not tell anyone what you really thought. It was too risky. You never knew who might be an informant." Although that conversation years ago, I can still see David's face as he told me his story. He was nervous and changed his tone when he spoke. At the time, it did not dawn on me that these stories and insights had been suppressed for decades.

In exchange for his education, he was required to teach others for three years in a location chosen by the government. In 1950, David was informed that he would soon be sent to Siberia to teach English. It was during this time that his first wife, fearful of the life she and their daughter would have in such a desolate place, took their daughter and left. Following his three years, he returned to a town near Moscow to continue his career as a teacher. It was during this time that he met and married his second wife, Katya. In 1961, he moved to Dubna to teach English. He taught for 20 years and then retired.[12]

In 1986, David received a "peace lantern," which included autobiographies from students who lived in La Crosse, Wisconsin. The lantern had come to him because the content, which included contact information, was written in English. The embellished paper lanterns were the brainchild of Dr. James and Mrs. Peggy Baumgartner. The La Crosse couple launched the Peace Lantern Project in the hope that the concept would create opportunities for peaceful dialogue.[13]

Based on his life experiences, David was deeply interested in any effort that would inspire and promote peace. Although he had wanted to travel back to the United States to see family throughout his lifetime, it was not until Gorbachev had relaxed travel restrictions that he was able to do so. In 1987, while on his trip, he went through La Crosse and met with Dr. Baumgartner. Based on the bond between the two, they decided that a formal friendship should be established between the cities of Dubna and La Crosse. Both men leveraged their influence to promote friendship and peace. In August of 1990, 20 delegates from La Crosse traveled to Dubna to sign an official sister city agreement.

Through this relationship, a steady stream of students, business leaders, artists, health care professionals, and politicians from Russia headed to La Crosse and vice versa. Meaningful and genuine friendships emerged, cultural understanding grew, and the quality of life was enhanced in both communities. When the Soviet Union collapsed and cities like Dubna, which were heavily dependent upon the government for support, were in need, their friends from the United States provided medicine and medical supplies.

Along the peaceful banks of the Volga River, on the outskirts of Dubna, there is an impressive and large rotunda built for outdoor events. In warmer months, it is an inviting location to sit and talk. It is among a handful of landmarks that are synonymous with the town. On Thursday, July 12th, 2007 a group of over 200 Americans and Russians gathered together at the Riverside Park in La Crosse, Wisconsin, where the Mississippi, Black and La Crosse Rivers converge. The group was there to dedicate the new Russian Gardens that had recently been completed. In addition, the citizens of La Crosse had built a much smaller, but no less inviting, version of Dubna's rotunda. The crowning jewel of the gardens was meant to be a physical reminder of the importance of the relationships between the two cities. It was during this event, that the dignitaries from both cities, dedicated the rotunda in the memory of the person who had served as the bridge between the two cities, David Natanovich Bell.

Later in life when David had been asked if he was bitter about the tragedies in his life, he replied honestly. He said, "I've been bitter all my life, especially when my father was arrested. I felt very sorry for him. He was a very honest man, a very conscientious man." But in Dubna, he said, "There's something I have done which I'm proud of."[14]

Due to reasons beyond his control, David, as a fourth grader, was uprooted from his home and school in Houston and placed in the heart of Moscow. Because of the ideologies of his government, his father and grandfather's lives were cut short, and his wife left him, taking his daughter too. It was not until he was in retirement that his greatest opportunity to make a difference would emerge. Fighting through fear and self-doubt, he found his voice. He could not change the past, but he could reframe his perspective on it. His bitterness regarding the loss of his father would remain, but he chose to use his pain as a catalyst for peace.

When I was in Russia, they used glass bottles for their drinks. Much like it had been in the United States in the past, the glass bottles could be exchanged or redeemed for money. David's choice to reframe his situation created a path to redeem or exchange the pain he had endured for the sake of peace. The pain he had endured throughout life could not be erased or removed, but it could be a catalyst for good.

What area of your life needs to be reconsidered from a new perspective?

If you cannot change the situation, how can you reframe your perspective about the situation?

The past cannot be erased, but it can be redeemed. However, it requires a choice to do so. Your entire life can be changed with a single decision. What kind of life would you like to have?

CHAPTER 7

"THE AWAKENING OF A GIANT"

The Voice of Movement

Mahalia Jackson was born on Thursday, October 26, 1911, to John Jackson Sr. and Charity Clark in the heart of New Orleans, Louisiana.[1] The "Big Easy," which is also known as the "Cradle of Jazz," has been the birthplace of numerous American musical icons, including: Louis "Satchmo" Armstrong[2], Al Hirt[3], Fats Domino[4], Sydney Bechet[5], and Wynton Marsalis[6]. Even among this list of musical royalty, Mahalia Jackson, who would become known as the "Queen of Gospel," stands alone.

The Jackson's three-bedroom, shotgun-style home was located in the Carrollton historic district, known as "The Black Pearl."[7] Thirteen people, including young Mahalia and her 5 siblings, shared the small house.[8, 9] Her father, John, was a hardworking man who was described as, "a longshoreman by day, a barber by night, and a clergyman on Sunday."[10] Her mother, Charity, worked as a maid and laundress, and when she died at the age of 25, Mahalia was sent to live with her namesake, Mahalia Clark-Paul, who went by Aunt Duke.[11]

It was at the tender age of 4 that Mahalia began singing at the Plymouth Rock Baptist Church on Hillary Street. In time, she would also sing in the Junior Choir at Mount Moriah Missionary Baptist Church on Millaudon Street. During these formative years, singing in the choir became a significant part of her life. It was said that by the age of 12, she "sang on Wednesday, Friday, and four times on Sunday."[12]

To help provide for her family, she left school in the eighth grade and began working as a cook and dishwasher. During that time, another influential figure, Aunt Bell, made a prediction about her niece's future. She said, "Halie, don't you worry. You going be famous in this world and walk with kings and queens." It was an awakening moment that challenged Mahalia's view of herself. She responded, "You think so, Aunt Bell?" She said, "That's right, baby. I seen it." Over time, Mahalia would ask her aunt again and again about her vision, and Aunt Bell's reply remained constant, "I seen it."[13]

At the age of 16, in the hope of finding better opportunities, Mahalia traveled north with an aunt to Chicago to live with an uncle and study nursing. It would not take long for her powerful voice to be recognized, and she was invited to join the Greater Salem Baptist Church Choir as a soloist. Soon thereafter, she was asked to tour with the famed Johnson Gospel Singers, who were among the first professional gospel groups. Traveling with them, she sang and performed in plays held in churches throughout the area.[14] While pursuing her career as a recording artist, she worked numerous jobs to make ends meet. Over the next several years, she worked as a nursemaid, packed dates in a factory, cleaned floors,[15] and was a laundress, and beautician.[16] Later, when she had become financially successful, she invested in real estate and opened both a beauty shop and florist shop in Chicago.[17]

In 1929, she met composer Thomas Dorsey. Dorsey, who is regarded as the "Father of Gospel Music," helped guide her life and career. The two toured together for over a decade. During that time, she was building the foundation for a fan base that would grow dramatically in future years. It was also during this time that she made a personal commitment to a life of purity—free of secular entertainment. In addition, she determined to only use her voice for spiritual songs.[18]

She signed her first recording contract in 1936 with Decca Records. As she transitioned to becoming a professional artist, she also changed the spelling of her name. Prior to this time, she spelled her name Mahala. She added an "i" to become Mahalia.

Her first record was only moderately successful. Sensing she would have more success by singing the blues, which had more popular appeal, the executives at Decca demanded she change her genre to stay under contract with them. She refused and stuck with her decision only to sing gospel. Her decision cost her the contract with Decca.[19]

She was married twice, but both unions ended in divorce. The first was in 1936 to Isaac Hockenhull, who sided with Decca and applied constant pressure for Mahalia to sing secular music. Addicted to gambling, it was thought his motivation for guiding Mahalia's career was to help fund his betting on racehorses.[20] Her first marriage ended in 1941. Her second marriage was to Minters Sigmund Galloway in 1964. The marriage ended in 1967, although there was speculation they were planning to reunite prior to her death in 1972.[21]

For the next 11 years, Mahalia honed her craft and became increasingly popular among the African American community and within churches. In 1947, she recorded, "Move On Up a Little Higher," which was released in 1948. With over two million copies sold, the song became the best-selling gospel song of all time.[22]

In what appeared to be an overnight success, she had been discovered. Audiences clamored for the opportunity to see and hear her perform. In 1950, she was invited to Carnegie Hall as the headliner for the First Negro Gospel Music Festival, a watershed moment in the history of gospel music.[23]

In 1952, she won a prize from the French Academy for her recording of "I Can Put My Trust in Jesus," which led to a tour of Europe. Her performance of the Christmas classic "Silent Night," was a hit in Norway, where it became one of the best-selling records of all time.[24] In 1961, Ms. Jackson was honored as the first gospel singer to win a Grammy. In that same year, she sang at the inaugural ball for President John F. Kennedy.

TELL THEM ABOUT THE DREAM

As the Civil Rights movement began to take shape, she was called upon to use her growing influence to help support the movement. In 1956, Civil Rights leader, Ralph Abernathy invited Jackson to travel to Montgomery, Alabama to sing at the first anniversary of Rosa Parks' act of defiance against institutional racism. She traveled by train to the epicenter of the conflict. In the midst of Klansmen, escalating violence, and hecklers, she arrived at the train station. Waiting for her was Abernathy and a young preacher named Martin Luther King Jr. His sermons inspired her, and the two became friends.[25]

The friendship between Dr. King and Mahalia was based upon mutual respect. They were both guided by their faith and found their voices in African American churches. In addition, they considered themselves to be messengers of a message given to humanity by God himself. They were not the authors of the message; they were the vessels through which it would be communicated. Although the way they shared the message was different, their motivation to do so appeared to be the same. They both sought to use their voices as a form of worship and devotion. According to Craig Werner, "King gave the movement a vision; Mahalia Jackson gave it a voice."[26]

Clarence Jones, a lawyer and trusted advisor to Dr. King, commented on the depth of their connection. Jones said: "When he was down—or the classic word that's thrown around today, that word 'depressed'—he would ask his secretary Dora McDonald, he would say, 'Dora, get Mahalia on the phone,'" Jones said. "And he would say, 'Mahalia, I'm having a rough day. Sing for me.' and Mahalia would sing to him in the phone. He would say, 'Sing, "Jesus Met the Woman at the Well," or "The Old Rugged Cross,"' or other favorites. He would listen to her voice through the phone, and sometimes tears would come down his face."[27]

In 1863, Abraham Lincoln had signed the Emancipation Proclamation, which ended the institution of slavery. One hundred years later, Mahalia, the granddaughter of a slave, was in Washington, D.C. at the request of Dr. King.[28] There was to be a March on Washington for Jobs and Freedom on August 28, and he wanted her there. It was one of the critical moments of the Civil Rights movement, and the world was watching.

The program for the event had several notable speakers, which led up to a speech to be given by King. With the 170-ton marble statue of Abraham Lincoln to her back, she stood in front of a sea of people and sang two spirituals, "I've Been 'Buked and I've Been Scorned" and

"How I Got Over." Rabbi Joachim Prinz spoke of life as a rabbi in Berlin under the rule of Hitler, and then King took the podium.[29]

Even at the age of 34 years old, King was considered a remarkable communicator. The speech had been thoughtfully crafted, and the message was scripted and clear. In an effort to navigate the complexity of the situation, however, it lacked the directness that those who had heard Dr. King in the past had come to expect. According to Clarence Jones, who had helped write the speech, that was when Mahalia changed the course of history.

> He was reading, and she just shouted to him, "Tell them about the dream, Martin. Tell them about the dream." I was standing about 50 feet behind him, to the right and the rear, and I watched him—this is all happening in real time—take the text of his speech and move it to the left side of the lectern, grab the lectern and look out.
>
> One of the world's greatest gospel singers shouting out to one of the world's greatest Baptist preachers. She may have ignored the fact that there were almost 300,000 other people there, and she just shouted out to Martin, "Tell them about the dream." Anybody else who would yell at him, he probably would've ignored it. He didn't ignore Mahalia Jackson.
>
> I said to somebody standing next to me, "These people don't know it, but they're about to go to church."[30]

As early as November 27, 1962, Dr. King had used the phrase, "I have a dream" in a speech given to an audience of 2,000 packed into a gymnasium at the Booker T. Washington High School, a segregated school, in Rocky Mount, North Carolina.[31] He picked up the theme again at the Freedom Rally in Detroit on June 23, 1963. This event was held to set the stage for the march in Washington, D.C. just a few months later. Ms. Jackson was at that event in Detroit and heard Dr. King speak about his dream.

It is worth noting that the Freedom Rally in Detroit nearly did not happen. The concept was due to the vision of Reverend C. L. Franklin, the father of the iconic singer Aretha Franklin, but he was struggling to gain momentum. He had shared the idea with other leaders in the community, but they were not convinced it was a good idea. When Dr. King made it clear to the leaders that he was in favor of the idea, the argument ended and the group unified. Reverend Franklin, according to his daughter, knew who needed to be involved in making the event a success. She said, "It started with Mahalia Jackson, who was a great friend of my dad's." She continued, "Harry Belafonte called Mahalia, and she called my dad." At the time, the rally in Detroit was likely the largest civil-rights demonstration in the history of the United States, until the rally in D.C. later that same year.[32]

Then, on that clear August day in Washington, D.C., Dr. King was giving a speech that was strong, but Mahalia knew he was capable of more. When she called out to him, he knew her voice, and he knew her heart. In the video recording of the event, he does not acknowledge her. He does not look her way, but he clearly heard her. Take the time to watch the recording, and you can see the moment. The first 12 minutes of the speech is the portion that was prepared and read by Dr. King. The final 5 minutes is his response to Mahalia's request to "tell them about the dream." After hearing her call out, he finished a few more sentences and was likely processing what to do. He then made his decision. He said, "And so even though we face the difficulties of today and tomorrow...," and then he stopped mid-sentence. He scanned the audience and made a choice to go off script. He resumed his speech with the words, "I still have a dream. It is a dream deeply rooted in the American dream."[33]

A meaningful speech given by a capable communicator became a timeless speech for the ages. The enduring greatness of the speech was due in large part to two people dedicated to a common purpose who were willing to push one another toward their greatest potential. This way of living, the choice to see the best in others, is not only the basis for great friendships but also the foundation for a meaningful life.

Upon her death on January 27, 1972, over 50,000 people passed by her casket. Harry Belafonte stated that Ms. Jackson was "the single most powerful black woman in the United States." He added that she was the "the womanpower for the grassroots" and there was not "a single field hand, a single black worker, a single black intellectual who did not respond to her civil rights message."[34]

There are times in life when you will be called upon to be the person who stands behind the podium and give your "I Have A Dream" speech. There will be times when you will be called upon to prompt someone else as they contemplate their path forward. From an early age, Mahalia knew her purpose, and she had pursued it for decades. She would often say, "Gospel songs are the songs of hope. When you sing gospel, you have the feeling there is a cure for what's wrong."[35] She sang to heal the soul, and she used her influence to help others who were dedicated to bringing healing as well.

ACTIVATION

Mahalia believed she was destined to do great things because of the encouragement she received from her family. When her Aunt Bell told her that she would be famous and "walk with kings and queens," it changed her. She trusted her aunt and believed that what she said could come true. She had been activated.

On August 28, 1963, Mahalia Jackson awakened a giant. In so doing, Dr. King gave voice to a movement. Because of Mahalia's insight and courage, the world would be changed forever. The following is an excerpt from a sermon delivered by Dr. King in 1968. The sermon was titled "The Drum Major Instinct." It is a remarkable example of a leader seeking to awaken the sleeping giants who were sitting in the church pews that evening. The people listening to him that night had believed they were powerless to change the world and that they lacked the ability to be great. Dr. King rejected this belief and offered a transformative alternative.

Everybody can be great because everybody can serve. You don't have to have a college degree to serve. You don't have to make your subject and your verb agree to serve. You don't have to know about Plato and Aristotle to serve. You don't have to know Einstein's 'Theory of Relativity' to serve. You don't have to know the Second Theory of Thermal Dynamics in Physics to serve. You only need a heart full of grace, a soul generated by love.[36]

The moment when Mahalia called out to Dr. King to tell the audience about the dream is a pivotal moment in history. It is also an example of how a single sentence, uttered by the right person at the right time, can redirect someone's entire life. Mahalia's mental model had been shaped by a sentence from her Aunt Bell who had believed her niece would walk with royalty. Dr. King's life was changed when Mahalia, who knew him and knew his capabilities, used her voice to encourage him to give voice to a movement. It is worth noting that she did not challenge Dr. King to tell the audience about *his* dream. She told him to tell the audience about *the* dream. She reminded him that he was the messenger, but the message was not his own. He heard her voice and when he looked out over the sea of people who were looking to him, he was transformed. He was not simply an orator, or a civil rights leader; he was a prophet of God proclaiming freedom. In one sentence, Mahalia had helped awaken a giant and the world would never be the same.

Who are you serving?

Who are you helping activate?

PART THREE

A NEW MINDSET

CHAPTER 8

"2M2N"

Freedom in Mile 2

If you appreciate good customer service, you are probably familiar with the Atlanta-based restaurant chain Chick-fil-A. According to research conducted by *QSR (Quick Service Restaurant) Magazine*, they are the friendliest drive-through of any chain in the United States.[1] In all honesty, I did not know much about them when I had the opportunity to meet the founder of the company, Mr. Truett Cathy, in 2008. Before that meeting, I would eat at Chick-fil-A on occasion and was impressed with their community involvement, but I did not know much of the backstory that had shaped their founder and his company.

It is worth noting that the reason I got to know Mr. Cathy was because of his generosity. At the time, I was working on a project designed to help develop future leaders. As is the case with virtually all non-profits, it can be difficult to find consistent funding. Consequently, when we received an unsolicited check from Chick-fil-A for $10,000, we were both surprised and extremely thankful. We connected with their corporate office to learn more about how they found out about the program and to express our appreciation.

Around the same time, we were planning to revive an awards event that had been launched a generation earlier. The original program had honored Oklahoma native Sam Walton. Based on the connection with Mr. Cathy, we invited him to receive the same honor. In addition, we asked if he would speak to a group of community leaders the next day. Amazingly, he accepted the invitation and waived any speaking fees.

I found him to be a fascinating person. Although he was already in his mid-80s when I met him, he retained his charm, enthusiasm, and energy level. When he took the stage at the event, he was a hit. The audience enjoyed every minute of his presentation.

When Mr. Cathy came to Oklahoma City, his son Dan accompanied him along with a few representatives from the company. Mr. Cathy was very proud of Dan, and when he was speaking to a small group of community leaders on the second day of his trip, he told them of Dan's musical ability. Unexpectedly, he asked Dan if he had his trumpet with him, and after a quick trip to the car to retrieve it, he returned and he played for the small group of leaders. Although Mr. Cathy shared some helpful insights, I think one of the biggest takeaways for me was the joy he had in being able to hear his son play the trumpet.

As Mr. Cathy departed, he said to our group, "If you are ever in Atlanta, drop by and say, 'hello.'" Over the next couple of years, a colleague and I would take him up on his offer twice. Both trips were memorable learning experiences.

The Chick-fil-A corporate office is just a few miles from the Hartsfield-Jackson Atlanta International Airport. Because of the office's proximity to the world's busiest airport, I was surprised when we drove onto the wooded campus. I was not expecting 73 acres complete with nature trails and a small lake.

We parked our car in a guest parking area and made our way toward the building. Among the first things one encounters on the way to the front doors is a plaque that states Chick-fil-A's famous corporate purpose. The purpose is widely known because of its connection to its founder's faith and because it does not mention chicken. The purpose includes two key thoughts: 1) to glorify God by being a faithful steward of all that is entrusted to us and 2) to have a positive influence on all who come in contact with Chick-fil-A.[2]

I opened the front door, and as I approached the front desk, the receptionist greeted us warmly and enthusiastically. She said, "Good morning! We are so glad you are here!" Although she was looking directly at us, I was confused by her hospitality. I could not recall having ever been greeted like this in any other corporate headquarters in my life. I nearly looked behind me to see if there was someone else, someone more worthy of such a warm welcome, before I clumsily responded, "Good morning to you. We are glad to be here!"

She asked who we were there to see, and I replied, "We are here to see Mr. Truett Cathy." As the words hit her ears, she stopped what she was doing and placed her hands in her lap. With amazing sincerity, she looked up at us and said, "Well…today is going to be a great day for you. He is a great man."

She made a quick phone call, and after talking with someone for a moment, she told us that he was running a few minutes behind but was on his way. She then said, "He loves cars and enjoys sharing some of his car collection with others. Would you like to see his cars?" I was not expecting this question. Once again, I have been in a lot of corporate headquarters and could not recall ever having been asked this type of question. We hesitated while trying to process what she just said. Noticing our hesitation, she added, "We have the Batmobile."

With our official nametags on our lapels, we began our mini-tour of the headquarters. From that moment until our departure a few hours later, every single person we saw greeted us by name. It was an amazing demonstration of their commitment to their culture.

Mr. Cathy was a car guy. He did not just have a few cars on display; he was a serious collector. While some executives like their artwork on canvas, it appeared that Mr. Cathy preferred his on wheels. Instead of hiding his passion for classic cars, he shared them with everyone. At that point, I thought, even if nothing comes from our meeting, this has been an incredible day.

When Mr. Cathy arrived, we were taken up to his office. The office felt more like a living room in a home than a corporate office. It was a beautiful and impressive space, but I had the distinct feeling that he was more interested in making people feel welcome than filling them with a sense of awe at meeting a billionaire entrepreneur. His office was filled with mementos, sculptures, pictures of family and friends, and artwork that had been collected over the course of a lifetime.

In front of his desk was an old wooden cart filled with vintage six-packs of Coca-Cola in glass bottles. This cart and the Coca-Colas had a very special meaning for Mr. Cathy. When he was 8, he began selling Coca-Colas door-to-door. He found he could buy a six-pack for a quarter, and if he was willing to do the work, he could sell each bottle for a nickel.[3]

He had a hard time making sales until a neighbor suggested he would sell more if the Cokes were cold. This was especially true in the heat of the Georgia summer. Not only did he enjoy making a profit, but he also genuinely enjoyed making his customers day. This approach to life would stick with him throughout his career.

When Chick-fil-A began to grow and Mr. Cathy began looking for people to go into business with him, it was clear that service was at the heart of his plan. He would ask people to think about how they would feel if the president of the United States came into their store. After giving them a moment to imagine the scenario, he would say, "Your voice and facial expressions would change. You'd be eager to serve the president well, make sure he had a clean table, then go up and see if everything was all right, or if he needed anything. If we're willing to do that for the president, why not treat every customer that well?"[4]

We fell into conversation easily. He had just gotten off a phone call about a situation that had been bothering him. There had been a break-in and vandalism at a home he owned, and the person responsible had been apprehended. The vandal was a young man and Mr. Cathy wanted to do something that would help, but was unsure how best to help. We talked about it for a few moments, and then the conversation turned to why he felt it was important to treat people well. He said, "Do you know why people come to my stores, even when they aren't hungry?" He paused for a moment, just in case we knew, which we did not. He continued, "Because of the way they are treated when they get there." He said, "We let people know we appreciate them. We express gratitude. That is why when someone says, 'Thank you,' we respond, 'It's my pleasure.'"

Mr. Cathy credited the Ritz-Carlton for changing how he and his company responded to someone who said, "Thank you" for the service they provided. When he stayed at a Ritz-Carlton, which would have been a long way from his upbringing, he was deeply impressed that when he said "Thank you," the Ritz-Carlton employee responded, "It's my pleasure."[5]

The second time we visited, we knew a little bit more about what to expect. When we got to his office this time, he invited us to sit down and asked if we would like anything to drink. Although I normally decline, I was unusually thirsty, and I said, "Thank you. I would appreciate something to drink." He asked what I would like, and I responded, "A Diet Coke would be great."

At that time, due to his age, he had a personal assistant who was on call to help whenever needed. The assistant was a great guy in his mid-20s who seemed to enjoy the opportunity to serve Mr. Cathy. I first met him when Mr. Cathy came to Oklahoma City, and I appreciated the important role he was playing in Mr. Cathy's life.

To my horror, instead of picking up the phone and asking his assistant to bring in a drink, Mr. Cathy got up from his desk, shuffled down the hallway, got a Chick-fil-A cup, and then filled it with ice and Diet Coke. With my drink in hand, the octogenarian shuffled back down the hallway and handed me my Diet Coke. It was humbling to have him serve me, and I wished I had not asked for the drink. I wondered how many soft drinks he had prepared over the course of a lifetime. It was clear why he could ask others to serve. It was not a strategy for his company; it was obviously a strategy for his life.

On the three occasions that I was to spend time with Mr. Cathy, he always gave me a gift. My experience with his generosity is not unique. Whether it was a wooden 12-inch ruler on which the Golden Rule was printed, a stuffed cow, or signed copies of his books, he was always seeking to give to others. He did not just give to others; he *looked* for opportunities to give to others. Perhaps that is why it is not a surprise that he quietly sent $10,000 checks to organizations trying to make a difference in the lives of future leaders, or why he taught a junior-high, boys, Sunday school class at his church for over 50 years, or why he invested so much of his time and money helping orphaned children and children in foster care.

Because of these experiences, when I was invited to a breakfast a few years later where Dan Cathy was going to be speaking, I was happy to attend the event. Although I did not have a relationship with Dan and had only interacted with him briefly when he was in Oklahoma City, my interest in Chick-fil-A's ability to consistently create a positive customer experience had grown.

When I arrived at the breakfast program, I smiled when I saw Chick-fil-A employees handing out free breakfast food in the lobby. I smiled again when I got inside the main auditorium and saw the iconic Chick-fil-A cows on every table. It was clear that the values that had made Chick-fil-A unique would continue beyond the life of its Founder. When Dan began to speak, I found his style was different from his father's, but his passion and focus was not.

At one point in the presentation, he shared something that I have found to be genuinely life-changing. He talked about what it meant to go beyond customer expectations. On the stage was a large whiteboard. He wrote the following, "2M2N." He explained that it was shorthand for "Second Mile, Second Nature."

Although the concept of "going the second mile" is commonly used, the origin of the idea is nearly 2,000 years old and attributed to the teaching of Christ. Specifically, it is from the fifth chapter of the book of Matthew. In the passage, Jesus states, "If anyone forces you to go one mile, go with them two miles."[6]

Jesus was a Jewish man living in a Roman world. He lived in a time in which his countrymen were continually reminded that they were not in power. One way to remind conquered people that they were subservient to Rome was to allow their soldiers to practice "impressment." Impressment meant imperial Roman army soldiers could conscript Jews to carry their equipment, which could weigh up to 100 pounds, for one Roman mile. Being forced to carry the supplies of a Roman soldier was an unmistakable reminder of the reach of Rome.

When Jesus told his followers to go two miles, it would have been shocking advice. Instead of fighting the Romans, they were being told to yield their rights. At first blush, going the second mile appears to be sound advice for avoiding conflict. At a deeper level, there is something else happening. By giving them the option of going the second mile, he is offering them freedom. You cannot enslave someone who chooses to serve.

Dan returned to the whiteboard, and using a dry erase marker, he drew what appeared to be a large capital T. Along the vertical or y-axis, he wrote the word, "expectation." Along the top of the horizontal x-axis, he wrote "transaction" on the left side and "transformation" on the right side.

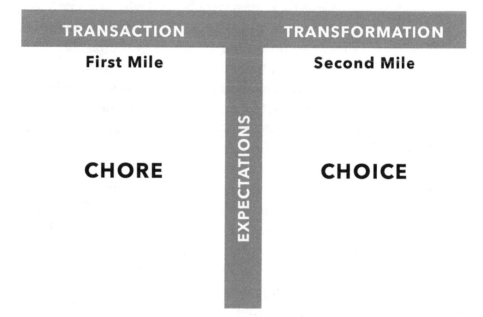

Using the model provided, transaction is a form of first-mile thinking, and transformation is second-mile thinking. He said the goal at Chick-fil-A was not transactions, but transformations. Accordingly, the team at Chick-fil-A was asked to consider the expectations of their customers. Using the perspective of the customer, they were asked, "What would you *not* expect for $5.95?" The answers came quickly and predictably; hot waffle fries, clean bathrooms, ketchup, etc. The question was then modified to, "What would you not expect for $5.95?" In essence, what actions would go beyond the normal expectations of a customer at Chick-fil-A? Energized by the concept, they responded with things like, they would not expect someone to come to your table and offer freshly ground pepper, to carry the trays of food to the table for moms, to refill drinks by asking, "May I refresh your beverage," or replying to a customer who has offered their thanks by saying, "It's my pleasure."

When expectations are met, a positive transaction occurs. When expectations are surpassed, the possibility for transformation emerges. Take a moment to think about the people who helped to transform your life positively. Did they meet your expectations or surpass them? For the vast majority of people I have known, they describe transformational people as those who went beyond what was expected of them. Through their words and actions, they did more than we would have asked them to do on our behalf. It is the teacher that pushed you to reach for more, the parent who went without so you would have what was needed. Transformational colleagues include the coworker who covered your shift so you could take care of a sick child or the boss who used their influence to help give you an opportunity you would not have been given otherwise.

There are numerous benefits to adopting a 2M2N mindset. One that is unexpected is how going the second mile energizes. When we go the second mile, it is no longer a chore; it is a choice. When I was a kid, every once in a while, my dad would call my brother and me into the living room and say, "Your mom had to run to the store. She has had a long day and is tired. Let's surprise her by cleaning up the living room and kitchen. We've got 30 minutes; let's make it happen." Something about anticipating her surprise motivated us. When we had the same job on Saturday morning as part of our chores, it took forever. When it was a choice and we wanted to surprise someone we loved, we had an entirely different level of energy.

I found the application of the 2M2N concept is indeed transformational. For example, one of the chores in our house is taking the trash from the kitchen to the garage where we have a larger trash can. Prior to applying the 2M2N concept, when the trash can in the kitchen was nearly full, I would become a human trash compactor and would compress the trash down as far as I could so the next person would have to take out the trash. After all, my job was to take the trash from the garage to the curb once a week. It seemed to me that if

I had to do this, the rest of the family could take care of the trash in the kitchen.

Prior to this revelation, I viewed taking out the trash as a chore. Instead of sticking with this approach, I decided to make it a choice. The next time the trash was full, I tied the top of the bag off and pulled it out of the can. I then reached under the sink and got another bag and replaced the one that I took out to the garage. I did not tell anyone that I had done it. The next time I saw the can was nearly full, I did the same thing again. On occasion, my wife will notice and express appreciation for what I have done, but that is not the point. The point is I went the second mile and by doing so something that I had viewed as a chore had become a choice. It changed my attitude, and it made me happy to surprise my wife with a small thing that I hope let her know how much she means to me.

TONY AND KATHY KENDALL

As mentioned, at the end of my sophomore year of high school, our family moved from Mobile, Alabama, to St. Louis, Missouri. My tenth-grade year in Mobile had been a special one for our family. Our varsity football team won the conference championship, and I was named an all-conference linebacker. It was a special day when we received our championship rings, and I have always treasured the fact that my dad and I both have one. He earned his as a coach, and mine was earned as a player.

The next year, while I was living in St. Louis, the team repeated as champions. I was happy for the team, but it was heart-breaking not to be there with them. My sophomore year, I had led the team in tackles, and if I had been able to play my junior year, I had a good shot at breaking the career record for tackles. Sensing my disappointment, I was amazed when my parents decided to allow me to go back to Mobile to play football my senior year.

They made arrangements for me to live with Tony and Kathy Kendall. In time, the couple would have two daughters, but at that time, they had no children and an unused guest bedroom. In an incredible act of kindness, they offered one of their guest bedrooms to me. I lived with them throughout the football season. Over the course of the few months I lived there, I forged a bond with the Kendall family that remains until this day.

Unfortunately, my senior year, the football team had a down year, and we only won three games. When the season came to a close, I moved back to St. Louis to finish out my senior year. Although going to two schools during my final year of high school was not ideal, it was the best option possible, and I remain grateful for the opportunity to have done so.

As the school year was nearing an end, I got an unexpected call from Mr. Kendall. He was calling to invite me to join my classmates on the senior class trip to Walt Disney World. Although I genuinely appreciated the kind invitation, I also knew our family did not have the money needed for me to take a trip to Orlando. I told him that I did not think it would work and tried to play it off. He said, "Well, I've already talked to your parents, and they said you could go."

I told him there was no way we could afford a trip like that. He said, "I understand. But there has been some extra money made available, and there would not be any cost for the trip." Overwhelmed by the generosity, I said, "Thank you," and agreed to join the group.

I would later learn where the "extra money" came from. When I moved to St. Louis, the seniors launched a fundraiser to help pay for the senior class trip. The primary fundraiser was selling candy, specifically M&M's, for $1 per box. Each senior that chose to do so, sold M&M's and used the proceeds to help defray the cost of their trip. Mr. Kendall saw an opportunity to help me raise money by selling M&M's under my name. He shamelessly used his position as a teacher to create a monopoly that makes me smile. He offered M&M's to his classes with the caveat that the only candy the students could eat in his classes were the M&M's he sold. Over the next few months, he sold hundreds of boxes.

Transforming lives requires going beyond what is expected. You cannot transform the culture of an organization by doing what is expected; it requires going the second mile. Are you living in mile one or mile two?

CHAPTER 9

"FLY FISHING AND D-DAY"

Keeping the Big Picture in Mind

A few years ago, I was asked to speak at a national education conference hosted in Birmingham, Alabama. While there, I had the opportunity to meet Dr. Steve Eckman, the president of York College. We were standing outside of the main hall, where the vendors had tables, and we struck up a conversation. It only took a few minutes to recognize that Steve was passionate about leadership development and education.

York, Nebraska is home to nearly 8,000 residents and is located 50 miles west of Lincoln. Founded in 1869, the town has long been a convenient place to stop for weary travelers headed north/south on Highway 81 or east/west on Highway 80.[1] The community boasts five parks, including Beaver Creek Park, which has a scenic walking trail. Most of the streets are tree-lined, and the majority of homes near the downtown are turn-of-the-century Victorians. The downtown is active with a handful of restaurants, a coffee shop, stores, offices, and banks. Surrounding the town, in all directions, are cornfields as far as the eye can see.

The United Brethren Church originally founded York College in 1890 in partnership with the city of York. In 1946, the United Brethren Church merged with the Evangelical Church to form a new denomination, the Evangelical United Brethren (EUB) Church. In 1954, the EUB decided to focus their support on an Iowa-based institution, which meant closing York College. Based on an agreement made in 1890, if the school closed, the control of the institution would be transferred to the City of York. In 1956, control of the institution was passed from the City of York to members of the Churches of Christ who sought to use the campus for its originally intended purpose. Consequently, the institution has been in existence since 1890, although its current affiliation began in 1956.[2]

Currently, York College is home to nearly 500 students from 30 states and 15 countries. The 50-acre campus includes several academic buildings, multi-storied dormitories, an expansive student center, a gym, a large field house, a performing arts center, and a prayer chapel. The chapel was initially constructed in another location in 1901 but was moved to the campus in 1999 and restored over the next five years. The peaceful and tree-lined campus is linked together by web of sidewalks. The grounds are well maintained, and the grass is lush and dark green in the warmer months. In the evenings, it is the ideal place for a stroll.

As Steve and I talked; we found that we had many shared interests. Among those interests was providing leadership development experiences for high school students. I felt an instant bond with him and decided to share an idea that I had been considering to see if he would be interested in partnering to make it happen.

To set the stage for the idea I wanted to share, I told him a story about an opportunity that my brother had when he was in high school. When Matt was a junior, he and a classmate were selected to participate in a program called the Presidential Classroom. The weeklong learning experience was hosted in Washington, D.C. and was designed for high school students from across the United States. Converging on the nation's capital, student leaders were given an opportunity to learn about themselves and the political process.

It was an honor to be selected for the program. Not only would he represent his family and friends, but he would also represent our school. As the younger brother, there are a few moments in life when you feel a sense of admiration for your older sibling, and this was one. What I remember most was his confidence. He was traveling to the nation's capital and did not seem fazed by it at all. It was a special moment for him and our family, and I have never forgotten how it felt to see him go.

I told Dr. Eckman that I wanted to help create similar moments for other families by launching a leadership program for students. Instead of hosting the program in Washington, D.C., however, I thought it would be interesting to partner with a presidential library. If we partnered with a college like York, we could host the bulk of the program on campus while spending a day visiting a presidential library. Finally, instead of asking individuals to attend the program, I thought it would be more impactful if we could design the experience for small groups of leaders from the same schools.

Leading a college or university is an incredibly challenging job. Among those challenges is the responsibility of balancing the needs and interests of a diverse constituency. To help avoid the fallout from political landmines, it is not uncommon for institutions to select presidents who are risk averse. Although this approach may be prudent, especially if the institution has experienced several missteps, it also means they are slow to consider new ways of doing things. Therefore, when I presented the idea to Dr. Eckman, my expectations were not too high. It would not have surprised me if he had responded with something like, "That is an interesting concept. Would you mind putting the concept on paper so I could share it with a committee that oversees these types of projects?"

Dr. Eckman listened to the idea. He paused for a moment and then said, "I think York would be interested in partnering." He looked me in the eye and said, "What do we need to do next?"

THE PRESIDENTIAL LEADERSHIP INSTITUTE

Within an hour, the core concepts had been formed, and over the next few weeks, the program took shape. An experienced leader, Dr. Eckman offered suggestions that enhanced and improved the original concept. Designed for ten high schools that would each send four to six students, along with sponsors, the program would bring together a sampling of schools from throughout the United States. During the weeklong program, each student group would focus on a specific challenge facing their school. At the end of the experience, each group would present to their peers what they planned to do in the upcoming school year to address the challenge. The program was named the Presidential Leadership Institute (PLI).

With York College on board, the next hurdle was trying to find a presidential library within driving distance of York that would be interested in partnering on the concept. To assist, I reached out to a friend, Mark Stansberry, whom I knew had a connection with Mary Eisenhower, President Eisenhower's granddaughter.

Among the many contributions President Eisenhower made to the betterment of the world was the creation of the non-profit People to People International (PTPI). Believing that "peaceful relations between nations requires understanding and mutual respect between individuals," he wanted to help create a way for people from around the world to connect with one another.[3] Launched on September 11, 1956, the PTPI mission was to "enhance international understanding and friendship through educational, cultural, and humanitarian activities involving the exchange of ideas and experiences directly among peoples of different countries and diverse cultures."[4] When I approached Mark about the concept of the Presidential Leadership Institute, he was volunteering as the chairman of the PTPI board, and Mary was the CEO.

Mark said he would be willing to connect with Mary to see if it was something that was of interest to her and PTPI. He relayed the concept, and she agreed to participate. Also, Mark connected with the Dwight D. Eisenhower Library, just under 3 hours away from York in Abilene, Kansas, to see if they would be interested in helping with the program as well. They both agreed.

One of the goals of PLI is to keep the cost as low as possible while maintaining a commitment to a world-class experience. Consequently, we ask each of our speakers to waive their standard speaking fees and donate their time as an investment in future leaders. Although we cannot offer an honorarium, we do provide a highly receptive audience of high school students and genuine appreciation for their contribution of time and effort. In addition to the generosity of the Eisenhower

Library and Museum and York College, we have also been inspired by the hospitality of the state of Nebraska. Not only does the state host PLI at the capitol building, but the governor also hosts the group for lunch and a presentation in the Nebraska Governor's Mansion.

Each day at PLI there are potentially life-changing moments. With that said, the day the group travels to Abilene, Kansas, to go to the Eisenhower Museum and Library is considered the highlight of the week. The night before, two talented faculty members from York College, Christi Lones, and Dr. Tim McNeese provide a compelling overview of the life of President Eisenhower.

To get to the library with plenty of time, the group leaves early in the morning. The students grab breakfast-to-go as they load on the tour bus. When they arrive at the library, the bus pulls in to a side parking lot from which the students can see the Eisenhower home, the museum, library, and gift shop. They can also see the Place of Meditation. This special site is where the 34th president and First Lady Eisenhower are buried alongside their firstborn son, Doud, who died at the age of 3 due to Scarlet Fever.

Although the students are looking forward to the overall experience, they are most excited about the opportunity to meet Mary Eisenhower. After watching an introductory video about the Eisenhower era, Mary welcomes the students. Following her welcome, she takes questions from the group. One student after another asks questions about what it was like living in the White House, questions about the Eisenhower family, and the pros and cons of growing up in a family known throughout the world.

THIS ONE IS SPECIAL

Following her presentation, which is in the library, the group crosses over a large courtyard to begin the tour of the museum. Although I am sure the docents are talented, there is nothing like being able to walk through the Eisenhower museum with an Eisenhower. Mary graciously leads the tour, and her stories transfix the students.

As the students make their way through the museum, I try to take photos of them, the faculty, and the staff interacting with Mary. I was standing a few feet from Mary when she stopped in front of a display that showcases an iconic picture with her grandfather and a paratrooper along with the paratrooper's uniform. She said, "This one is special."

She pointed to the soldier in the picture[5] who wore a simple placard around his neck with the number "23" on it. The man to whom she was pointing was 1st Lieutenant Wallace "Wally" Strobel from Saginaw, Michigan. Strobel was from Company E, 502nd Parachute Infantry Regiment of the 101st Airborne Division. The uniform preserved in the display was the one he was wearing when the picture was taken. As the jumpmaster, he was assigned to plane number 23, which was why he had the sign around his neck.[6]

The photo was taken about 8:30 p.m. on Monday, June 5, 1944, at the Greenham Common Airfield in England. A little more than four hours later, Strobel and the 15 to 18 paratroopers assigned to him would be dropped in Zone A, which was behind enemy lines.[7] Amazingly, June 5th was not only the day before D-Day, but it was also Wally's 22nd birthday.

"I grew up looking at that picture," Mary said. "I got to meet number 23. When I met him, I told him that I had looked at his picture my entire life, and I had wondered what he and granddad were talking about. He told me that granddad had asked him where he was from, and when he replied 'Michigan,' he followed up by asking him about the fishing there."

In the iconic photo, General Eisenhower is gesturing with his right arm. In Mary's conversation with Strobel, she learned that this moment is not entirely what it appears to be. Her grandfather's gesture, which many assumed was the general making an important point to the men, was in fact, the general demonstrating his form with an imaginary fly rod.

Although Wally knew the picture of him with the general was a famous photo, he did not make too much of it nor did he go out of his way to let people know he was the one to whom General Eisenhower was speaking. It was not until 1984 that he was officially identified in the photo when a Defense Department employee saw the picture sitting on a table and commented, "That's Wally Strobel. He's a neighbor of my brother's in Saginaw."[8]

THE DECISION

General Eisenhower believed that an airborne landing strategy would play the critical role in the success or failure of the amphibious landings. The paratroopers and glider troops would be dropped behind enemy lines to disrupt the German response and to protect bridges and other strategic targets. The plan was bold, but the strength and effectiveness of the German response remained unknown.

Just 6 days earlier, British Air Chief Marshal Sir Trafford Leigh-Mallory met with Eisenhower to ask him to reconsider the use of the airborne landing strategy. Assigned to the Allies, Leigh-Mallory had the title of Air Commander in Chief, which made him responsible for what happened in the skies on D-Day. Conflicted by how close his appeal was to the actual event, Leigh-Mallory had gone through the scenario time and again and was convinced the cost would not outweigh the benefit. He estimated, "casualties to glider troops would be 90% before they ever reached the ground," and "the killed and wounded among the paratroopers would be 75%."[9]

It was windy, cold, and drizzling when General Eisenhower was driven the one-mile distance from his sleeping quarters to the Southwick House for his daily 4:00 a.m. meeting. Southwick is a grand manor house built in the late Georgian style. When he arrived, Eisenhower and the others convened in the conference room. Before the war, the 25-by-50-foot meeting room had been a stately library.

On the morning of June 5th, there were a few maps on boards behind the group, but the room, much like Eisenhower, was understated. The sturdy, wooden, conference room tables were covered in blue fabric. The chairs positioned around the table were simple wooden or metal office chairs. Even at this early hour, the air would soon be thick with cigarette smoke. In nearly every photo of the room, there are ashtrays within reach of everyone. There was a blue rug on the wooden floor, where Eisenhower was known to pace back and forth as he mulled over decisions. The bookshelves were empty, and the walls were covered in oak wood paneling. Along the outer wall were floor-to-ceiling French doors, which opened onto the home's front portico.[10]

When General Eisenhower had been named Supreme Commander of Allied Forces, he stressed the importance of morale. He outlawed negativity and used his formidable skills as a mediator to keep the Allied leadership focused on their objectives. Throughout this time, he had personally set the pace for his fellow leaders. His unflappable and direct approach to problem solving had been a source of inspiration. The stress of the job, however, was taking its toll. He was smoking four packs of Camels and was drinking 15 or more cups of coffee per day. His blood pressure was high, and he was dealing with insomnia.

D-Day had been initially scheduled for June 5, but due to the forecast of poor weather, which proved to be accurate, the original date had been scrubbed. In consideration of the distances the ships crossing the English Channel would have to travel, the decision to go on the morning of June 6 would now need to be made that morning. After hearing the weather forecasts, Eisenhower went around the room getting the thoughts of each person. Everyone said they wanted to go, but the decision remained his to make. He processed the options once more and said, "Ok. Let's go."

WITH THE SOLDIERS

It says a great deal about Eisenhower that when he made the decision that D-Day was a go, he spent the final hours before the invasion with the men that he knew would pay the ultimate price for his decision. He wanted to be among the troops, to see their faces and gauge their readiness. The paratroopers in the photo are elite soldiers from the 101st Airborne Division, and each had volunteered to serve in this important role. When the group encountered General Eisenhower, they had been confined to the tented assembly area for nearly 5 days due to security concerns. At the moment captured on film, they are about to go to their assigned planes in preparation for takeoff at dusk. Their faces have been darkened with a concoction of burned cork, cocoa, and cooking oil to help them blend into the darkness of the night.[11]

Following the war, author Val Lauder was on a speaking tour about World War II. As part of her presentation, she discussed the stress placed on General Eisenhower due to the gravity of the decision to be made about D-Day. Following one of the presentations, a woman approached and said that she had been a Red Cross worker in England during the war. She said that she was at the airfield on the night before D-Day, passing out coffee and doughnuts to the paratroopers. When General Eisenhower arrived, she gave him a cup of coffee, and he took it. It was only after placing the coffee in his hand that she noticed "his hand was shaking so badly the coffee threatened to spill over." To keep him from being burned, she "eased the cup out of his hand."[12]

In an article written by Wally Strobel about that day for the Eisenhower Birthplace State Historical Site, he shared the following about his brief encounter with General Eisenhower:

We were waiting for orders to leave for the planes when the word was passed, "Eisenhower is in the area." At that point in time this did not cause a great deal of excitement because all of us had seen him before when he had visited the division and, besides, we were all pretty well preoccupied with our thoughts of our equipment and the operation ahead.

A short time later, we heard some noise, and we all went into the streets between the tents to see what was going on. Down the street came the General, surrounded by his staff and a large number of photographers, both still and movie. As he came toward our group, we straightened up, and suddenly he came directly toward me and stopped in front of me. He asked my name and which state I was from. I gave him my name and that I was from Michigan. He then said, "Oh yes, Michigan, great fishing there. Been there several times and like it." He then asked if I felt we were ready for the operation, did I feel we had been well briefed and were we all ready for the drop. I replied we were all set and didn't think we would have too much of a problem. He seemed in good spirits. He chatted a little more, which I believe was intended to relax us, and I think that all of us being keyed up and ready to go buoyed him somewhat.

You must remember that the men of the 101st and the 502nd Parachute Infantry especially were exceptionally well trained. We all felt we had outstanding senior and field grade officers. We had the best arms and equipment available, and we had been very well briefed for the operation. We were at a peak physically and emotionally. We were ready to go and to do our job.

While I think the General thought his visit would boost the morale of our men, I honestly believe it was his morale that was improved by being such a remarkably 'high' group of troops. The General's later writings confirmed this.[13]

REMIND THEM OF HOME

Mary continued on the tour, but I was not ready to move on from the display. I found every part of the story compelling. I wanted to know more about Lieutenant Strobel and his experience in the war. I was amazed by General Eisenhower's presence of mind and love for the soldiers under his command. Specifically, I was struck by where he chose to focus in times of uncertainty.

He knew that everything had been done that could be done to prepare the troops for what was to come. The paratroopers knew what to do and had been trained well. He also knew they, and he, needed to be reminded why it mattered and who would be impacted by their courage. Instead of focusing on the enemy or the inherent danger, he transported Lieutenant Strobel from England to a fishing spot in Michigan. He took him home. For a moment, the two were just a couple of men talking about the joy of fishing.[14]

Commenting years later on the famous June 5th photo of his father with the 101st, John Eisenhower said, "He was always trying to talk to troops about things back home, things that were familiar to them. If he found out that someone was from Kansas, he'd talk about cattle and farming, so it's natural that with Wally he discussed fishing."[15]

On the same day, June 5th, 1944, General Eisenhower recorded a historic speech about D-Day that would be heard throughout the world via radio. It was an inspirational rally cry for those involved in Operation Overlord. After delivering the message that morning, he sat down in his trailer and composed a second one to be given if D-Day proved to be unsuccessful.

He folded the note, which had been scrawled on a 4.5 by 7-inch piece of nondescript notebook paper, and placed it in his wallet. It remained there until July 11th. When he discovered it, he casually showed it to his naval aide, Captain Harry C. Butcher. Butcher, sensing its historical importance, asked if he could have the note, and General Eisenhower gave it to him. The message is now preserved at the Eisenhower Library.[16]

The "In Case of Failure" note speaks volumes about General Eisenhower's approach to leadership and life. He wanted it to be clear that if the invasion did not work, the blame rested squarely on his shoulders. It is a clear example of someone who has a strong internal locus of control. He does not offer excuses nor does he assign blame. He owns it.

The note states the following:

> Our landings in the Cherbourg-Havre area have failed to gain a satisfactory foothold, and I have withdrawn the troops. My decision to attack at this time and place was based upon the best information available. The troops, the air, and the Navy did all that bravery and devotion to duty could do. If any blame or fault attaches to the attempt, it is mine alone. July 5[17, 18]

There are a handful of things to notice in the image of the handwritten note, and I will highlight two. The first is that he used the wrong date. Although he stated it was July 5, it was June 5. He was exhausted. The second is that historians have suggested that he underlined the words "mine alone." Whether he did so intentionally or the straight line below the words was simply meant to imply the end of the message, the fact remains he used the words "mine alone."

MINE ALONE

When contemplating your life, there will likely be some significant decisions that must be made for you to regain control of your life. The decision to change direction in life can be made in an instant, but the process of actually changing your mindset may take months or years. The difference between success and failure is often the willingness to take ownership of the situation. You cannot move forward in life until you claim control of it. Claiming control of your life requires accepting responsibility for it.

General Eisenhower was willing to look the soldiers he was sending into battle in the eye because he believed in what he was asking them to do. When he reminded them of home, he was being reminded too. He concluded that fighting for freedom was worth the sacrifice.

What are you willing to sacrifice to experience freedom?

How are you reminding other people of "home?" What does "home" look like for you?

CHAPTER 10

"WE WILL START THE WAR FROM HERE"

Intentionally Courageous

Ted Roosevelt (Theodore Roosevelt III) was born on Tuesday, September 13, 1887, at his family's home in the village of Cove Neck, New York. He was the eldest son of T.R. (Theodore Roosevelt Jr.) and Edith Kermit Carow. Ted's siblings included Kermit (born 1889), Ethel (born 1891), Archibald (born 1893), and Quentin (born 1897). In addition to his three brothers and a sister, he also had a half-sister, Alice Lee (born 1884).[1] She was the daughter of his father and his first wife, Alice Hathaway Lee, who died due to Bright's disease on February 14, 1884.

Although Ted would never meet his paternal grandparents, who both had died before he was born, they impacted his mental model nonetheless. His grandfather, Thee (Theodore Roosevelt Sr.), was born on Thursday, September 22, 1831, in New York City. By the time Thee was born, the Roosevelt family was well on its way to becoming one of the most prominent families in New York. Thee's father, who went by C.V.S., grew the wealth of the family significantly by importing plate glass, which was used to help build buildings of all sizes in the growing city. C.V.S. was among the founders of the Chemical Bank (now Chase Bank). He was a real estate investor in Manhattan, and by the end of his career, considered among "the five richest men in town."[2]

Martha "Mittie" Bulloch was born on Wednesday, July 8, 1835. Mittie and Thee were married at Bulloch Hall, the family estate, in

Roswell, Georgia, on December 22, 1853. Their home, which had been constructed in 1839, was a Greek Revival mansion, which was purported to have been "the model for Margaret Mitchell's Tara Plantation in *Gone With the Wind*."[3] In addition to Ted's father, the couple had three other children including Anna "Bamie" (born 1855), Elliott Bulloch (born 1860), and Corinne (born 1861).

When C.V.S. died on July 17, 1871, he left behind a sizable inheritance to his family. These resources gave Thee the freedom to focus his efforts on philanthropic pursuits. Although C.V.S. had provided him access to wealth, Thee's mother, Margaret Barnhill Roosevelt, had instilled in him a great sense of purpose and responsibility. An English-Irish Quaker, she taught each of her children that those who have influence should use their power to help others.

GREAT HEART

Thee did not use his wealth to provide a life of leisure. He worked tirelessly to help build and strengthen institutions that enhanced life. In recognition of his efforts, friends and family bestowed upon him the name "Great Heart." The moniker was a nod to the character in John Bunyan's classic, The Pilgrim's Progress. In the story, Mr. Great-heart is a strong and brave man who fights lions to clear the way for the pilgrims to continue on their journey.[4]

Great Heart set the pace for service and generosity in his family. Each week, he set aside time to visit poorhouses, assist the needy, and personally teach mission school. He was involved in the establishment of organizations such as the American Museum of Natural History, the American Museum of Art, the Children's Aid Society, and the New York Orthopedic Hospital. On Sunday evenings, Thee took his children with him when he visited the Newsboys Lodging House. From the earliest moments in their lives, they watched as their father used his considerable power and wealth to serve others.[5]

Thee was just 46 years old when he died of stomach cancer on February 9, 1878. The loss was devastating to the family. In a letter written years later, T.R. provides Edward S. Martin, a noted journalist and fellow Harvard graduate, a description of his father. The following is an excerpt from that 1900 letter. He said:

> I was fortunate enough in having a father whom I have always been able to regard as an ideal man. It sounds a little like cant to say what I am going to say, but he did combine the strength and courage and will and energy of the strongest man with the tenderness, cleanness, and purity of a woman. I was a sickly and timid boy. He not only took great and untiring care of me—some of my earliest remembrances are of nights when he would walk up and down with me for an hour at a time in his arms when I was a wretched mite suffering acutely with asthma—but he also most wisely refused to coddle me, and made me feel that I must force myself to hold my own with other boys and prepare to do the rough work of the world. I cannot say that he ever put it into words, but he certainly gave me the feeling that I was always to be both decent and manly, and that if I were manly nobody would laugh at my being decent. In all my childhood he never laid a hand on me but once, but I always knew perfectly well that in case it became necessary he would not have the slightest hesitancy in doing so again, and alike from my love and respect, and in a certain sense, my fear of him, I would have hated and dreaded beyond measure to have him know that I had been guilty of a lie, or of cruelty, or of bullying, or of uncleanness or cowardice. Gradually I grew to have the feeling on my account, and not merely on his.[6]

Noted presidential historian Douglas Brinkley, ranked fathers of U.S. Presidents from best to worst. He ranked Thee as the best. Declaring, "He's in a league of his own," he stated, "The elder Roosevelt took Young Teddy to the Amazon, instilling in him a love and respect of the outdoors. He got his son private tutors in foreign languages, taxidermy lessons with a student of Audubon, and weights after a bully beat up

Teddy." In many ways, it was Thee that activated his son for greatness by teaching him to serve.[7]

A HOUSE DIVIDED

The only part of his father's life T.R. found difficult to reconcile was his unwillingness to fight in the Civil War. To avoid being drafted following the 1863 conscription bill, Thee utilized a broker to secure a replacement to fight on his behalf. He paid the broker $1,000, of which his replacement Abraham Graf received $38.

Graf was described as a "slight, fair, blue-eyed, thirty-six-year-old German just off the boat."[8] Within two months of enlisting with the 7th New York Infantry, he was taken prisoner, paroled, and then placed in a Union hospital at Point Lookout, Maryland.[9] He died the next year on March 31, 1865. Upon his passing, no one claimed his effects, which included a knapsack, shirt, hammock, underwear, a woolen blanket, towel, knife, fork, and a spoon.[10] He had passed alone and nearly penniless.

The reason Thee used a replacement was not likely cowardice; it was much more a matter of devotion to Mittie. His wife's family owned slaves and lived on a plantation. To fight against the South would mean he would be fighting against his wife's family, and she could not bear this thought. As a compromise, he would not fight but would use his considerable influence to promote the North, and he would send a replacement on his behalf.

His staunch support of the North could not have been misinterpreted. He was a charter member of the Union League Club of New York, which raised funds for food and supplies for the Union forces. In 1864, the Union League provided Thanksgiving dinner for the entire Army of the Potomac.

In addition, he campaigned for legislation intended to prevent price gouging of sales made to the Union forces. He also lobbied for an allotment system, which created a process that allowed soldiers to forward their pay to their families, and helped relieve the financial stress created by their service. When the allotment system was enacted,

Thee was named New York's allotment commissioner. He toured all New York divisions of the Army of the Potomac, at his own cost, to explain and promote the system.[11]

According to family members, Thee regretted his decision to not fight for the rest of his life. This regret appears to be among the key influencers in T.R.'s mental model, which would in turn influence Ted's choices. In adulthood, T.R. sought opportunities to prove himself through war. When the chance to do so presented itself in 1898, through the Spanish American War, T.R. emphatically demonstrated his capacity as a leader and warrior. Ted was ten years old when his father and the Rough Riders fought the Spanish in what T.R. would often describe as his "crowded hour."[12]

When he returned to the United States, T.R.'s postwar fame propelled him to the vice presidency. When President William McKinley succumbed to an assassin's bullet on September 14, 1901, he became the 26th President of the United States. Ted turned 14 the day before.

Not only did President Roosevelt have high expectations for himself, he expected the same from his children. The intensity was hard on Ted, and his frequent migraines were attributed to the constant pressure being placed on him by his father. President Roosevelt was warned by a family friend and physician to change course with how he was rearing his children.[13]

As he grew, Ted was given access to high-quality educational opportunities. He attended Groton School, and following graduation, he enrolled at Harvard, where he graduated in 1909. While in college, Ted played football and was selected for membership in the prestigious Porcellian Club. After receiving his diploma, Ted became a partner in the Philadelphia banking firm of Montgomery, Clothier, and Tyler. The Tyler family were cousins of his mother, Edith.[14]

THE GREAT WAR

When World War I began, the Roosevelt family responded by enlisting. Ted seized the opportunity to become an officer in the U.S.

Army. Although he had been successful as an investment banker, he had long-desired to serve in the military.

The Roosevelt family served with distinction in the Great War, but it came at a high price. Ted's lungs were damaged when he inhaled poisonous gas. While still recovering, he made his way back to the battlefield and was shot in the left leg, a wound from which he would never recover feeling in his left heel. His youngest brother, Quentin, who was engaged to marry the granddaughter of Cornelius Vanderbilt, was a pilot for the British when he was shot down and killed on July 14, 1918. While leading a platoon of troops against a German position, his brother Archie was severely wounded when shrapnel broke his arm, leaving his arm paralyzed, and shattered his kneecap.[15] The only sibling that was neither wounded nor killed was Kermit. A remarkable linguist, he learned Arabic while serving in Iraq. He commanded an armored car, and in an impressive display of courage, knocked down a door during the battle for Baghdad. When he entered, he used his British swagger stick to demand the surrender of the Turkish soldiers inside. Confused, they complied.[16]

The former president learned of the death of his son, Quentin, on July 17, 1918, when it was confirmed through the Red Cross. In honor of his service, German airmen buried him with full honors. When T.R. was given the news, he responded, "But Mrs. Roosevelt, how am I going to break it to her?" The next day, in what can only be described as a blend of shock and defiance, T.R., who was racked by grief and in poor health, traveled from his home to Saratoga, New York, to speak to an awestruck audience at a program where he had committed to speak.[17]

Following WWI, Ted continued as an officer with the Army Reserves and pursued public service. He was elected to the New York Assembly in 1919 and remained in this position until President Warren Harding requested that he serve as the Assistant Secretary of the Navy. Ted's father had served in the same role from 1897-1898, as had his cousin, Franklin D. Roosevelt who served from 1913-1920. He ran for governor of New York in 1924, and although he won the Republican Party nomination, he lost the race to Governor Al Smith.

He was named the Governor of Puerto Rico (1929-1932) and then Governor General of the Philippines (1932-33). He resigned his post in the Philippines following the election of his cousin Franklin, as the president of the United States. Upon his return to New York, he served as vice president at Doubleday Publishing Company and would later serve as the chairman of the board of the American Express Company, as Vice President for the Boy Scouts of America, and as President of the National Health Council.[18]

WORLD WAR II

Ted was initially opposed to entering World War II, but when it became clear the war was unavoidable, he looked for an opportunity to do his part. As a reservist, he had participated in annual training programs, and when the war began, he started active duty as a colonel and was soon promoted to brigadier general with the command of the 26th Infantry Regiment, a part of the 1st Infantry Division. This Division is also known as the Big Red One, due to their distinctive insignia, which is in fact a red number one.

For World War II historians, Generals Terry Allen and Ted Roosevelt will forever be linked. Allen was the commander of the "Big Red One," which was considered the most effective fighting division against the Germans in North Africa and Sicily. Beginning in 1943, Ted was the Assistant Division Commander (ADC). Recovering from the initial setbacks in North Africa, the 1st Infantry Division fought two German panzer divisions to a stalemate. By checking the German advance, the "Desert Fox," German General Erwin Rommel, was forced to withdraw. Rommel stated, "I was forced to the conclusion that the enemy had grown too strong for our attack to be maintained."[19]

A decorated war hero from WWI, Ted was already known for his courage, but he quickly proved he was not content to rest upon the successes of the past. His first assignment was in North Africa, and it appeared he had only grown bolder with time. In recognition of his efforts, Roosevelt was awarded the Croix de Guerre. The award stated:

> As commander of a Franco-American detachment on the Ousseltia plain in the region of Pichon, in the face of a very aggressive enemy, he showed the finest qualities of decision and determination in defense of his sector.
>
> Showing complete contempt for personal danger, he never ceased during the period of 28 Jan-21 Feb, visiting troops in the front lines, making vital decisions on the spot, winning the esteem and admiration of the units under his command and developing throughout his detachment the finest fraternity of arms.[20]

Although their courage was never questioned, there was concern regarding a lack of discipline in the 1st Infantry Division, which was the responsibility of Allen and Roosevelt. For example, when in combat, the soldiers had learned not to salute officers as a matter of safety. Even when they were not in combat, the soldiers in the "Big Red One" had continued the practice of not saluting. In addition, Allen and Roosevelt were very close to the soldiers under their command and were criticized for their approach to leadership, which relied on inspiration and strength of relationship.

When General Bedell "Beetle" Smith, General Eisenhower's Chief of Staff, was told that Allen made the 1st Division one of the best in the Army, Smith exclaimed:

> Made the 1st Division! He ruined the 1st Division. He started out to make it a rough, tough outfit that would win battles. He thought it was enough to win battles, to have battlefield discipline. He didn't realize the importance of discipline when the troops are out of the line.[21]

The Sicily campaign was coming to a successful close in 1943 when Allen and Roosevelt were relieved of command. It remains unclear who made the decision to remove them, but it appears that General George Patton recommended the removal with concurrence from General Omar Bradley and General Dwight Eisenhower.[22] Although the decision was challenging to accept, both Allen and Roosevelt would quickly find their footing, and their actions in 1944 would further prove their value as leaders.

D-DAY

As a result of the change, Ted was eventually sent to the European Theater of Operations. When he learned of the Allied plan to invade Europe through Normandy, he asked to be included in the invasion. At 56 years of age, with an arthritic knee that required the use of a cane, and other health issues, the request was denied. Undeterred, he requested a second time but was denied again. The third request was a written petition to Major General Raymond "Tubby" Barton, the 4th Infantry Division commanding general. Ted's argument was straightforward and transparent. He said:

> The force and skill with which the first elements hit the beach and proceed may determine the ultimate success of the operation. With troops engaged for the first time, the behavior pattern of all is apt to be set by those first engagements. [It is] considered that accurate information of the existing situation should be available for each succeeding element as it lands. You should have, when you get to shore, an overall picture in which you can place confidence. I believe I can contribute materially on all of the above by going in with the assault companies. Furthermore, I personally know both officers and men of these advance units and believe that it will steady them to know that I am with them.[23]

His request was approved, and soon after that, he began training with the troops for the invasion. It is worth noting that during this time, Ted was not in good health. Concerned that he would be removed from the invasion, he chose not to reveal that he was having mini-heart attacks in the weeks preceding D-Day.

On the early morning of June 6th, Ted's troop transport pushed toward Utah Beach. When they hit the beach around 6:30 a.m., not only was Ted in the first wave of soldiers, but he was also among the first three off the landing craft. Because he had to use his cane, he could not carry a rifle. Instead, he carried a .45-caliber pistol. Once he was on the beach, he refused to duck, even when under direct fire.

WE WILL START THE WAR FROM HERE

Due to a strong current, Ted's landing craft had been pushed south nearly 2,000 yards away from their intended target. When he recognized they were out of position, Ted personally scouted the area and determined where they had landed was a better location than the one that had been planned initially. While still under fire, there was a quick meeting among the leaders about what to do. Ted was reported to say, "Get word to the Navy and bring them in. We'll start the war from here." Following his lead, they redirected the additional waves of soldiers to land in the same place. As they communicated with the Navy, he began to lead multiple groups over the seawall and helped get his soldiers organized inland.[24]

Major General Barton, who had approved Ted's request to be in the first wave, landed at Utah later that day. He met Ted near the beach, and he would later write the following about the exchange:

> While I was mentally framing [orders], Ted Roosevelt came up. He had landed with the first wave, had put my troops across the beach, and had a perfect picture (just as Roosevelt had earlier promised if allowed to go ashore with the first wave) of the entire situation. I loved Ted. When I finally agreed to his landing with the first wave, I felt sure he would be killed. When I had bid him goodbye, I never expected to see him alive. You can imagine then the emotion with which I greeted him when he came out to meet me [near La Grande Dune]. He was bursting with information.[25]

When General Omar Bradley, who had relieved Ted of command less than a year earlier, for "loving his division too much," was asked what he considered the most heroic action of the war, he responded, "Ted Roosevelt on Utah Beach." General Bradley said, "He braved death with an indifference that destroyed its terror for thousands of thousands of younger men. I have never known a braver man nor a more devoted soldier."[26]

The thought of the son of a U.S. president using his influence to get into battle versus avoiding it is inspiring. Roosevelt was the only general to land in the first wave on D-Day, and at the age of 56, he was also the oldest. While these facts are compelling, the most amazing bit of trivia is that Ted and his son, Quentin II, were the only father and son combination of soldiers who would land together on D-Day. As Ted was fighting on the more lightly defended Utah Beach, Quentin II, who was named after Ted's brother who had been shot down and killed over France in WWI, was landing in the first wave on Omaha Beach. Omaha was considered to be the most heavily fortified of the sectors to be attacked on D-Day.

On the final day of his life, July 12, 1944, Ted was able to spend two hours with his son, Quentin II, talking about life.[27] That evening, he died in his sleep following a heart attack. On the same day, General Eisenhower had approved General Omar Bradley's request to promote Ted from a one-star to a two-star general. When Eisenhower called the next morning to share the approval, he learned of his passing.[28]

THE MEDAL OF HONOR

In recognition of his service to his country, Ted was awarded the Medal of Honor on September 28, 1944. The citation states the following:

> The President of the United States of America, in the name of Congress, takes pride in presenting the Medal of Honor (Posthumously) to Brigadier General Theodore Roosevelt, Jr., United States Army, for gallantry and intrepidity at the risk of his life above and

beyond the call of duty on 6 June 1944, while serving as a commander in the 4th Infantry Division in France.

After two verbal requests to accompany the leading assault elements in the Normandy invasion had been denied, Brigadier General Roosevelt's written request for this mission was approved, and he landed with the first wave of the forces assaulting the enemy-held beaches. He repeatedly led groups from the beach, over the seawall and established them inland. His valor, courage, and presence in the very front of the attack and his complete unconcern at being under heavy fire inspired the troops to heights of enthusiasm and self-sacrifice. Although the enemy had the beach under constant direct fire, Brigadier General Roosevelt moved from one locality to another, rallying men around him, directed and personally led them against the enemy. Under his seasoned, precise, calm, and unfaltering leadership, assault troops reduced beach strong points and rapidly moved inland with minimum casualties. He thus contributed substantially to the successful establishment of the beachhead in France.[29]

GETTING INTO THE FIGHT

It is always inspiring when people use their power and influence to get into the fight versus avoiding it. Utilizing a mindset that began with his grandfather, and was nuanced through his father, Ted recognized the importance of using his personal example to inspire others. He understood that his story was part of a larger story that included those who had gone before him and those who would come after him. Consequently, he was willing to sacrifice himself in the pursuit of what he considered to be more valuable than his life.

How are you using your influence for the benefit of others?

How are you using your influence to pursue difficult or challenging things versus avoiding them?

CHAPTER 11

"RAWHIDE DOWN"

Remapping Your Brain

I have always been drawn to biographies and history. Reading about the lives of others has proven to be a great source of inspiration and instruction. When I first started reading about the experiences of leaders, I was drawn to U.S. presidents. Although their leadership styles, personalities, and interests varied greatly, they are forever linked by the role they have played in shaping U.S. history. In time, I began reading about the presidents in chronological order. I found it fascinating to see how each leader dealt with the challenges created by their predecessors and how they attempted to forge their own path forward.

The 20th century is often referred to as the "American Century." As the United States began to take a larger role in global leadership, the role of the president on the global stage expanded as well. Debates about which presidents were among the most effective of all time will never be fully resolved, but there are a handful from the 20th century who promise to stand the test of time. If I were to create a list of the top five from the past century, I would include: Theodore Roosevelt, Franklin D. Roosevelt, Harry Truman, Dwight Eisenhower, and Ronald Reagan.

When we moved to southern California so I could pursue graduate degrees at Pepperdine, our rental house was located in Westlake Village about 15 miles from Simi Valley, which is the home of the Ronald Reagan Presidential Library and Museum. If you have never been to the Reagan Library, it is unique for a handful of reasons. Built upon a hill, the library overlooks the valley with a distant view of the Pacific Ocean and it is surprisingly peaceful. It is the final resting place for the president and first lady, Nancy Reagan. With a red-tile roof and large central courtyard, it is a large complex in the Spanish mission style, which is a nod toward the history of the area. In addition to being entrusted with the artifacts pertaining to the Reagan family and Reagan administration, the library is also the home of the Boeing 707 used as Air Force One during his administration.

I spent a great deal of time at the Reagan Library, due in part to the fact that Ronald Reagan and Theodore Roosevelt were the primary subjects of my doctoral dissertation. My research focused on the use of mediation as a leadership style. I examined President Reagan's interactions with Mikhail Gorbachev at Reykjavik in October of 1986. I also reviewed Theodore Roosevelt's role as mediator between Russia and Japan in 1905, which led to the Portsmouth Treaty, for which he would become the first American given the Nobel Peace Prize.

Just as I find the presidential biographies to be a great learning tool, I find the presidential libraries to be the same. Even if you do not agree with the policies of the president being remembered, I always find visiting the presidential libraries to be thought-provoking. This is definitely the case with the Reagan Library. Although a significant portion of the library is specifically about Ronald Reagan's life, there is a great deal about the global issues that contributed to the Cold War, the tensions in the Middle East, and the social challenges that helped define the 1980s.

To become a official researcher is not difficult and requires filling out an application that explains why you need access to the archives. Once approved, a researcher card is issued, and after going through an orientation, researchers are allowed access to the Research Room. The archivists who work in the room are typically very helpful in providing guidance and assisting in research.

One afternoon, I was working in the Research Room, and one of the archivists motioned me to come to the desk where he was working. At the time, he was processing some of the legal pads in which President Reagan used to write the content for his radio programs in the years before being elected president. I was thankful for the opportunity to see firsthand the writings of the future president. Each page was filled with his handwriting, and it was fascinating to see the process by which he would organize his thoughts.

Although I enjoyed the feeling of being an "official researcher," after a few weeks of researching, I found that much of the information I needed could be found online. I still found being there was helpful to my writing process, and I enjoyed sitting outside at one of the tables used by patrons of the restaurant connected to the library. If I needed to go into the Research Room, it was available, but more often than not, I was able to do my work independently.

On a handful of occasions, when I got to the library, special events were being hosted of which I was unaware. An example of this was the day I arrived and the entire complex was abuzz with activity. At the time, the library was much smaller than it is now, and I would often walk through the museum portion for inspiration before getting down to work. When I got to the entrance of the museum on this day, the docent told me they were closing the museum for a special event. The cars that had been part of Reagan's presidential motorcade were being driven to the library in anticipation of the pavilion that would later hold Air Force One, Marine One, and the motorcade. There were a number of VIPs who would be attending the event. I replied, "Not a problem. I can come back later." Surprised by my lack of protest, she followed up by asking if I came to the library often, and I told her that I was a researcher who was using President Reagan as part of my dissertation. She expressed her appreciation for people who had an interest in the former President and then said, "Do you think you could make it through the museum quickly?" I assured her that I could and amazingly, she waved me through.

Because the museum portion of the library was closing, there were very few people in it. It felt very odd to be walking through nearly alone, and I considered it a privilege to be there. When I got to the replica of the Oval Office, I was alone, save another docent who stood nearby. The docent looked at me and said, "This is a special place." I nodded my head in agreement. He said, "Enjoy the moment." He stepped out into the hallway leaving me alone with my thoughts. All alone, I reached for my phone to take a picture. Sadly, the battery died, and I did not get a picture of the moment. Although it would have been fun to have the picture, in some ways, it made the moment all the better. Without the distraction of my phone, I stood there in silence and did as the docent suggested and enjoyed the moment.

ASSASSINATION ATTEMPT

The Library is designed to tell the story of Reagan's life chronologically. There are a handful of moments in Reagan's story that stand out to me as especially meaningful or poignant. One of those moments is the section of the museum dedicated to telling the story of what happened when Reagan nearly died at the hand of a would-be assassin, John Hinckley Jr., who would later be declared legally insane.

It was on a Monday afternoon on March 30, 1981, at 2:27 p.m. when President Reagan exited the Washington Hilton following a luncheon speech given to the AFL-CIO. He had been president for 69 days and was looking to build momentum for his vision for America. The president appeared confident as he departed the building and began to make his way toward the open door of his limousine, which was just 30 feet away. When the crowds began to cheer, he waved with his right arm to the bystanders who had lined up across the street. On his left was another group of bystanders and reporters standing just 15 feet away behind a roped off area. In what was later considered a "colossal mistake," the group had not been screened.[1] As he was within feet of the vehicle, he raised his left arm to wave to the smaller and closer crowd to his left. In that crowd, stood 25-year-old John Hinckley Jr., who recognized this moment as his best chance of hitting the president. Clasping his hands together and pushing forward, he raised his .22-caliber revolver toward the president and began to fire.

The first shot struck White House Press Secretary James Brady in the forehead, just above his left eye, and he instantly dropped to the ground. The gun used by Hinckley was an inexpensive, small caliber, short-barreled revolver. Due to its lack of relative power, it was an unlikely choice of weapons for a would-be assassin. With that said, he had chosen to use "Devastator" cartridges, which were designed to explode on impact to maximize damage. Of the six shots taken by Hinckley, the only one that detonated on impact was the one that hit Brady.[2]

Although he would survive, Brady had permanent brain damage that left him with several neurological-based challenges and would require him to use a wheelchair for the remainder of his life. Using his experience as a platform, he and his wife, Sarah, would dedicate the remainder of their lives to preventing gun violence. When he died on August 4, 2014, his death was ruled a homicide, as the cause of death was directly related to the bullet wound he received during the attempted assassination.[3]

The second shot hit D.C. police officer Thomas Delahanty. He was facing the president, and the bullet struck him from behind. The path of the bullet remains unclear, but it appears to have struck him in his back-left shoulder and then traveled toward his neck, possibly hitting his spinal cord and coming to rest an eighth of an inch from his spine.[4] He instantly fell to the ground and yelled out, "I'm hit!"[5]

In total, Hinckley would fire six shots at the president. The entire episode only lasted 1.7 seconds. To put that in perspective, the last sentence takes about 1.7 seconds to read aloud.

When I first began going to the Reagan Library, the section about the attempted assassination was much smaller than it is today. Now, the experience has been enhanced significantly to help make it more personal to the growing number of visitors who were either too young to remember the shooting or were not yet born. Today, the exhibit includes being led into a small room designed to make the visitor feel as if they were there were among the group waiting outside of the Hilton when the president emerged. While standing in the small room, the footage of the moment begins. The experience is memorable and it brings the gravity of the event into focus.

Although watching the video from that afternoon is not for everyone, I have found it to be a surprising source of inspiration. You will notice that once the firing begins, the majority of the people in the footage instinctively flinch and duck for safety. There are a few people, however, whose response is noticeably different. Instead of ducking for cover, which is the prescribed training for the police and the military, the Secret Service is trained to do the opposite.[6]

According to Jerry Parr, the Secret Service agent assigned to the president: "The first shot, the first thing that you see, the first yell, the first scream, the first violence, you go into action. Cover. Cover and evacuate. Cover and evacuate. You gotta get it embedded in your head as the muscle memory."[7] He had been trained for this moment, and his response and the response of his fellow agents was instantaneous.

When Hinckley fired the third bullet, he had an unobstructed path to the president. Instead of hitting his intended target, the shot went high. It struck a window in a building across the street but did not injure anyone.

As Hinckley took the fourth shot, Agent Tim McCarthy moved back toward the president to become a human shield. Although he was not wearing body armor, he spread his arms out wide in an effort to make himself as big of a target as possible. Entirely exposed, he was struck in the chest. The impact of the bullet pushed him backward, and he fell to the ground clutching his abdomen.

He stated later, "I was hit in the chest, and the bullet went into the lung, liver, and diaphragm. The common picture shows me grabbing my abdomen, but that's down where the liver was when it went through the liver. That's where the pain was at the time, but actually, I was shot in the chest."[8]

In a later interview, McCarthy echoed Agent Parr's explanation about how he was able to respond in the face of danger. He said, "In the Secret Service, we're trained to cover and evacuate the president. And to cover the president, you have to get as large as you can, rather than hitting the deck. So I have to say people have asked me, and I said quite frankly, it probably had little to do with bravery and an awful lot to do with the reaction based upon the training."[9]

As Agent McCarthy moved back to stand in the way of bullet four, Agent Jerry Parr had already grabbed the president and was forcibly pushing him into the limousine. The two were nearly in the car when the fifth shot hit the bulletproof window of the open door. The bullet cracked the glass, but the window held.

The sixth shot hit the limousine as Parr, who was draped over the president in an effort to shield him, landed hard in the back of the car. Amazingly, the bullet, which had ricocheted off the car, flew through the gap between the A-frame pillar of the car and the open door. The bullet, which had flattened like a dime when it hit the car, struck the president on his left side near his underarm. A fraction of a second earlier, the bullet would have hit the president in the head. Instead, it hit a rib, which was broken by the impact, and then traveled through the lung and caused a partial collapse. It finally came to rest less than an inch from Reagan's heart.

As the presidential limousine sped away toward the safety of the White House, both Parr and Reagan were unaware that Reagan had been hit. Parr quickly examined Reagan, but he could not find evidence of a wound. He said:

> What made me change the course was that there was a profuse amount of blood coming out of his mouth, and I knew [this was bad] from the training I had in a 10-minute medicine course. I thought maybe I broke a rib when I came down on top of him. So I spoke to the president, and I said, "I'm taking you to the hospital," and he basically agreed with me. He said OK, and he nodded or something. His blood worried me, and his demeanor worried me, though I have often said he was perfectly lucid during the whole ride.[10]

Agent Parr ordered that the limo be redirected to the nearby George Washington University Hospital. According to the doctors responsible for saving his life, this quick decision was the reason Reagan would survive. Mrs. Reagan would later comment, "If Jerry hadn't made the change, I wouldn't have a husband."[11]

INSPIRED ROLES

An interesting side note is that Jerry Parr's interest in the Secret Service began after he watched the 1939 movie *Code of the Secret Service,* which starred Ronald Reagan as Agent "Brass" Bancroft. Parr was 9 years old when he "gripped his father's arm as Brass survived one cliff-hanging moment after another, one narrow escape after another, before finally beating the bad guys and winning the girl. As he left the theater that night, young Jerry thought, *I want to be a lifesaver, too!*"[12]

On Monday, March 30, 1981, Parr was playing the part he chose to play in life. His childhood had been tough due to instability at home. His father was an alcoholic, and his mother divorced him. She married twice more, but both men proved to be violent. The family would end up moving often, which made Jack the target of bullies. In response to the turmoil, he learned he could either be a victim to his circumstances or he could make his own way.[13] He chose to become the very person he wished would have intervened in his life.

Interestingly, Ronald Reagan was playing a part he had chosen as well. He too was the son of an alcoholic and had moved often as a child. At 10 or 11 years old he picked up the book *That Printer of Udell's,* written by Harold Bell Wright, that changed his life. In a 1984 letter sent to Wright's daughter-in-law, he described the impact of the book. He stated, "The term 'role model,' was not a familiar term in that time and place, but looking back, I know that I had found a role model in that traveling printer Harold Bell Wright had brought to life. He set me on a course I've tried to follow even unto this day. I shall always be grateful."[14]

That Printer of Udell's is primarily about Dick Falkner. Subjected to extreme poverty and a physically abusive father, he ran away from his dire situation in the hope of finding a better future. Homeless and destitute, he arrives in the Midwestern town of Boyd City. He reasoned that the Christians in the town would show him compassion and that he would not go hungry. He was disappointed when the church members appeared disinterested in helping him. When he found an opportunity to work for a local printer named Udell, he was determined to make the most of it.

In time, both Udell and Falkner would come to faith and become Christians. Falkner found he could use his plainspoken oratory skills and a positive outlook on life for the benefit of others. He called upon his fellow citizens to do what was right and to fight against evil. Through his persuasive efforts, he became recognized as a community leader. The book concludes with the young man who came from a challenging background leaving the Midwest on his way to making a difference in Washington, D.C.

Reagan decided to be like Falkner. He developed his skills as a speaker, learned to use stories and humor to connect with others, and determined to adopt a positive outlook on life. Not only can this learned approach to life be seen throughout his career, but it can also be seen very clearly in how he responded when his life was in danger.

He was not acting like someone he was not. He had chosen to act like the person he wished to be. Much like Parr had been trained to respond to danger by the Secret Service, Reagan had trained himself how to respond to life's challenges. He was not going to allow himself to be a victim. He was going to respond. *TIME Magazine* compiled a handful of Reagan's quips following the assassination attempt. Below are a few that capture Reagan's attempt to maintain control in a situation in which he had none. He was continually aware that, as a leader, he had a role to fill, and after years of training, he responded with a level of grace and confidence that even his critics had to admire. The article quotes:

> To surgeons, as he entered the operating room, "Please tell me you're Republicans."
>
> In a note written while surrounded by medical staff, "If I had this much attention in Hollywood, I'd have stayed there."
>
> To an attentive nurse, "Does Nancy know about us?"
>
> To daughter Maureen, the attempted assassination "ruined one of my best suits."

Greeting White House aides the morning after surgery, "Hi, fellas. I knew it would be too much to hope that we could skip a staff meeting."

When told by Aide Lyn Nofziger that the government was running normally, "What makes you think I'd be happy about that?"[15]

I am inspired by actions of the Secret Service agents who served at the president's side that day, the response of the medical professionals who attended to those injured, and by the attitude of the president in his recovery. It is a testament to the will and training of everyone involved that they demonstrated such bravery and professionalism in the face of a life-threatening crisis. It is also a reminder that how we choose to think and the behaviors that are reinforced can, in time, override our natural response in favor of the one we choose.

REMAPPING

To be effective in a time of crisis, the Secret Service agents who saved the life of President Reagan chose to respond to danger in a way that is very different from the response that would normally be anticipated. To react in the way they did required significant training—to be able to exchange one way of thinking for another. Doing so meant remapping their brains to override the natural instinct for self-preservation. The discipline needed to accomplish this goal is staggering, but it provides a real-life example of how it can be done.

In addition to the Secret Service, President Reagan had also chosen to develop his brain in a way that was equally important to reach his goals. At every phase of his life, as a lifeguard, an actor, a governor, and as president, he cultivated his ability to step into the role he needed to play. He intentionally shaped his mental model to fit the image of the leader that he discovered as a young boy reading *That Printer of Udell's*.

At any point in your life, you can choose to think differently. Doing so is challenging and difficult, but with intentionality and practice, you can remap your brain to learn in new ways. You are never too old to chart a new course and learn new things. In fact, pushing yourself to consider a new perspectives and to force your brain to work in new ways can help significantly in keeping your brain sharp and flexible throughout your lifetime.

What areas of life would you like to explore, but have considered yourself too old or too set in your ways to pursue? (For example, playing the piano, learning a foreign language, learning to paint, etc.)

If the statement, "I am set in my ways and can't learn new ways of doing things" does not have to be true, in what areas of your life would you like to see improvement?

PART FOUR

A NEW LIFE

CHAPTER 12

"THE SONGBOOKS AT THE CHURCH"

Small Moments Matter

I was grateful for the opportunity to travel to Marietta, Ohio, to see my grandmother a few months before her passing. When I climbed the back steps of her home and opened the door into her small kitchen, I was instantly filled with emotion. We normally saw her at special events like graduations and weddings or when she would come to visit during the holidays. When I had moved to California for graduate school, there had been a gap in our visits, and I knew that she had wanted to see her family, especially her great-grandchildren, more.

As I stood in her kitchen, I looked at the small table where I sometimes ate breakfast as a child. One of the last times I had sat at this table was with my dad, my uncle, and my granddad. I did not see my uncle often, and the gathering was made all the more meaningful to me as it was the first time in my life that I had been invited to join in a meal with them as an adult. My grandfather was in poor health at the time, but I did not realize it would be the last time that I would see him or my uncle. Granddad died on Friday, August 4, 1995. My grandmother's grief was compounded when my uncle was killed in a motorcycle accident 11 days later on Tuesday, August 15, 1995. With the sun in her eyes, a motorist driving a pick-up truck did not see him as he rode down the highway toward her. She tragically pulled out directly in his path, and he died on the scene.

My grandmother seemed much smaller than she had the last time I stood in her kitchen. She had lost weight, and her white hair had thinned considerably. Although her heart was failing, her mind remained remarkably sharp. Her heart trouble was related to her valves, which meant the heart was not pumping efficiently, and, due to her age, there was nothing that could be done to prolong her life. As a result of her condition, she moved slowly, and it took a great deal of effort to complete tasks that would have been routine in recent years.

Family and friends had been on notice that she would likely pass away soon. Although it is always a shock to hear a loved one has died, it was something we expected. A few minutes after noon on Monday, March 22, 2010, she quietly passed away. She had decided that she wanted the memorial service to be held the day after her passing. Those who were able to do so scrambled to find a way to get to Marietta in time for the 2:30 p.m. service on Tuesday. It was held indoors in a small mausoleum at East Lawn Memorial Park on the edge of town. On the day of her memorial, the thermometer never rose above 44 degrees, it rained, and there was a steady breeze.[1]

When someone lives for a long time, especially when they have been ill for a prolonged period, they will often have a very small crowd at their memorial service. The size of the crowd is not necessarily indicative of the impact they had in life but is more often than not a recognition they outlived their friends and loved ones. Considering grandma's obituary had only been in the paper for a few hours before her service, we were not expecting many in attendance. Therefore, it was a pleasant surprise to see so many people file in to offer their respects.

A TREASURE TROVE

After the funeral, we gathered back at grandma's house. Over the next day or two, we packed up family photos, mementos, and any important documents that did not need to be left in an empty home while dad made arrangements for its sale. Before her passing, grandma had either given away or designated most of the things she thought might be meaningful to friends and family. I doubt she owned any one item that was worth more than a few hundred dollars. It was humbling to consider how generous she and granddad had been over the years with birthday and Christmas gifts. What mostly remained now were pieces of furniture and personal items that had not been thrown away.

My grandparents' home had been built in 1900, and its 1,320 square feet consisted of two floors and a basement. The living room and the kitchen were on the first floor. A half bath had been added when granddad had gotten sick, and the sitting room downstairs had been converted into a bedroom. On the second floor, there were two bedrooms and a full bathroom.

In my grandparent's second story bedroom was a bedroom suite, their bed, and two antique wooden trunks. The floors in the upstairs bedrooms were painted wood. The trunks were full and would have been too heavy to move easily. Consequently they had sat in the same spot for decades. Grandma considered them to be family heirlooms and a direct connection to our past, although it was not entirely clear which family members had owned them or in what era they might have been used.

The first trunk was a flattop steamer. It was sturdy and made to withstand abuse. Even when it was empty, it was heavy. When we opened the trunk, we were surprised by its contents. She had saved every single handwritten thank you note and special-occasion card she had ever received throughout her lifetime. She treasured them and had dutifully collected them for years.

The second trunk was a dome-top trunk of seemingly equal age. Inside the trunk was an upholstered tray, which held a few letters and small items. Beneath the tray, we found the trunk had been carefully filled with old photographs and documents, a few items of clothing, and other odds and ends that had been preserved for their sentimental value. We put the tray back into the trunk and carried it downstairs to be taken to my parent's home for safekeeping.

Later when I was at my parent's home, I asked to go through the items in the dome-top trunk. I removed the tray that was resting inside the trunk and began sorting through the next few layers. The contents were a time capsule for our family. Among the treasures, which would not have meant much to others, but were extremely valuable to us, was a colorized photo of my granddad on the Marietta High School football team in 1939. Another was a certificate stating he had earned his high school letter in football. Finally, we found his football pants that he had last worn 70 years earlier.

My grandfather was among the many veterans who took home war trophies and mementos from World War II. In addition to an Arisaka Type 99 rifle and bayonet, he also brought home a Japanese samurai sword. I knew of these items, and, amazingly, as children, my brother and I would play with the gun, with the firing pin removed, around the house and in the backyard. It never crossed our minds that it might have been unsettling for granddad to see his grandchildren running around "playing war" with a rifle he brought home from a very real war.

Searching deeper, I found mementos from WWII that neither my father nor I had ever seen before. They were small items that appeared to have been possessions of Japanese soldiers. Along with the artifacts was a handwritten letter of explanation left behind for posterity by grandma. Written in her distinctive cursive, she stated that she and granddad had tried to return the personal effects to the Japanese government, but they were told that it was not possible to do so. It was clear my grandparents did not know what to do with them, so they placed them carefully in the trunk. Much like granddad's memories from the war, these items were purposefully tucked away. His memories and those artifacts remained a part of his life, but once stored away, neither would ever see the light of day during his lifetime.

Another item that caught my attention was a document on thick parchment paper that was rolled up like a scroll. When I picked up the scroll, I was surprised by how heavy it felt in my hands. I took it over to the nearby bed to examine it. It was in the early afternoon, and the light from the windows was plenty to see the paper clearly. I carefully rolled it out to reveal what was written on the document.

The words that emerged were printed in the traditional blackletter style. The document was a high school diploma, and once unrolled, the thick paper was 18 inches tall and 2 feet wide. Affixed vertically along the left side of the diploma was a yellow satin ribbon that was about a foot long and an inch wide. On the ribbon was placed a gold seal with the words, "Board of Education Marietta Ohio" embossed in a circle. The diploma stated, "This certifies that C. Ben Mellor having completed the English Course of Study prescribed by the Board of Education is hereby declared a Graduate of the Marietta High

School and is awarded this Diploma as an honorable testimonial of the excellence of his character and scholarship. Dated, Marietta, Ohio, June 5, 1908."

The diploma was my great-grandfather's. Benjamin Charles Mellor was 19 years old when he had earned it. It was an especially meaningful find, as this document is the only possession of his that has survived. It was also significant that he had graduated from high school, considering this was not the norm at the time. Although the number of high school graduates would steadily increase through the first half of the 20th century, the percentage of 17-year-olds graduating from high school in 1899-1900 was just 6.4%. A decade later, 1909-1910, the number had grown to 8.8%.[2] It would not be until 1940 that the number of high school graduates would exceed 50%.[3]

The final treasures that meant the most to me were my grandparent's high school yearbooks from 1940. When I visited my grandmother for the last time, I had noticed them on the bookshelf in the guest bedroom. At that time, I had thumbed through each page. What I found most interesting were my grandfather's responses to the questions in the back of the yearbook. He had taken time to respond to a series of questions like, "Where would you like to be in five years?" and "What profession would you like to pursue?" His dream had been to be either a machinist or a mechanic.

GLEN MELLOR

Glen's father, Charles Benjamin, was born in 1889. Tall and lean, he went by the name Ben. According to the 1910 census, Ben was working as a butcher in a local slaughterhouse two years after graduating from the Marietta High School. By 1920, he was a letter carrier for the United States Postal Service, and he would continue in this job until his death in 1947. Glen's mother, Clara, was born in Pennsylvania in 1895 and then moved to Ohio where she would live until her death in 1985.

Glen enlisted in the Army on August 20, 1944. He had been drafted earlier, but his service had been deferred due to the hardship it would bring upon his young family, which included one son and a daughter who would be born in October 1944. Once deployed, he was assigned to the 164th Infantry, Company G in the Pacific Theater. He served until he was honorably discharged on February 16, 1946.

Based on a few clues found in some of the documents that were preserved from that time, it appears that he entered the war as a cook, but upon arrival in the Philippines, he served as a rifleman. Grandma kept the documents that pertained to his service and a few pictures from that time. The only insights I have about his service are harvested from these items. His Separation Qualification Record includes the following description:

> Served in Pacific theatre of operations for 11 months. Worked with Company G, 164th infantry. Worked as rifleman, used M-1 rifle in combat. Loaded, aimed, and fired at enemy troops and installations. Used all small arms and hand weapons. Captured and imprisoned enemy personnel.

The photos below were apparently about a year apart from one another. The photo on the left is from his enlistment in 1944, and the one on the right is near the end of the war in 1945. From my perspective, his eyes tell the story about the impact of war on the mind of a young husband and father who was doing his best to get home safely.

When Glen came home from the war, he had hoped to pursue his dream of becoming a mechanic or a machinist. Unfortunately for him, due to the war, there was an abundance of mechanics and machinists available. He found the best job he could and became a letter carrier. Later, he would take on additional work as a janitor at a downtown bank and a local church.

Although he did not have money, Glen was known as a man of his word. When my dad wanted to go to college, it would have been impossible unless he could get a loan. My dad and his parents did not know much, if anything, about the financial aid process, and they did not know anything about student loans, which were just becoming available. So, when dad was accepted into college, he and granddad went down to the bank—the same one where granddad would work as a janitor—to see if they could borrow the money. My dad said:

> Dad and I went down to the bank, and dad told the guy working there that he needed a loan so his son could go to college. The people at the bank knew him, and they knew he was good for the money. They listened to him, and then a few minutes later, they were making out a check that would let me get started. I felt really proud of my dad. It meant a lot to me that he was the kind of person that the people at the bank trusted.

A year ago, I was invited to speak at a university located just across the river from Marietta in Vienna, West Virginia. I was thrilled to get the invitation for a couple of reasons. The first was because I enjoy working with institutions of higher education, and this was one that impressed me. The second was due to its proximity to Marietta.

I called my dad and asked if he wanted to join me, and he agreed. While there, we planned to go see some sights, and then on Sunday, we would go to the church he had attended while growing up, which was the same one that granddad cleaned as the janitor. Dad made arrangements to present the work he was a part of in Guatemala. I kept to myself the reason I was interested in going until we got there.

When my grandfather would clean the church, he did something that I thought was unusual. He took the time to make sure every songbook was facing the same direction. I asked him about it once, and he said, "When people come in here, if they notice that someone took enough care to get the details right, maybe it will help them know that what happens here is important." This approach to life is one that I have adopted. Consequently, if you ever attend a Strata Leadership event, hosted anywhere in the United States or abroad, you might notice our attention to the details. When someone walks into one of our programs, we want to set the tone for the event by taking care of the details. Not only is this a reflection of our belief in the "2M2N" approach to life, but it is also a nod to my grandfather's memory.

When we decided to attend the church where he had worked, I was curious to see if his small gesture persisted after his passing. At that time, it had likely been 25 years since he had cleaned the building. I parked my rental car on the curb, got out, and crossed the brick-lined street. I opened the front door, was hit with the familiar smell of the church, and was instantly transported back to my childhood. I crossed over the lobby and made my way to one of the wooden double doors that opened into the auditorium. I pushed the door open and scanned the pews. Although the songbooks that I had known as a child had been exchanged for new ones, I smiled when I noticed that every single one of them was facing the same direction. If they had not been, I would not have been surprised, but the fact they were meant a lot to me. Specifically, it meant that when someone serves with excellence, they are sometimes able to set a standard that the next generation chooses to keep. I do not know who is responsible for cleaning the auditorium at the church on the corner of Sixth and Washington streets, but I would imagine they do not know why they make sure the songbooks are all facing the same direction. I do, and it makes me happy.

By watching my grandfather, I learned that he took pride in doing things the right way. He never used those words, but his actions revealed his beliefs. For several years, he would make wooden rocking horses and sell them in his front yard. They were rustic and sturdy and a source of pride for him. I know he was proud of his work because, on the underbelly of those rocking horses, he would take the time to carve, sometimes in cursive:

Glen Mellor
107 Wooster Street
Marietta, Ohio

You do not take the time to carve your name into wood if you are not proud of your work. It is because of people like my granddad that I would come to realize that your title does not define you, but the way you do your job does. If we are defined by how we do our jobs, what is the legacy you are leaving behind?

In my office, you can see the inheritance my grandfather left me. Three small hammers are stacked on top of one another on the top shelf of my bookshelf. The bookshelf is an old barrister style, and the three hammers sit behind a thin pane of glass. They represent an attitude that he took to work and to life, and it is a foundational piece of the mental model I have chosen.

Another connection to my granddad is that my computer bag is different from most. Due to its age and fragility, I do not always carry it, but the bag is something special to me. It is a leather U.S. Mail Bag that was used in the U.S. Navy during World War II. I carry it to remember my roots and as an expression of gratitude to those who have gone before me. One of the main reasons why I like to carry it is because I like to feel the full weight of the bag on my shoulder. When I carry it for a longtime, it gets uncomfortable. When it does, I am reminded of the miles and miles that my grandfather carried his mailbag to provide for our family. It makes me think of those who went before me. In those moments, I stand a little taller, because I am standing on the shoulders of giants.

Who are the giants in your life?

Why do you consider them to be giants?

CHAPTER 13

"30 MILES CHANGES YOUR PERSPECTIVE"

Making Hard Choices

Each summer, our family tries to spend some time in one or more of the national parks. In addition to seeing amazing places, we also use this time to make memories with my parents. They enjoy traveling, and we are always glad when they are able to join the journey. Over the years, our little family, representing three generations, has hiked trails in beautiful places like the Grand Tetons, Yosemite, and Olympic National Park.

Because my dad seemed to enjoy hiking on these trips, it did not surprise me too much when he began talking to me about backpacking gear. Nor did I think much of it when he began telling me about the books he had been reading about hiking. It was a surprise, however, when he announced that he had been researching the Appalachian Trail (A.T.) and that he and my uncle were planning on hiking part of it. In my experience, most people do not begin their hiking careers in his or her 70s, but my dad and uncle were intrigued by the idea and decided to make it happen.

The A.T. is 2,190 miles long and traverses 14 states. The southern terminus of the trail is in Georgia's Springer Mountain. The northern terminus is at Mount Katahdin in Maine. The A.T. is the longest hiking-only footpath in the world.[1]

Some will hike the A.T. in one season as thru-hikers. For most, it takes 5 to 7 months to complete the journey, although the odds of completion are typically only one in four.[2] Others will hike the A.T. in multi-day or section hikes. Section hikers may take years to complete the entire journey. This approach is popular among those who do not have flexibility in their schedule to take off months at a time.

My dad and uncle decided to begin their trek on the A.T. with a multi-day hike. It is suggested that section hikers begin in Georgia instead of Maine. By starting in the south, it helps avoid some of the knee problems that can emerge on the rocky terrain of the New Hampshire and Maine sections.[3]

Beginning at Springer Mountain, they planned to hike north for a week. During the trip, they hoped to become more familiar with hiking and backpacking. The first major stopping point on the A.T. is a historic stone building that was completed in 1937 by the Civil Conservation Corps (CCC). The building was named the Walasi-Yi Interpretive Center (pronounced Wa La See Yee) in recognition of the Cherokee who had lived in the area prior to their forced removal in 1838. According to Cherokee mythology, the gap was the home of a giant frog, and the term Walasi-Yi is believed to mean the "place of the great frog."[4] The area was known as "Frogtown Gap" until 1946 when it was renamed Neel's Gap in honor of the chief engineer of U.S. Highway 129, which connected the area to the outside world.[5]

The center served as a dining hall, inn, and dancehall for the first few decades of its existence until it was closed in 1965. For the next few years, it was a studio for a local artist, and it then was abandoned for some years in the 1970s. Recognizing its historical significance, locals stepped in to preserve the building and were able to get it listed on the National Registry of Historical Places in 1977. In 1983, the building became the home of Mountain Crossings, a store dedicated to serving hikers and those interested in outdoor adventure gear and supplies. Since that time, it has become a nearly mythical friend to hikers.[6]

One of the services Mountain Crossings is famous for is providing a "Shake Down" for hikers' backpacks. Each year, they do hundreds of "Shake Downs," and nearly ten thousand pounds of gear is sent home. Keep in mind that each member of the staff is extremely qualified, and all but one have thru-hiked the entire A.T. According to their website, "Our varied staff of former thru-hikers have made all the mistakes you can imagine over our collective 27,000 miles of hiking, but we have learned a lot from those miles!"[7] The process is straightforward; one of the members of the staff will go through each item in your pack and provide suggestions about what you could leave behind and what you might need to pick up for the remainder of the trip.

Recently, Mountain Crossings has begun offering a "Virtual Shake Down" service. The online service is available at the cost of $100, but this amount can be applied toward anything offered in the shop. Anticipating questions about the fee, the store's website offers its rationale for why hikers should make the investment. In a section titled "Why do I need a Shake Down" the site offers the following:

> There is so much information out there about lightweight backpacking, but nothing teaches you as well as experience. After three days of walking on the AT, you have a much better sense of what you need to carry and what you can leave behind than when you were standing on Springer. If you're still unsure, our staff make of former thru-hikers can help you trim down on the unneeded items. Take it from those who have already learned the hard way, carrying everything you think you want 1,500 miles and then finally dumping it only to realize you wish you had done it, in the beginning, is a tough pill to swallow. Don't make your thru-hike tougher than it has to be. Get a Shake Down![8]

I have often been told there are two primary reasons people are willing to change: opportunity or pain. As much as we may wish that the promise of a better situation would cause us to change, this is typically not the case. Most people are open to change when the pain of their current situation is too great, and they are seeking relief.

The location of the Mountain Crossings store is one of the primary reasons I think it is so successful. Located 31.7 miles down the trail, it takes most hikers at least three days to get there. After hiking for just three days, a hiker will know all too well how much their pack weighs. I have never been to the store, but I am assuming there is little marketing needed to convince weary hikers of the value of the service.

THE SHAKE DOWN

One of the experiences offered by Strata Leadership is an intensive learning experience known as the Institute for Emerging Leaders (IEL). Each program is limited to 30 high potentials that forge deep friendships with one another through the event. On the final day of the program, when trust has been established, we offer our version of the pack shake down.

In a group-coaching format, we ask each member of the program to consider their future and identify what they need to leave behind in order to succeed. In addition, we ask them to describe what they will need to pick up for the remainder of the trip. Although I have participated in this exercise on multiple occasions, I always look forward to it. It is an awakening experience for many.

It can be tough to recognize that you need to leave something behind to be able to get where you want to go. Sometimes the reason we have carried something in our pack for so long is because someone we trusted told us we would need it. Even when it has become obvious the advice given us does not match our experience, it can be difficult to reconcile the advice with the reality of our situation. Consequently, many will continue carrying unnecessary burdens. While this added weight might be manageable walking on flat ground, when the terrain becomes more demanding and the pace more important, it will become increasingly difficult to keep up. This is why an approach to life that worked at one point does not always work at another point. If you are seeking to maximize your life, you cannot do so without making tough choices.

One of the key reasons so many people are unwilling to make the difficult choice is that they are locked into a survival mentality and have a hard time seeing the bigger picture. Tunnel vision is a common challenge for people who get so focused on the immediate threat or goal. They cannot see the bigger picture. When someone is trapped in this loop, I like to remind him or her there is more than "one bear in the woods."

GLACIER NATIONAL PARK

It has been said that America's greatest idea was the constitution, and its second was the creation of the national parks. From my perspective, there is something to this argument. If you grew up like me and did not live near any of the parks in the national system, it may be time for a road trip.

People experience the national parks in different ways. Some prefer to see them on a tour bus, others in a vehicle, on a bike, and still others on foot. There is really not a bad option, but my favorite way to explore is on foot. Life is good when I have a pack on my back and hiking boots on my feet. Since our family's first trip to the Grand Tetons when I was in my mid-30s, I have hiked about three thousand miles. While some of those miles have been with friends and family, often they are alone.

When hiking in most of the parks, there are several signs posted about the danger of solo hiking. There are numerous risks involved when dealing with nature. To mitigate those risks, I take as many precautions as possible. When hiking alone, I stay on the trail and carry a pack that has the gear needed to be able to manage inclement weather, self-administer first aid, navigate, and survive.

While on the trail, I have experienced some amazing things. Among the most memorable moments are the times when I have encountered bears in the wild. Thus far, I have seen about 15 bears while in the national parks. While some have seen that number in a single day in one of the Alaskan parks, for me, each sighting has been a special moment. Of that group, 13 were black bears, and two were grizzlies.

When I told friends that I was headed to Glacier National Park, they shared with me that the bears there were bigger than those in the Tetons, Yellowstone, or Sequoia national parks. I took that under advisement but did not really know what to expect. Glacier is located in northern Montana and shares the border with Canada. It is the home of some of the most scenic views on the planet. Not surprisingly, the famed "Going to the Sun" road is considered one of the top 10 most beautiful drives on the planet. The road is narrow and not intended for those who have issues with heights.

One afternoon, I decided to go for a hike, but I was limited on time. So, I looked for something that was near the western entrance of the park. I found a few spots on the map and made my way there. I parked the car, put on my pack, and got to the trailhead. Most of the trailheads have posted warnings about any unusual threats you may encounter while on the trail. This one had several warnings about bears and about not hiking alone. I took note that I needed to stay alert and then began up the trail.

There had been a large fire in the area a few years earlier, which had left some parts of the park uneven. For example, during the first part of the hike, there were not as many trees, and the foliage was green and full of life. Once I got past where the fire had been, the forest was thick with trees. It was in the heat of the summer, and the added shade felt great.

As the trail began to get steep, to help manage the elevation, there were multiple switchbacks to make the trail more enjoyable for hikers like me. When hiking, I like to use hiking or trekking poles. The poles help with balance, reduce pressure on your knees, and provide a workout for your arms. When I'm hiking alone, every hundred yards or so, I will strike the poles together a few times to make a clicking sound that I hope will warn any animals of my presence.

I had just "clicked" the poles together when I heard a noise above me. I looked up quickly, and about 30 yards above was the largest bear I had ever seen. I instinctively stopped in my tracks as the massive grizzly turned away from me and ran into the forest. You would think that a bear of this size would be easy to see among the trees, but you would be wrong. I was standing in the middle of the trail scanning for the bear that I had just watched run into the forest, but I could not find him.

It was at that moment that I decided my hike was over. With my bear repellent spray at the ready, I began to make my way back down the trail carefully. As I was walking, I kept trying to locate the bear, but I was not having any luck. A couple of days earlier, there had been a national park employee killed by a bear within a few miles of my location, and at that point, they had not yet been able to find the bear. I told myself that this bear was unlikely to be the same one. Furthermore, the employee who been killed was riding a mountain bike when he surprised the bear, and I was on foot and unlikely to be considered a threat. As carefully as possible, I continued making my way down the trail and had gotten maybe 50 yards when a western terrestrial garter snake slithered across the trail, and I nearly stepped on it.

It is amazing to me how the brain works. Normally, nearly stepping on an unexpected snake while hiking through the woods would have caused me to jump. In this situation, in an instant, I saw the snake, avoided stepping on it, and simultaneously remembered there were no poisonous snakes in this part of the park. Instead of responding to the snake, I continued my descent while looking for the bear in the area I saw him enter the forest.

The problem with seeing one bear is that you tend to be so focused on it that you become less aware of the other threats around you. There is something about seeing a grizzly that inspires tunnel vision. While this level of focus may be helpful in the short-term, it can become a significant problem in the long-term. The grizzly that I saw was not the only bear in the forest. After the snake went by, I realized I was only looking in one direction and that I needed to be attentive to what was both in front and behind me. I expanded my area of focus and continued down the trail toward my car.

Sometimes we are so focused on what is directly in front of us that we become too focused. When this happens, we are only focused on the immediate. While this may help us get through the moment, it can also keep us from seeing the big picture.

If you are serious about pursuing a life that matters, it will require seeing the big picture and adjusting accordingly. If you are only hiking a mile or two, carrying a pack that is weighted down may not matter much. If you are considering hiking the A.T., it matters a lot. If you are interested in a life that matters, it requires a long haul. Consequently, it is time for a mental shakedown.

What do you need to leave behind? What do you need to stop believing to be able to get where you want to go?

What do you need for the journey ahead? What changes need to be made to your mental model to keep moving forward?

CHAPTER 14

"A GRADUATION OF ONE"

Claiming What Is Yours

Although the natural and rugged beauty of Arkansas is undeniable, it is a long way away from my dad's home in the mid-Ohio Valley. It was in September of 1966 that Glen and Helen Mellor proudly drove their 19-year-old son, my dad, to enroll in college. From the front steps of their home in Marietta, Ohio, it was 825 miles to Harding College, which is located in Central Arkansas.

The windows were down for most of the trip, and they were making good time. The family car was a brown, four-door, 1963 AMC Rambler. Glen pushed the six-cylinder engine to the speed limit, and the morning air circulated through the vehicle. It was an adventure, and every mile was taking them farther and farther from home.

The trip would take the better part of three days. Each night, they would find a motel along the way. One evening, they stopped at a motel with a pool. It was an unexpected luxury that none of them had ever experienced before.

During the day, they would eat food brought from home, but in the evenings, they stopped at sit-down restaurants. Like many families at the time, restaurants were a novelty. In fact, the first time dad had ever been to a restaurant was the year before. He was a senior in high school and had been recognized as the player of the week on his football team, which meant he and one of his coaches received a complimentary steak dinner at a local establishment. When he got to the restaurant, he was nervous. He and his coach were seated and given menus, but dad was not sure what he was supposed to do. The waiter approached their table to take their order and he was relieved when the coach ordered first. When the waiter turned to him, my dad said, "I would like the same thing."

The last stop before Arkansas was a motel in Cairo, Illinois. The next morning, the smell of coffee mingled with the smell of the gasoline engine as they made the final push to Harding. As they headed south, they passed one farm after another. Eventually, they started seeing signs for Searcy, which was their destination.

Searcy became a college town in 1889 with the opening of Galloway Women's College. The college, affiliated with the Methodists, had a respectable, new campus with impressive facilities that would have resembled something found in the more established schools in the northeast. The grounds were manicured, and the pathways were lined with oak trees. Although the school was beloved by its faculty, staff, and students, it was not immune to the financial challenges that gripped the United States during the Great Depression. Due to declining enrollment, it was with great sadness that the doors were closed in 1933. Galloway merged with nearby Hendrix College, a school that was also affiliated with the Methodists. Although the choice to merge was undoubtedly difficult, Hendrix has thrived since and remains a highly respected institution.

The once-promising campus sat empty and silent for a year until the leaders at Harding College, which was located in the town of Morrilton, 70 miles to the west, was able to buy the campus in an auction. Against the odds, the cash-poor school had been able to secure a mortgage of $75,000 to buy the campus, which was thought to have been worth nearly $500,000 prior to the depression.[1] Although Searcy was grateful to have another school, Harding was not a sure bet, and the news would have likely caused more than a few raised eyebrows.

Harding, which had been founded in 1924, was a relatively new school and had significant financial challenges of its own. The school had been the result of a merger between two junior colleges, Harper College, which had been founded in 1915 in Harper, Kansas, and Arkansas Christian College, which had been organized in 1919 and opened for its first students in 1922. The new institution was affiliated with the Churches of Christ, but considering the Churches of Christ are not organized as a denomination and do not have a centralized hierarchy, this meant that if the school did not have the ability to pay its bills, there was not a larger entity that could step in to assist.

Whether he was aware of it or not, when dad arrived at Harding, it was an institution in transition. George Benson, had just retired as president after serving in the role from 1936-1964, and a new president was at the helm. The new leader, Dr. Clifton Ganus Jr., had graduated from Harding in 1943 with a degree in Bible and history. He returned to Harding to teach in 1946 after earning an M.A. in history from Tulane and quickly became a student favorite at Harding. He completed his Ph.D. in history from Tulane in 1953.[2]

One of the reasons for his popularity was that he was a storyteller. When Ganus told a story, he did not seem to be in a hurry. An educator at heart, his stories were detailed and layered with meaning. Also, he possessed a distinctive voice that was reminiscent of James Earl Jones. Even in his 90s, Dr. Ganus is routinely asked by Harding University's football and basketball teams to star in their recruiting videos. The request is not meant to simply be an honor for a revered man in the twilight of his life; it is because his voice and presence, even at his advanced age, is still that commanding.

As Dr. Ganus took the helm in 1965, the school, which was on relatively strong footing, began experiencing unprecedented growth. From the fall of 1964 until the fall of 1966, student enrollment had grown by 40%. In the fall of 1966, my dad would be one of 850 first-time college students at a school with a total enrollment of 1,750 students.[3]

Of the 29 major buildings on campus, 24 had been built since 1950. Although many of the facilities were new, the campus felt much older than the collective age of its structures. This was due in part to the classical design of its red brick buildings but also because of the natural features of the property itself.

The core of the campus is designed around a large quad area. From east to west, the quad is approximately a football field wide. From north to south, the area was two and a half to three football fields long. The American Heritage Center anchored the northern end of the quad. The center, which had recently been completed, included a four-story hotel and a 500-seat auditorium. When guests arrived at the hotel, they pulled in under a large canopy that was wide enough for two or three cars to fit comfortably. The lobby would have still smelled of fresh paint and new carpet the first time my dad walked through it. At the southern end of the quad was the Administration Building, which was the most prominent building on campus. The entrance of the building is flanked by four columns, each 40 feet tall, and is intended to impress. In addition to housing several offices and classrooms, it was also home to a 1,350-seat auditorium along with a smaller 200-seat venue.

Near the northern end of the quad is an area known as the "Front Lawn." It is an ideal place for students to throw a Frisbee or play a pick-up game of touch football. Several large oak trees that created islands of shade on the grass below canopied the remaining two thirds of the quad. The most mature trees were already old and tall before the first buildings were constructed. Nestled below the branches of the trees, there were occasional pink and white dogwoods and numerous decorative shrubs. For generations, the quad has been a place to enjoy a pleasant afternoon.

Under the shade of the trees are the famous, "Harding Swings." Made of wood and painted white, their distinctive design is timeless. They are inviting and have universal appeal. Each freestanding swing comfortably seats two people. The structure that holds the swing is made of 4x4 beams, and there is a simple pergola above the seating area to provide shade. The design of the swings is credited to a Harding employee who began building them soon after the school moved to Searcy in 1934.[4]

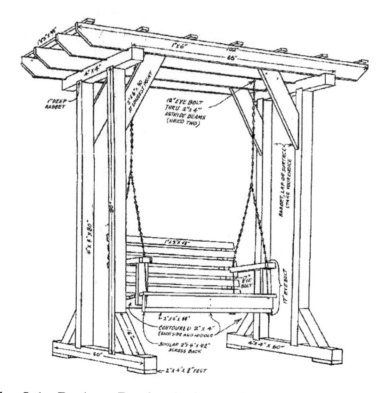

The Lily Pool or Pond, which stood directly in front of the Administration Building, would have definitely caught his eye. An oval-shaped pool, it was about 50 feet long and 30 feet wide. The friendliness of the water feature helped offset the seriousness of the tall granite columns that created a sense of drama when entering the Administration Building.

The Lily Pool had been constructed in 1952 as a replacement of the original Lily Pond, which had been built decades earlier a few hundred yards away when the school was still Galloway College. As the name suggests, the original pond, which was a shallow earthen pond circled by stones, had lily pads and a few goldfish. The new concrete pool was painted pale blue to enhance the beauty of the water; lily pads were added along with a small birdbath placed in the middle of the pool. In 1968, the Student Association raised $1,100 to add a lighted fountain and benches nearby.[5]

Once installed, the fountain dutifully propelled streams of chlorinated water a few feet into the sky before gravity eventually pulled it heavily back into the pool. Although the lily pads would eventually be removed, the original name stuck, and it would forever be known as the "Lily Pool." Little did my father know at the time, but this spot would end up being a place of great importance for his future.

As the sun went down on the first night in his new home, it was a warm evening. The year before, the first dormitory with air-conditioning had been opened, but he was not assigned the new dorm. Life without AC would not be too much of a hardship, however, as he, and likely many of his classmates, did not have it at home either. The hum of box fans throughout the dorms muffled but did not erase the sounds of nature's orchestra that filtered into the open windows of the dorm. In time, the music of the cicadas, crickets, and katydids; the calls of distant frogs and the melodies of the songbirds would fade into the background. During the first few nights, everything was new.

Sports had been a refuge for my dad since childhood. In high school, wrestling was likely his best sport with football coming in second. When he learned that Harding did not have a wrestling team, he decided to play football instead. His first year, he played on the freshman (or junior varsity) team. After completing his first season, he had expected to continue playing at the varsity level, but he was told that he could not play varsity while also working. He would have to choose between playing football or working. Whether this was a rule for collegiate athletes or a team rule was unclear, but considering he could not afford to stay in school unless he was working to help pay his bills, the choice was obvious. Without a viable option, he reluctantly hung up his cleats and walked away from a sport that had been a mainstay in his life since the sixth grade.

Marietta High School did not have a swim team, but he had worked at the YMCA throughout high school and had been a competitive swimmer and diver there. When he learned that he could be on the swim team while also working a part-time job, he joined. Practice was at 6:00 a.m., which made it possible for him to go to class during the day, unload trucks at a local warehouse late at night, and still make it to practice. His commitment was noticed, and he was eventually named team captain by his teammates.

SUSAN HANKINS

Susan Elaine Hankins was born on Sunday, August 14, 1949, in Topeka, Kansas. She was the second daughter of Hank and Arvoca Hankins. Her sister, Jana Lee, was born two years earlier, and the two have always been best friends.

Her father went by Hank, but his given name was Willis Dorven Hankins. Born in Kansas City, Missouri, on Friday, April 21, 1922, he had jet-black hair, was usually the tallest person in the room, and had a calming presence. A dedicated family man, he enjoyed people as well as outdoor sports like hunting and fishing. After graduating from high school, he had a few odd jobs before serving stateside in the U.S. Naval Reserve (USNR) as an Aviation Chief Machinist's Mate (ACMM) in World War II. Following the war, he attended a small business school in Kansas City to learn business basics. Due to his ability to connect with others, it was suggested he focus his efforts on sales and he spent the majority of his adult life selling International Harvester products.

Susan's mother was born Ona Arvoca Phillips on Wednesday, January 9, 1918, to Jeston and Margaret Phillips in the small Missouri town of Braymer. She went by her middle name throughout her life. It is unclear why her parents chose the name Arvoca, but the word is a Chippewa term that means, "meeting place."

Although she was a product of the Great Depression and came from a small rural town, Arvoca had an uncanny sense of style. Confident and creative, she enjoyed traveling and learning. She drove fast, had a great sense of humor, and had an optimistic outlook throughout her lifetime. In her final years, when Alzheimer's had robbed her of much of her memory and personality, the caregivers and family would ask how she was doing, and her response was always the same. She would smile and say, "Better."

Married on December 5, 1942, Hank and Arvoca were deeply committed to one another. Their marriage would provide a model of what married life could be for their daughters, Jana and Susan. Susan was born in Kansas, but in the first 18 years of life, she had called Kansas, Texas, New Mexico, and Missouri home.

Susan's parents were loving and devout, and they had high expectations for their children. They were the kind of people who did not argue in front of their children, and much of their social life was built around their friends from church. The pictures of them from those years are of people who appear genuinely happy. Moving so often was not easy, but it had helped bond the Hankins family together. They learned to rely on each other and would do so the rest of their lives. Although they were not a wealthy family, they had broken into the middle-class, drove good cars, and were able to take family vacations. When Hank had his first heart attack at the age of 38, their world was shaken.

Hank made as many lifestyle changes as he knew how to reduce his risks but there was little the cardiologists could do to help. In the pictures of Hank in the years that followed his first attack, as well as the subsequent attacks, it was clear he was not well. He was only in his 40s, but he could have passed for someone a generation older. He put his things in order, and although it was left unsaid, he was obviously hoping to live long enough to see his children chart their own course.

A generation earlier, Hank and Arvoca had longed to attend college at Harding, but World War II and other practical matters made it unfeasible. As a result, sending their two daughters there was a dream come true. Susan graduated from Glendale High School in 1967 in Springfield, Missouri, and started at Harding that fall.

My mother, Susan, recalled the first time she noticed my dad. He was playing with a little boy who appeared to be 3 or 4 years old. Standing near the Lily Pool, he was swinging the child over the water and acting as if he might let go. The boy screamed in delight as if it were the best Disneyland had to offer. She noticed the way he interacted with the boy and thought, "That guy is going to be a great dad." Considering her dad was the greatest man she knew, the fact that this had been her first impression was significant.

The two became friends, but they did not date. My dad was in a serious relationship that he thought would lead to marriage. When the person he thought would become his wife broke up with him, he was surprised by his feelings. Instead of wanting to fight for the relationship, he found himself walking to my mother's dorm to see if she would like to go on a date. She said "yes," and the two began dating in the spring of 1968.

For some people, if they were asked to identify the turning point moment in their lives, they would have to stop and think about it. This would not be the case for dad. From the moment he started dating, Susan Hankins, he charted a new course.

Frustrated by his inability to take her on what he considered a "real" date, due to a lack of funds, one afternoon, while standing near the edge of the Lily Pool, he jokingly said to a friend, "If I do a flip into this water, will you give me a quarter?" Considering the water was less than 18 inches deep, his friend was intrigued. He said, "Sure!" There was a bench near the edge of the pool, and a few moments later, he successfully made the dive. A crowd began to form, and he offered new spectators the same deal. In a few minutes, he had the money needed to take her out.

Life was good for the couple, but there were issues that threatened the budding relationship. One was uncertainty about the Vietnam War. Like most men during that time, David wrestled with what to do. He wanted to do what he thought was right, but for a host of reasons, discerning what was right was complicated. Although there were some at that time who were enrolling in college to avoid service, this had not been his motivation. Being in college would defer his service as long as he was successfully pursuing his undergraduate degree, but once he was no longer a student, he would immediately become eligible for the draft.

In anticipation of finishing school, he had a few options to consider. One option was to enlist. His brother, who was nearly five years older, had enlisted in the Army a few years prior. He served stateside and in Germany before being honorably discharged prior to the escalation of the Vietnam War. If he chose this option, he could be more selective about which branch of the Armed Forces to join. The problem was that, although he had respect for those who served in this capacity, he would only be choosing to serve because of Vietnam. Based on his life experiences, he knew the impact that he could make in the lives of young people through athletics, and he wanted to choose a path that allowed him to follow his passion through coaching.

Another option would be to wait to see if he was drafted. Considering one, if not both of his grandfathers, had been drafted for World War I and his father had been drafted for World War II, he knew the possibility of him being drafted for Vietnam was very real. If he waited for the draft board to decide his fate, he would lose control over choosing the branch in which he would serve. After a great deal of consideration, he chose not to enlist. He concluded that he would not do anything to avoid the draft, and if he were required to serve, he would do so to the best of his ability.

In an effort to make the draft more equitable, in 1970, the Nixon administration adopted a lottery process. On December 1, 1969, young men, specifically those born from 1944-1950, along with their friends and family, gathered anxiously around televisions and radios to listen to a life-changing broadcast. The process was straightforward: 366 plastic capsules were placed in a large glass bowl. Inside each of the small containers was a slip of paper on which one day of the year (including February 29) had been written. Drawn one at a time, each capsule was opened and then announced. The first date to be announced was September 14th. Consequently, the men born from 1944-1950 on September 14th were assigned the number 001. This "low number" meant they would be the first to be drafted. The second slip of paper read April 24th, which meant those born on the 24th would be assigned the number 002. The process continued until every day had been assigned a lottery number. My dad's birthday, April 20th was a "high number," and he was assigned number 345, which meant it was nearly certain he would not be drafted.[6]

The couple's second hurdle was that my dad was struggling to stay in school. His undiagnosed learning disabilities required he put in more and more effort as he progressed through college. Often, he fully grasped the concept being taught, but when he attempted to transcribe to paper what was in his head, it was a disaster. He would never be tested or receive an official diagnosis, but the evidence strongly suggests that he had dyslexia.

Initially, he was placed on academic probation, which was meant to let a student know that they were beginning to fall behind. Eventually, he was placed on strict academic probation, which was the status given just before a student was dismissed for their grades. Susan recognized the problem was not his level of intelligence but something deeper. Armed with this awareness, she began assisting him by helping edit and type his papers. With help, he felt he had a fighting chance. Not only did his confidence begin to rebound, but his grades also improved.

There are numerous forms of leadership, but the approach my mother used with my father, and would later use on her sons, says a great deal about her personal character. She saw an opportunity to help my father realize his potential, and she used an amazing amount of wisdom in helping him find his way. Recognizing the challenges he was facing could not be fixed by simply working harder, she used quiet leadership to help bridge the gap.

He viewed himself as lacking intelligence, but she did not see him that way at all. She knew he was smart, but she also knew that judging his potential using the traditional academic standard was neither fair nor accurate. From her perspective, someone who was willing to work as hard as he was willing to work was bound to be successful. His tenacity and sheer determination was something to behold. Most people with challenges like his would have given up years earlier.

TRANSITIONS

As the relationship grew, he knew she was the one but he was not as confident that she felt the same way. He decided he was going to ask her to marry him but was not sure how she would respond. After thinking about it, he decided to pop the question on April 1st. His rationale was simple. If she said "no" he would play it off as an April Fool's joke. If she said "yes," he would be the happiest man in the world. When he asked, her answer was "yes," and the two were married on Thursday, March 26, 1970.

He finished the spring semester in 1970 and had just two courses remaining before graduation when he got a call from a mentor, Gene Bell. Dad had worked part-time with "Mr. Bell" at the YMCA in Marietta for five years while in high school and college. Mr. Bell had recently moved to Vincennes, Indiana, to become the director of the YMCA, and he offered my dad the role of Youth and Aquatic Instructor.

He had not yet graduated, but he was so close they were willing to hire him anyway. The job would be a chance to launch his career with the "Y" and an opportunity to work alongside a mentor. In addition to his title at the "Y," he would also be named the Knox County Water Safety Chairman and the swimming instructor for the Vincennes University's swimming classes.

He accepted the offer. Before long, he and my mother moved to Vincennes to start their new life together. The local paper printed a picture of him with Mr. Bell and another colleague and incorrectly stated that he was a graduate of Harding. It was the first of many times he would be reminded that he had come close but had not yet finished his degree.

Although he planned to finish the last couple of classes, life quickly got in the way. The newlyweds had only been married for four months when my mother became pregnant. It was a time of celebration for the family, especially my mother's family, as this would be the first grandchild for Hank and Arvoca.

Everything changed on Friday, March 12, 1971, when Susan's dad passed away. He was just 48 years old. Although his heart condition had been serious for nearly a decade, his passing was crushing. The family assembled in Springfield and did their best to console one another. The funeral was massive as people from throughout the area gathered to express both their grief and respect for Hank. They were comforted by Hank's abiding faith in God, but the loss was profound.

Sixty-six days after the death of her father, on Monday, May 17, 1971, Susan gave birth to Matthew Willis Mellor. The birth of a child is always a reason for celebration, but the arrival of this child was truly a gift from God. He was an island of joy in a sea of grief. Of all of the pictures of my grandmother, the ones I treasure the most are those from this time of life. She is holding my brother tightly, and her face is filled with genuine happiness. Her resilience was nothing short of remarkable. The same could be said for my mother and aunt, who had loved their father so deeply. My brother's birth was a reminder of why people must go on, even in the face of great loss.

GRADUATES

With work and family obligations mounting, Dad's dream of completing his degree began to fade. Money was tight, and he doubted that he could pass the courses. Furthermore, his career had already begun and getting the degree did not seem to be the highest priority. He focused his efforts on his family and his career and before long, the years began to pass by. If my dad harbored any hope of finishing his diploma, it was put on pause when my brother started college.

Matthew graduated from college in May of 1995. All of the family who could make it for the occasion sat in the Benson Auditorium at Harding University in anticipation. When his name was eventually called, it was the first time in history that someone with our last name had ever received a college diploma. While finishing his undergraduate degree, Matthew had also been taking several graduate courses that could be applied toward a Master of Education. Consequently, after finishing his undergraduate degree, he earned a graduate degree in August of the same year.

To complete the trifecta, I graduated from Harding in December of 1995. Although it was not as historic as my brother's moment, it was a great moment nonetheless. A year later, in December of 1996, I asked Christie Bishop to be my wife. She said "yes," and we decided to get married on Saturday, May 17, 1997.

In anticipation of coming to campus for the wedding, my mother called the registrar's office at Harding to check on which classes my dad would need to complete in order to receive his degree. I am not sure what prompted her to make the call, but I can only assume that since she had gotten her sons through college, it was now time to finally get her husband through too. She gave them the information needed, and they replied that they did not yet have the records from that era in the current computer system. They would have to go into the "vault" to find the paper copies.

A few hours later, the registrar returned her call. He shared they had been able to find my dad's transcript without any problems, but when reviewing it, they found something unexpected. Although it was true that he did not have enough credit hours to receive a degree in kinesiology, he did have enough credit hours to receive a degree in general studies. On behalf of people who likely no longer worked at Harding, he said, "We should have caught this a long time ago, and I am very sorry."

When my dad came home later that day, my mother sat him down to explain what had happened. She was not sure how he would take the news. Would it be cause for celebration or cause for anger or sadness? She relayed the conversation she had with the registrar. It took a moment to register fully. When it did, his eyes filled with tears of gratitude and relief. It is an amazing moment when you have believed something for years that was not true. For years he had believed he did not have what it took to finish school when in reality it had already been done.

The evening before our wedding, Christie and I had a traditional rehearsal dinner. The dinner was hosted in the heart of the Harding campus on the second floor of the Student Center. About halfway through the dinner, Dr. Burks slipped out unnoticed. A few minutes later, he reemerged dressed in his full academic regalia. In one hand, he held a framed diploma.

My dad noticed him walking in, but he did not think it odd and assumed he must have been on his way to or from an event. Dr. Burks walked to the front of the room and began telling the group about a special graduate. It was then that my dad began to put it together. Our rehearsal dinner was also his college graduation. He called my father to the front of the room and presented David Russell Mellor his diploma. I have been witness to my fair share of special moments, but this one was among my favorites.

In an instant, my father had displaced my brother as the first Mellor to have ever earned a college degree. I am confident that my brother could not have been happier. Not only had dad received his degree, but he had also received it in a graduation of one. It is always nice to have someone in the family who graduated first in their class.

WHAT DO YOU NEED TO STOP BELIEVING?

My dad is much better at buying cars today than he was earlier in life, but I think it is safe to say the 1970s represented a dark period in car buying for the Mellor family. We were among a precious few Americans who could say we had owned three different models of the AMC brands—Rambler, Gremlin, and Hornet. With that said, there was one purchase that he got right during that time period. He hit a home run when he brought home a Buick station wagon. Even by the standards of the pre-fuel crisis cars, the Buick Century was huge. It was a little over 19 feet long, and at a width of 6 and a half feet, it provided enough interior space to compete with a school bus. Weighing in at a curb weight of 5,400 lbs., it remains one of the heaviest cars ever produced.

Evidently in the 1970s, if your parents loved you, they would leave you in the car when they went into a store. One day, my mother had to grab a few things at a grocery store and left my brother, our foster sister, and me in the car for a few minutes. What happened next is one of the reasons why parents no longer leave their children in the car when they have to run an errand.

My brother is one of the most creative people I know. I have always admired his work ethic and willingness to learn how to build and repair things. Even when he was in elementary school when an appliance would stop working, he would take it apart, diagnose the problem, and if possible, fix it. In high school, he learned to work on cars and did his best to restore a 1964 Chevrolet truck and a 1965

Plymouth Valiant convertible. He learned to rebuild the engines, fix the bodywork, and reupholster the interior.

I mention his inquisitive nature and proclivity for all things mechanical because cars during that era were built for utility versus safety. For example, there were three rows of seats, but I do not ever recall using a seat belt. There were no cup holders, but there was a more-than-ample ashtray. Of all the mechanical devices on the car, the one that grabbed my brother's attention the most was the cigarette lighter.

When mom went into the store, my brother went for the lighter. Borrowing from what I assume to be technology similar to a toaster, once the lighter is activated, it remains depressed until it reaches a certain temperature and then releases. When the lighter was ready, it would make a distinct popping sound. Amazingly, one end of the lighter remains cool enough to hold, while the other end is so hot that it turns the metal coil bright orange.

I am not sure what went through my brother's mind when he was holding the lighter. He looked at the lighter in his hand, and then he looked at the vinyl dashboard. Without saying a word, he placed the lighter firmly on the dashboard and held it there. After holding it in place for a moment, it began smoking. He pulled the lighter back to see what had happened. The result was a perfect circle melted into the dashboard.

We were never abused, but I knew this one was going to cost him. He could see the fear in my eyes and I said, "You are dead." Instead of changing course, he doubled down. He put the warm lighter back in the receptacle and pushed it again. A few moments later, it popped, and he pulled it out. He proceeded to make a straight line of circles across the dashboard.

When mom made it back to the car, my brother was trying to play it cool, but it was obvious that something had happened. I am not sure if it was the toxic smoke or the burnt plastic smell, but she instantly saw the circles. After a moment of silence, she looked at my brother and asked him two questions.

The first question was straightforward. She said, "What were you thinking?" An important lesson in life is recognizing that not every question asked should be answered. My brother chose wisely and did not swing at the pitch. He lowered his head a bit and sat in silence.

Her second question was brilliant. In fact, although the question was not even directed at me, I have remembered it for decades. She looked at him and said in a steady voice, "When you realized what it did...why didn't you just stop?"

He looked up and said, "I thought if I made a pattern, you wouldn't notice." The earnestness in his eyes and the honesty of his response caught her off guard. She looked at him and started laughing. We sat stunned with awkward half-smiles trying to understand what was happening. She loved that car, but not nearly as she loved her son. It was a message that got through loud and clear. Her question however, was brilliant and important. "When you realized what it did...why didn't you just stop?" What do you need to stop believing?

RALPH THOMPSON

Ralph Thompson was born on Friday, June 27, 1947, to Elmer and Isabel Thompson of Beersheba Springs, Tennessee. His dad was a logger turned construction worker, who also farmed on the side. Known for his work ethic, Elmer would travel as far north as Detroit in pursuit of construction work when the local economy faltered in the 1950s.[7] Ralph's mother, Isabel Scruggs, was a schoolteacher. Among her first teaching assignments was an elementary school that met in a one-room, log cabin schoolhouse in nearby Savage Gulf, Tennessee. In the cooler months, the students would walk to school early in the morning to gather wood and start the fire, so by the time their teacher arrived, the room was already warm. She taught throughout the 1930s in the nearby community of Tarlton, which is located just north of Beersheba.[8]

Among the more notable members of Ralph's family was his great-great paternal grandfather, Thomas "Tommy" Thompson. Tommy was born in Louisiana in 1808 but relocated to the hills of Eastern Tennessee in his early 20s. Renowned for his hunting ability, the outdoorsman helped keep numerous families in the area fed. According to the stories passed down:

> Tommy went to Big Bear Cave and reach inside to get a feel for the hibernating bear's position. When he found the right spot, he stuck the bear with his knife, dragged him out and dressed him for the meat and fur. After a bountiful supply of meats were gathered, Tommy came down to a bluff near his home in Tarlton and raised the white flag yelling, "Meat aplenty, meat aplenty!" Folks from all over saddled up their mules and horses and headed for "Tommy's Outdoor Meat Market." Deer, turkey, rabbit, squirrel—whatever your taste buds wanted and your wallet could afford, Tommy had it.[9]

It was in 1833 that Mrs. Beersheba Porter Cain, the wife of a McMinnville doctor, discovered the springs that made her the town's namesake. Located at an altitude of 2,000 feet, the town, which was incorporated in 1839, was a bit cooler in the summer months than the surrounding communities. As a result, Beersheba Springs became the preferred resting place for stagecoaches and travelers making the trek from Chattanooga to McMinnville.

To accommodate the guests, George Smartt and Dr. Alfred Paine of McMinnville built a few log cabins and a tavern. In 1854, John Armfield acquired the property. The former slave trader and financier used a blend of slaves and white construction workers to upgrade and enlarge the resort over the next two years. The popularity of the resort was short lived, however, due to the outbreak of the Civil War in 1861. During the war, the resort was subject to numerous raids by both the Union army and area Bushwhackers. Following the war, the resort would never regain its former prominence.[10]

Ralph attended Panhandle, Beersheba, and Altamont Elementary Schools. By the time he graduated from Grundy County High School in 1965, he had grown to be the tallest student in his class. Following graduation, he moved north about 65 miles to the much larger community of Cookeville, where he enrolled at Tennessee Technological University, which is referred to by most as Tennessee Tech. He graduated four years later in 1969 with a degree in Industrial Engineering.

On Saturday, September 12, 1970, Ralph married Susan Simpson of McMinnville. In time, the couple was blessed with a daughter and a son. Their firstborn, Jennifer, followed in her grandmother's footsteps and became an educator. Their son Jeremy also chose to attend Tennessee Tech and is employed by the Tennessee Valley Authority (TVA) as a mechanical engineer.

Ralph would often express gratitude for the chance to work as the plant manager at Alcoa Aluminum (Ingot Plant—Tennessee Operations), as a project engineer for Union Carbide Nuclear at Oak Ridge, and as project manager over various areas for the TVA. He never took for granted the opportunity to have access to steady work.

Grundy County's unofficial poet laureate was Leonard Tate, who was born in Beersheba in 1912 and was laid to rest in the same town in 1989. Considering Tate's life overlapped Ralph's, he provides valuable insight into what it meant to be from the area during Ralph's most formative years. In a description of the people of Gundy County, Tate once wrote:

> We are mountain people.
> We are a boorish set, they tell us-
> Hard-bitten, coarse of feature and speech,
> Shallow and brawling as the mountain streams,
> With morale friable as our sandstone.
> All my life I have wanted to tell them:
> That we are mountain people,
> That mountain streams have pools of deep quietness,
> And that beneath the sandstone of our hills
> There is granite.[11]

COACH

My friendship with Ralph began in the summer of 1999 when he invited me to lunch. I jumped into his SUV, and we drove down the street to an aging Chinese food restaurant. At the time, I did not realize it was going to be a place where we would eat often over the next few years. Once we got comfortable in our booth, we began talking about life. It was early in the conversation that he told me that he had retired from TVA four years earlier due to Amyotrophic Lateral Sclerosis (ALS). His type of ALS was extremely rare; there are only five families in the world known to have the specific genetic mutation.[12] He told me the doctors had estimated he had five years or less to live. It was his intention to make as many memories with his loved ones as possible while being positive and embracing life.

Ralph had a background in law enforcement, and one of his roles at TVA had been Manager of Personnel Security. Before asking me a challenging question, he liked to tell me that he had been trained to detect when someone was not telling the truth. Smiling, the interrogation would begin. He would start with something like, "So… Nathan…tell me about who you want to be."

As our friendship deepened, I am not sure why, but I started calling him "Coach." Due to my family history, I regard this title as among the highest compliments I could bestow. In fact, as an adult, he is the only person that I have ever called Coach.

TALK LIKE A REAL PERSON

At that time, I had an interest in leadership but did not know it would end up being my career. Ironically, Ralph was in the first leadership class I ever taught. The class was designed for a group of about 40 volunteer leaders. The one-hour class met once a week over the course of three months. I was either 26 or 27 years old at the time, and many in the group were decades older than me. Considering I did not have a great deal of life experience, I was nervous and insecure about teaching. To help establish credibility, I spent a lot of time preparing and researching. I wanted to make sure that I had good sources to underscore each point I would be making. As a result, every time I introduced a key concept, I would say something like, "According to the research of…" or "The following is based upon the insights of…" Following the first class, Ralph suggested we get together for lunch.

We sat down at our restaurant and Ralph asked, "So...How do you think the class is going?" I told him that I thought it was going well, but based on his facial expressions, I sensed he did not agree. He listened and then asked another question. He said, "Why do you keep referencing all of your sources?" I told him my rationale, and he said, "It is not having the effect you are wanting. We don't care about the sources. They are in the handout." He paused for a moment and said, "You sound like an academic. Just talk like a real person."

Ralph was not anti-intellectual. If I had been presenting in an academic environment, he would have given me different counsel. His actual concern was that he sensed that I either lacked the self-confidence needed to have my own opinion or I was misreading the audience. He felt the approach that I was taking would work in an academic context, but it was not connecting in what he considered a "real world" environment. He had longstanding and deep relationships with several people in the people in the class, and he assured me that I was missing the mark. The conversation was a breakthrough day for me. I knew him well enough to know his motive. Ralph loved me and wanted me to succeed. He felt it was his responsibility to tell me what I was doing was not working. For him, it was a matter of loyalty. He felt loyalty often required telling people you care about something that they would rather not hear and you would rather not tell them, but your love for them demands it. You do not let people you care about walk into oncoming traffic if you can stop them from doing so.

My relationship with Ralph was not always easy. His form of "encouragement" often included uninvited assessments of my life or work. In addition, his version of a "good discussion" could look and feel a lot like a good old-fashioned disagreement. He was not above claiming both sides of an argument and then claiming victory.

Just in case you wondered, getting into a dispute with someone from Grundy County is not a good idea. Although it may be true that many "Mountain People" have not historically had access to formal education, this does not mean they lack intelligence. These "Mountain People" are the same people who consciously chose not to retreat to the relative safety of the cities when it would have been easy to do so. They had the strength of body and mind to carve out a life for themselves and their families in the wilderness that others considered too difficult to tame.

When arguments got heated, Ralph would sometimes break into a smile, and for years, I could not understand why. With the passing of time, I think I now know. Ralph was not as concerned that we were in agreement as much as he was concerned that I was learning to think for myself. He was pushing me from a single loop to a double loop learning mindset. It is a gift that I will value for the rest of my life.

Coach passed away on Friday, February 10, 2017. It had been nearly 18 years since our first discussion, when he told me he thought he had five years left. In addition to the advances being made in healthcare and the quality of care provided to him by Susan and healthcare professionals, I believe he also lived longer because of his mindset. He told me that he was determined to hold on as long as possible because the doctors were using his case to better understand how to fight the hereditary disease. It was his hope that by working closely with the researchers, they might find a breakthrough that could benefit future generations.

As I was writing this book, I often heard Ralph's voice in my head. I found it helpful to imagine we were going to our Chinese restaurant to meet and talk about the book. If he had read it, I think he would have said, "It was good. I liked it." After a few seconds, he would have then said, "The only thing I thought you could do better was the conclusion. You should have summarized some of the key points. Through the book, you took the readers on several journeys, told us good things and asked insightful questions, but you never told us what we are supposed to do with all of it." I would have countered, "That's the point. I didn't want to tell people what to do, I wanted them to make their own choices." He would have then replied, "It's not about what you want. People want to know how they are supposed to apply this to real life, and you need to give them what they want."

I miss Coach. I loved him very much. He was one-of-a-kind, and I am grateful for my time with him. In honor of him and in recognition of the investment he made in my life, I have attempted to summarize three key concepts shared in the book with the goal of practical application. If Ralph and I were having lunch together, this list would have been written on a napkin or on the back of a receipt. My intent is not to tell you what to do but to provide a practical example or two that might help prompt you to take action.

1. YOU ARE THE ONLY ONE WHO CAN CHANGE YOUR MENTAL MODEL

Everyone has a unique mental model. It may be similar to others, but it is not the same. From a broad perspective, it is the lens through which we process the world and the process by which we create mental representations of it. Our mental model, or worldview, helps us identify our place in the world and provides a context through which we experience life.

Mental models are shaped by genetics, access to nutrition and health care, and our life experiences. From the first moments of life, we instinctively begin grasping for understanding. With amazing speed, our mental model and our neural network takes form. In the early years of infancy and childhood, those within our social circles influence our mental model profoundly.

Our mental model is not fixed, but as we mature, our perspectives tend to become increasingly durable. Because the brain seeks to use the least amount of energy possible, once a mental model is adopted, it tends to be the filter we use until there is a compelling reason to change course. This approach to life is usually helpful, as it allows us to function in a world in which we do not have all the information needed. Our mental model allows us to "fill in the gaps" and make decisions accordingly. It helps us decide if we should stop at the dimly lit gas station on the side of the road or keep going. It helps us choose if we should greet a stranger on an elevator or keep to ourselves. It helps us determine where we should sit in class, which jobs we should pursue, and whether or not we should speak up in a company meeting.

In my dad's story, from an early age, he believed he was dumb. This mental model was impacted significantly by an undiagnosed learning disability (dyslexia), which was exacerbated by instability at home. Whatever the reason, he adopted a perspective that he believed was accurate and began to see the world through this lens. Every time he struggled to grasp a concept, misspelled a word, or could not recall something he had studied, he considered it to be proof that his perspective was accurate.

Like a cancer growing unchecked, his negative mental model grew throughout his childhood. It was first confronted in the sixth grade when Mr. Casto, someone he considered an authority figure, challenged it. When Mr. Casto asked my dad to teach Daniel how to read, the request did not compute. Mr. Casto believed my dad could teach Daniel to read. My dad did not. It was a collision of mental models. From my father's perspective, the role of teacher was designated for "smart people." Considering he was not part of that group, he concluded the request must have been a mistake. He dismissed it. To my dad, what Mr. Casto was asking was not possible, because he did not *believe* he was capable. Whether he was *actually* capable or not was not really the issue. In that moment, Mr. Casto, whether he knew it or not, had challenged my father's mental model and identity and, in so doing, changed the course of his life.

I would like to think that my father stopped believing he was dumb, but at that moment, I do not think this was the case. His breakthrough was that he concluded he did not have to be the smartest person to make a difference. In short, he concluded that he had enough intellectual capacity to get the job done. On an intellectual level, he has come to understand that one can be bright while also being impacted by learning disabilities that make some aspects of life more challenging. Interestingly, I believe he has gained a sense of quiet confidence by recognizing that some of his achievements, like earning a college degree, are made all the more meaningful because of the added level of difficulty he had to overcome to realize his goals.

At any point in your life, your mental model can be changed. The way you think is not fixed or concrete. Changing your mind, literally changing how your brain processes information, is possible because of neuroplasticity. Neuroplasticity is an umbrella term that describes the process by which the brain is organized, both functionally and physically. Throughout life, when we successfully learn to perform an action, a pattern emerges. This pattern becomes the brain's preferred pathway or a habit. To help conserve energy, the brain uses the path of least resistance and will continue to use the preferred pathway unless there is a reason to do otherwise. At any point in life, it is possible to change or alter the preferred pathway, but it requires deliberate, focused, and repeated effort.

A negative person can learn to see the world from a positive perspective, but it will require purposefully and intentionally looking for the positive. An impatient person can learn to be patient, but it will require disciplined effort. The secret service agents who were assigned to Ronald Reagan's detail are examples of people who were committed to remapping their brains. During the assassination attempt on Reagan's life, the agents went into action as soon as the threat emerged. Considering the attack tool less than two seconds, their response was nearly instantaneous. Through their extensive training, they had learned to think and act differently than would normally be expected. When the agents who were closest to the president were interviewed about their reaction times, they stated their actions were a reflection of their training and did not require conscious thought. If an agent can learn to deny their most basic self-preservation instincts, it gives helpful insight into the flexibility of a willing mind to learn to think and act differently.

The first step toward changing your mental model is ownership. You are literally the only one who can do it. It cannot be assigned to someone else. You cannot hide behind the notion "That's just the way I am." Your perspective, your mental model, can be changed, but only if you are willing to make the change.

When Mo Anderson said to the group, "My 70s have been my best decade, and I cannot imagine what is going to happen in my 80s," she was demonstrating an internal locus of control and ownership of her mental model. She was connecting her age to positive outcomes. She was choosing to be positive.

When Eric Baird decided he was "not going to waste this" when referring to his terminal diagnosis, he was demonstrating ownership of his mental model. His decision to view his cancer as a key to opening doors of opportunity was intentional. He knew exactly what he was doing, and in so doing, even at the end of his life, he was living a life of meaning. He was choosing to live a life of meaning by connecting his suffering with a deeper purpose.

When Adam placed his little hand under the bathtub faucet and found the water did not burn, he was remapping his brain. The choice to place him in scalding hot water had been made by someone else, but the choice to crawl up into my mother's lap was his alone. His choice to surrender from a life of rage and to be held in my mother's arms was among the earliest and most important decisions he would ever make. His choice to surrender was his path to liberation. In that moment, he was pushing back against a mental model in which "mom" was the cause of pain and was exchanging it with the idea that "mom" could be the source of comfort.

2. USE YOUR INFLUENCE TO ACTIVATE OTHERS AND PROVIDE ACCESS

Two important gifts we can give others are: 1) activation and 2) access. For the purpose of our conversation, *activation* is helping make someone aware of what makes them unique. *Access* is helping open doors of opportunity to use their abilities as important gifts in life. Activation without access is highly frustrating. It is the awareness that you can do something but denial of the opportunity to try. Access without activation is a tragedy. It is painful to watch someone who has the ability but does not believe they have what is needed miss opportunity when it is within their grasp.

I was raised in a loving family and was surrounded by encouraging coaches and teachers, but I had never considered myself to be someone who could succeed in an academic context until I met an activator, Dr. Dee Carson. When she said, "I think you are gifted and do not know it," she challenged a core belief. She said the right thing at the right time, and it changed my life.

What I find all the more humbling is that Dr. Carson's actions were not in isolation. There were several people who contributed to that breakthrough moment. For example, I would have never been in Dr. Carson's class if Dr. David Burks had not helped provide me access to graduate school. I would have never known Dr. Burks if I had not been Student Association President. I would have never been Student Association President if Dr. Duane Warden had not chosen to give me a D for my effort versus an F. I could go on, but I think you get the idea. There are no self-made people. This is why we should express gratitude and a posture of humility when considering the opportunities that have been given to us.

Mahalia activated Dr. King when she called out to him and said, "Tell them about the dream, Martin." He knew her voice, and he trusted her judgment. In the midst of the most important speech of his life, Dr. King went off script because of Mahalia Jackson's encouragement to do so. When Clarence Jones, who had helped Dr. King write the original script, saw what was happening, he looked to the person next to him and said, "These people don't know it, but they're about to go to church."

Mike O'Neal used his position as a university president as a platform to serve. He opened the doors of opportunity for Rwandan students who had the ability to succeed but lacked access. Instead of using the prestige of his family name to avoid getting involved in World War II, Ted Roosevelt used it to gain access. His argument was simple; if I am on the beach on D-Day, the soldiers will see my example and will not lose heart. He used his influence to activate the soldiers.

3. THE SHAKE DOWN—STOP BELIEVING

I am drawn to the idea of the pack shake down at Mountain Crossings. It is compelling to think of a place where experienced guides are helping remove the burdens of others. A long hike is enhanced when we lighten our load and leave behind what is no longer needed or wanted. Sometimes, however, what is left behind is something that we would have preferred to keep, but for reasons beyond our control, we must let go. I think of my forefathers who made the decision in 1795 to leave behind their prized farming implements to be able to make the journey from Baltimore to Fort Pitt. It was not without a great sense of loss, but it was the right choice when considering the distance to their ultimate destination. If the family was going to survive, hard choices had to be made. I asked the question at the conclusion of Chapter 13, but I will ask it again at the conclusion of the book, "What do you need to leave behind to get where you want to go?"

For most people, the struggles they have today are the result of decisions made long ago. Not only do you have permission to change your mental model, but you also have the responsibility to do so. Sometimes, this requires believing new things, but more often than not, it means laying something down that you have carried for too long and walking away. It would have excruciating to leave behind the farming implements and keep traveling. I am assuming they looked back over their shoulder a time or two, but they kept moving until what they left behind was so small it could no longer be seen.

COUNSEL FROM COACH

After Coach received the diagnosis that he had ALS, he began the process of researching the disease. In time, he created a website that offered guidance to those who also had the illness and their families. Due to his expertise and willingness to help, he became the person who people would call after they had been diagnosed and were grappling with what to do next. In Ralph's trademark style, he offered advice that was straightforward and direct. He would tell them what to expect physically and explain how important it was to accept reality and choose a positive outlook. His counsel was to not waste time but to use their time wisely by making memories with their loved one and friends. Ralph's advice was for fellow travelers who had the same disease, but it can be applied to us all. As the website he created said, "Be positive, be aggressive and embrace life."[13]

WHERE DO WE GO FROM HERE?

Writing this book has been a journey for me. I hope it has been helpful for you. It was definitely helpful for me. Through the stories told, it gave me an opportunity to visit people and places from the past and to consider my own path forward. As I wrote each page, I became increasingly aware of how indebted I am to so many people who have been a source of encouragement along the way. It has been a humbling endeavor for which I am grateful to have had the opportunity.

I have breakfast often with my friend, Shad Glass. He is a dedicated husband, father and leader and I value his insights. As the book was coming together, I asked him to read through a rough draft and provide feedback. While eating breakfast and drinking a cup of coffee, he shared with me some of his thoughts about the book. As we were wrapping up, he said, "Your book covers several generations of people over the course of a few centuries." I was unsure where he was headed, but I nodded in agreement. He continued, "Although it covers a long period of time, I noticed that the key themes remain constant. The context in which people were living changed, but what was truly important remained the same." I smiled and said, "I think you're right."

He was right. Whether the stories shared in the book took place a decade ago or a century in the past, the key concepts remain remarkably durable. Evidently, throughout human history, living a life of meaning has always required intentionality and a willingness to serve others.

I would like for you to imagine we are having breakfast together. We are sitting in a corner booth that is filled with some of the key people in your life. Imagine who you would most like to be there. See them in your mind's eye. Now imagine one of them, someone who means the world to you, looks up, makes eye contact with you and says, "So... tell me about who you want to be." I look forward to hearing your response.

PHOTOS

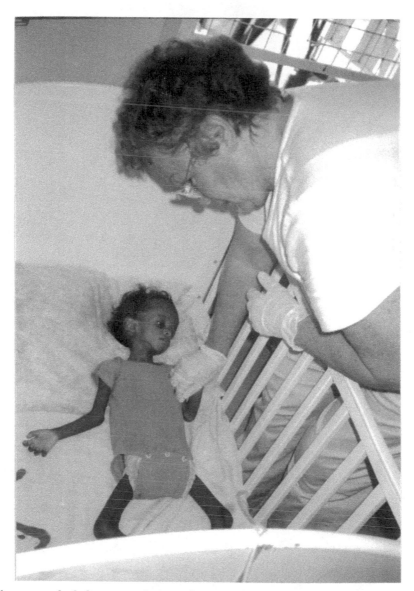

When my dad first traveled to Guyana in 1982, he went with Benny and Kitty Mullins. This picture is of Kitty Mullins providing comfort to an infant in the children's ward. I traveled to Guyana for the first time in 1988.

Susan graduated from Glendale High in Springfield, Missouri in 1967. Upon graduation, she enrolled at Harding College where her sister, Jana, was already attending.

This picture was taken in 1969 while my parents were students at Harding College. They married on March 26, 1970.

Church was a big part of our life and dad had a hand in buying, driving and painting the buses. Each week, the busses were filled with kids who wanted to go to church, but did not have transportation.

147 happy kids on one bus headed to the Central Church of Christ in Vincennes, Indiana. Dad was one of the ministers as well as a bus captain. Mom taught the second grade class.

Matt (left), Kristi (middle) and Nathan (right) sit for a family portrait. This picture was taken around 1980.

On the left is Katya Bell, I am standing in the middle and David Natanovich Bell is on my right. We are standing in their apartment in Dubna, Russia. David was born in Houston and moved to Russia at the age of the age of 10 in 1931. He was among the key reasons why I was able to teach English in Dubna in the summers of 1993-1995. This photo was taken in 1993.

Dubna is the home of the Joint Institute for Nuclear Research (JINR) and was originally launched as one of the Soviet Union's "Science Cities." This mosaic is located at the entrance of the town. Those below include the English teachers in the summer of 1993. The group includes (left to right): David Pratt (host), Chris Barker, Anissa Carlyle Falconer, Nathan Mellor, Jessica Beltzer Henman, Jerry Higgs and Michelle Morgan.

Our classroom was usually a school cafeteria or a large open room. Each day, we would work with men and women who wanted to improve their conversational English skills. I taught in Dubna, Russia in the summers of 1993-1995.

On May 16, 1997, in a surprise graduation, the President of Harding University Dr. David Burks (left), presents a diploma to my dad, David Russell Mellor (right). Dad left Harding College in the spring of 1970 without graduating. It was later discovered that although he did not have enough credits to graduate with a degree in kinesiology, he did have enough credits for a general studies degree.

Dad getting in the Buick Century in what likely the summer of 1976. This was the car in which Matt used the lighter to create a design on the dashboard. The white house in the background is our duplex at 109 Wooster Street in Marietta. Grandma Mellor is standing under the tree with her grandchildren with their home in the background.

ENDNOTES

Introduction

1   Senge, P. M. (1990). *The fifth discipline: The art and practice of the learning organization.* NY: Doubleday Currency.

Chapter 1

1   Marietta-Washington County Convention & Visitors Bureau. (n.d.). History. Retrieved September 1, 2018, from https://mariettaohio.org/about-marietta/history

2   Ohio History Central. (n.d.). Shawnee Indians. Retrieved September 2, 2018, http://www.ohiohistorycentral.org/w/Shawnee_Indians

3   Health Talents International. (n.d.). General overview of HTI. Retrieved September 2, 2018, from http://www.healthtalents.org/index.php?page=brochures

4   Ohio State University. (n.d.). Script Ohio. Retrieved September 9, 2018, from https://tbdbitl.osu.edu/marching-band/traditions

5   The Computer UFO Network. (n.d.). Selective service system classifications for WWI, WWII, and PWWII through 1976. Retrieved April 13, 2018 from http://www.cufon.org/CRG/memo/74911231.html

6   Ohio History Central. (n.d.). Category: Great Depression and World War II. Retrieved March 30, 2018, from http://www.ohiohistorycentral.org/w/Category:Great_Depression_and_World_War_II -

7   Hebb, D. O. (1949). *The organization of behavior: A neuropsychological theory.* NY: John Wiley & Sons.

Chapter 2

1   City of Vincennes. (n.d.). History. Retrieved September 5, 2018, from http://www.vincennes.org/dev/history

2   Retrieved September 5, 2018, from http://population.us/in/vincennes/

3   Central Church of Christ. (n.d.). Our history. Retrieved

September 5, 2018, from https://www.churchofchristvincennes. com/history

4 Retrieved August 26, 2018, from https://www.landsofamerica. com/property/1750-acres-in-Johnston-County- Oklahoma/5071788

5 Retrieved August 26, 2018, from https://www.adventureroad. com/destinations/blue-river

6 Keller Williams. (n.d.) Mo Anderson: Vice Chairman. Retrieved September 6, 2018, from https://www.kw.com/kw/mo-anderson. html

Chapter 3

1 Page, A. W. (1908, January). The statesmanship of forestry. *The World's Work* (p. 9757). Retrieved May 8, 2018, from https:// foresthistory.org/research-explore/us-forest-service-history/ people/national-forests/forest-ranger-life/ranger-qualifications

2 Page, A. W. (1908, January). The statesmanship of forestry. *The World's Work* (p. 9757). Retrieved May 8, 2018, from https:// foresthistory.org/research-explore/us-forest-service-history/ people/national-forests/forest-ranger-life/ranger-qualifications

3 Albright, H. (2005, Fall). Cover letter for ranger applicants to Yellowstone National Park, 1926. *Ranger: The Journal of the Association of National Park Rangers Newsletter, 21*(4), 4.

4 McGoff, B. (2015, May 5). 100 famous short men everyone can look up to. *The Modest Man*. Retrieved September 10, 2018, from https://www.themodestman.com/100-famous-short-men

5 Miller, H. (1940, October). Park service rangers. *Region III Quarterly, 2*(4). Retrieved May 12, 2018, from https://www.nps. gov/parkhistory/online_books/region_111/vol2-4g.htm

6 Kaufman, P. W. (1985, Fall). Women in the National Park Service. *Ranger: The Journal of the Association of National Park Rangers, 1*(4). Retrieved May 12, 2018, from http://npshistory. com/centennial/0916/article.htm.

7 Wilson, L. D. (n.d.). Antlers. *Oklahoma Historical Society*. Retrieved September 11, 2018, from http://www.okhistory.org/

publications/enc/entry.php?entry=AN015

8   Retrieved September 10, 2018, from http://population.us/ok/
    antlers

9   Wilson, L. D. (n.d.) Antlers. *Oklahoma Historical Society.*
    Retrieved September 12, 2018, from http://www.okhistory.org/
    publications/enc/entry.php?entry=AN015

10 Staff. (1968). Straight A's earned by 51 students. *Harding Bulletin
    July 1968, 43*(21), 3. Retrieved September 10, 2018, from http://
    scholarworks.harding.edu/hubulletins/283

11 Staff. (1967). 29 students merit Who's Who Recognition; Faculty
    names 6 juniors, 23 seniors to list. *Harding Bulletin October
    1967, 43*(9), 2. Retrieved September 10, 2018, from http://
    scholarworks.harding.edu/hubulletins/289

12 Staff. (1968). Business team triumphs again. *Harding Bulletin
    June 1968, 43*(20), 1. Retrieved September 10, 2018, from http://
    scholarworks.harding.edu/hubulletins/282

13 Staff. (1969). Ranks among nation's best: Gold medal winner.
    Harding Bulletin September 1969, 45(3), 11. Retrieved September
    10, 2018, from http://scholarworks.harding.edu/hubulletins/304

14 Staff. (1975, March 1). Marriages. *Harding College Bulletin, 50*(9),
    6. Retrieved September 10, 2018, from https://scholarworks.
    harding.edu/hubulletins/369/

15 Oklahoma Christian University. (n.d.). Emeritus Mike O'Neal.
    Retrieved September 10, 2018, from https://oc.edu/president/
    emeritus

16 Oklahoma Christian University. (2011). Richard Lawson.
    Retrieved July 25 2018, from http://www.oc.edu/about/history/
    event/richard-lawson

17 BBC staff. (2014, April 7). Rwanda genocide: 100 days of
    slaughter. *BBC.* Retrieved September 12, 2018, from https://
    www.bbc.com/news/world-africa-26875506

18 Jehl, D. (1994, June 10). Officials told to avoid calling Rwanda
    killings "genocide." *The New York Times.* Retrieved September
    13, 2018, from https://www.nytimes.com/1994/06/10/world/
    officials-told-to-avoid-calling-rwanda-killings-genocide.html

19 Landler, M. (2014, June 3). Declassified U.N. cables reveal turning point in Rwanda crisis of 1994. *The New York Times.* Retrieved September 13, 2018, from https://www.nytimes.com/2014/06/04/world/africa/un-cables-reveal-a-turning-point-in-rwanda-crisis.html

20 Marks, D. (2008, July 20). Investing in their nation's future: Group of 15 Rwandan women learning how to help their home. *The Oklahoman.* Retrieved July 24, 2018, from https://newsok.com/article/3272392/investing-in-their-nations-futurebrspan-classhl2group-of-15-rwandan-women-learning-how-to-help-their-homespan

21 Hixon. (2010). Hearts interwoven. *Vision: Oklahoma Christian University,* Summer. Retrieved September 14, 2018, from https://www.oc.edu/stories/content/hearts-interwoven

22 Kwibuka, E. (2013, October 17). Profile: Who is who at University of Rwanda. *The New Times.* Retrieved July 25, 2018, from http://www.newtimes.co.rw/section/read/70006

23 University of Rwanda. (2017). *Facts and Figures, June 2017.* Retrieved July 25, 2018, from http://ur.ac.rw/sites/default/files/Facts%20and%20Figures-2017-Final%20to%20be%20published.pdf#overlay-context

24 Kagame, P. (2017, February 10). Rwanda–Oklahoma Christian University Decade of Gratitude Gala. Retrieved July 25, 2018, from http://paulkagame.com/?p=5269

Chapter 4

1   Smith, M. K. (2001, 2013). Chris Argyris: Theories of action, double-loop learning and organizational learning. *The Encyclopedia of Informal Education.* Retrieved September 23, 2018, from http://infed.org/mobi/chris-argyris-theories-of-action-double-loop-learning-and-organizational-learning

2   Smith, M. K. (2001, 2011). Donald Schön: Learning, reflection and change. *The Encyclopedia of Informal Education.* Retrieved September 23, 2018, from www.infed.org/thinkers/et-schon.htm

3   Argyris, M., & Schön, D. (1974). *Theory in practice: Increasing*

professional effectiveness. San Francisco, CA: Jossey-Bass.

4 Argyris, C., Putnam, R., & McLain Smith, D. (1985). Action Science: Concepts, methods, and skills for research and intervention (pp. 81–82). San Francisco, CA: Jossey-Bass. Retrieved September 23, 2018, from https://actiondesign.com/assets/pdf/AScha3.pdf

5 Argyris, C., Putnam, R., & McLain Smith, D. (1985). Action Science: Concepts, methods, and skills for research and intervention (p. 82). San Francisco, CA: Jossey-Bass. Retrieved September 23, 2018, from https://actiondesign.com/assets/pdf/AScha3.pdf

6 Argyris, C., Putnam, R., & McLain Smith, D. (1985). Action Science: Concepts, methods, and skills for research and intervention (p. 82). San Francisco, CA: Jossey-Bass. Retrieved September 23, 2018, from https://actiondesign.com/assets/pdf/AScha3.pdf

7 Burks, D. B. (2014). *Camaraderie: Celebrating faith, learning & living at Harding University* (p. 9). Searcy, AR: Harding University Press.

8 Ryan, M. (2013, March 21). Beginning of a legacy. *The Bison.* Retrieved September 19, 2018, from https://thelink.harding.edu/the-bison/2013/03/21/beginning-of-a-legacy

9 Burks, D. B. (2014). *Camaraderie: Celebrating faith, learning & living at Harding University* (p. 9). Searcy, AR: Harding University Press.

10 Burks, D. B. (2014). *Camaraderie: Celebrating faith, learning & living at Harding University* (p. 9). Searcy, AR: Harding University Press.

11 Hannigan, J. (2017, May 17). First ladies garden party. *Harding Alumni Magazine.* Retrieved September 19, 2018, from https://hunet.harding.edu/wordpress/harding/2017/05/17/first-ladies-garden-party

12 Cleveland Clinic. (n.d.). Attention deficit hyperactivity disorder (ADHD): Stimulant therapy. Retrieved May 19, 2018, from https://my.clevelandclinic.org/health/treatments/11766-

attention-deficit-hyperactivity-disorder-adhd-stimulant-therapy

13   Klein, R. G., Mannuzza, S., Ramos Olazagasti, M. A., Roizen, R., Hutchison, J. A., Lashua, E. C., & Castellanos, F. X. (2012, December). Clinical and functional outcome of childhood attention-deficit/hyperactivity disorder 33 years later. *Arch Gen Psychiatry, 69*(12), 1295–1303. Retrieved May 19, 2018. doi:10.1001/archgenpsychiatry.2012.271

Chapter 5

1   National Park Service. (n.d.). Judge Isaac C. Parker. Retrieved August 15, 2018, from https://www.nps.gov/fosm/learn/historyculture/judge-parker.htm

2   Todd, J. L. (2014, March 3). Veteran recalls nearly starving to death as German POW: Interview of Pendleton Woods on Nov 14, 1984. *Bartlesville Examiner-Enterprise*. Retrieved February 15, 2018, from http://www.examiner-enterprise.com/living/military/veteran-recalls-nearly-starving-death-german-pow

3   Todd, J. L. (2014, March 3). Veteran recalls nearly starving to death as German POW: Interview of Pendleton Woods on Nov 14, 1984. *Bartlesville Examiner-Enterprise*. Retrieved February 15, 2018, from http://www.examiner-enterprise.com/living/military/veteran-recalls-nearly-starving-death-german-pow

4   BSA Order of the Arrow. (n.d.). First BSA National Jamboree – 1937. Retrieved February 15, 2018, from https://history.oa-bsa.org/node/3154

5   Todd, J. L. (2014, March 3). Veteran recalls nearly starving to death as German POW: Interview of Pendleton Woods on Nov 14, 1984. *Bartlesville Examiner-Enterprise*. Retrieved February 15, 2018, from http://www.examiner-enterprise.com/living/military/veteran-recalls-nearly-starving-death-german-pow

6   U.S. Army Heritage and Education Center. (2010, February 17). 99th Infantry Division World War II veterans survey inventory. Retrieved January 1, 2018, from http://cdm16635.contentdm.oclc.org/cdm/ref/collection/p16635coll21/id/300

7   U.S. Army Center of Military History. (n.d.). Order of Battle of

the US Army - WWII - ETO 99th Infantry Division. Retrieved January 7, 2018, from https://history.army.mil/documents/ETO-OB/99ID-ETO.htm

8   Lauer, W. E. (1951). *Battle babies: The story of the 99th Infantry Division in World War II* (p. 6). Baton Rouge, LA: Halldin.

9   Todd, J. L. (2014, March 3). Veteran recalls nearly starving to death as German POW: Interview of Pendleton Woods on Nov 14, 1984. *Bartlesville Examiner-Enterprise*. Retrieved February 15, 2018, from http://www.examiner-enterprise.com/living/military/veteran-recalls-nearly-starving-death-german-pow

10 Todd, J. L. (2014, March 3). Veteran recalls nearly starving to death as German POW: Interview of Pendleton Woods on Nov 14, 1984. *Bartlesville Examiner-Enterprise*. Retrieved February 15, 2018, from http://www.examiner-enterprise.com/living/military/veteran-recalls-nearly-starving-death-german-pow

11 Todd, J. L. (2014, March 3). Veteran recalls nearly starving to death as German POW: Interview of Pendleton Woods on Nov 14, 1984. *Bartlesville Examiner-Enterprise*. Retrieved February 15, 2018, from http://www.examiner-enterprise.com/living/military/veteran-recalls-nearly-starving-death-german-pow

12 Humphrey, R. (2014). *Once Upon a Time in War: The 99th Division in World War II* (244–245). Norman, OK: University of Oklahoma Press.

13 Todd, J. L. (2014, March 3). Veteran recalls nearly starving to death as German POW: Interview of Pendleton Woods on Nov 14, 1984. *Bartlesville Examiner-Enterprise*. Retrieved February 15, 2018, from http://www.examiner-enterprise.com/living/military/veteran-recalls-nearly-starving-death-german-pow

14 Parton, J. (1946, January). AAF's tactics and how they worked (reprinted from Army Air Force's *Impact*). *Flying Magazine, 8*(1), 70. Retrieved January 7, 2018, fromhttps://books.google.com/books?id=Uz9Tdfe8FWEC&lpg=PA52&ots=rJC68M5n7z&dq=duren%20allied%20air%20bombings%20november%2016%201944&pg=PA79#v=onepage&q&f=true

15 Stadt Düren. (n.d.). History of the city of Duren. Retrieved

January 7, 2018, from https://www.dueren.de/sprachversionen/english/history-of-the-city-of-dueren/)

16 Humphrey, R. (2014). *Once Upon a Time in War: The 99th Division in World War II* (244–245). Norman, OK: University of Oklahoma Press.

17 Musee De La Bataille Des Ardennes. (n.d.). The Battle of the Bulge. Retrieved January 7, 2018, from http://www.batarden.be/site/en/histoire-de-la-bataille-des-ardennes/10.html

18 Todd, J. L. (2014, March 3). Veteran recalls nearly starving to death as German POW: Interview of Pendleton Woods on Nov 14, 1984. *Bartlesville Examiner-Enterprise*. Retrieved February 15, 2018, from http://www.examiner-enterprise.com/living/military/veteran-recalls-nearly-starving-death-german-pow

19 Lauer, W. E. (1951). *Battle babies: The story of the 99th Infantry Division in World War II* (pp. 18, 20). Baton Rouge: Halldin.

20 Nelson, J. G. (1995). Transcript of an oral history interview with Jerome G. Nelson, rifleman, Army, World War II (p. 15). *Wisconsin Veterans Museum Research Center*. Retrieved from https://www.wisvetsmuseum.com/wp-content/uploads/2017/03/NelsonJerome-_OH183.pdf

21 Todd, J. L. (2014, March 3). Veteran recalls nearly starving to death as German POW: Interview of Pendleton Woods on Nov 14, 1984. *Bartlesville Examiner-Enterprise*. Retrieved February 15, 2018, from http://www.examiner-enterprise.com/living/military/veteran-recalls-nearly-starving-death-german-pow

22 Admin. (2002, September 27). Prisoners of War remembered, honored. *Tinker Take Off,* 60(38). Retrieved January 1, 2018, from http://journalrecord.com/tinkertakeoff/2002/09/27/prisoners-of-war-remembered-honored

23 Humphrey, R. (2014). *Once Upon a Time in War: The 99th Division in World War II* (244–245). Norman, OK: University of Oklahoma Press.

24 Winfrey, N. (2009, January). POW makes the great escape. *Edmond Outlook*. Retrieved January 30, 2018, from http://www.outlookoklahoma.com/archives/m.blog/27/2009-january-pow-

makes-the-great-escape

25 Admin. (2002, September 27). Prisoners of War remembered, honored. *Tinker Take Off, 60*(38). Retrieved January 1, 2018, from http://journalrecord.com/tinkertakeoff/2002/09/27/prisoners-of-war-remembered-honored

26 Winfrey, N. (2009, January). POW makes the great escape. *Edmond Outlook*. Retrieved January 30, 2018, from http://www.outlookoklahoma.com/archives/m.blog/27/2009-january-pow-makes-the-great-escape

27 Todd, J. L. (2014, March 3). Veteran recalls nearly starving to death as German POW: Interview of Pendleton Woods on Nov 14, 1984. *Bartlesville Examiner-Enterprise*. Retrieved February 15, 2018, from http://www.examiner-enterprise.com/living/military/veteran-recalls-nearly-starving-death-german-pow

28 Carter, J. (1999, July 5). Loss of freedom inspires concern for others. *The Oklahoman*. Retrieved May 22, 2018, from https://newsok.com/article/2659339/loss-of-freedom-inspires-concern-for-other-people

29 Oklahoman Video Archive. (2017, November 29). An interview with Pendleton Woods part 3 (2007-09-12). Retrieved from https://www.youtube.com/watch?v=UamEb19Xkv0

30 Staff. (1984, January 2). Pendleton Woods winds up distinguished National Guard career. *The Oklahoman*. Retrieved January 1, 2018, from http://newsok.com/article/2052382

31 Woods, P. (n.d.). We captured a town. *The Patriot Files*. Retrieved from http://www.patriotfiles.com/index.php?name=News&file=article&sid=391

32 Admin. (2002, September 27). Prisoners of War remembered, honored. *Tinker Take Off, 60*(38). Retrieved January 1, 2018, from http://journalrecord.com/tinkertakeoff/2002/09/27/prisoners-of-war-remembered-honored

33 Raymond, K. (2011, June 16). Oklahoma City volunteer, POW to receive national award. *The Oklahoman*. Retrieved May 25, 2018, from https://newsok.com/article/3577468/oklahoma-city-volunteer-pow-to-receive-national-award

34 Winfrey, N. (2009, January). POW makes the great escape. *Edmond Outlook*. Retrieved January 30, 2018, from http://www. outlookoklahoma.com/archives/m.blog/27/2009-january-pow-makes-the-great-escape

35 Oklahoma History Center. (n.d.). Pendleton Woods. Retrieved February 15, 2018, from http://www.okhistory.org/historycenter/militaryhof/inductee.php?id=116

36 Winfrey, N. (2009, January). POW makes the great escape. *Edmond Outlook*. Retrieved January 30, 2018, from http://www. outlookoklahoma.com/archives/m.blog/27/2009-january-pow-makes-the-great-escape

37 Slipke, D. (2014, December 3). Family, friends remember veteran Pendleton Woods in Oklahoma City. *The Oklahoman*. Retrieved January 1, 2018, from http://newsok.com/article/5372291

38 Staff. (1984, January 2). Pendleton Woods winds up distinguished National Guard career. *The Oklahoman*. Retrieved January 1, 2018, from http://newsok.com/article/2052382

39 Staff. (2015, January 11). Obituary of Pendleton Woods. *The Oklahoman*. Retrieved May 25, 2018, from http://legacy. newsok.com/obituaries/oklahoman/obituary.aspx?n=pendleton-woods&pid=173808234

40 Winfrey, N. (2009, January). POW makes the great escape. *Edmond Outlook*. Retrieved January 30, 2018, from http://www. outlookoklahoma.com/archives/m.blog/27/2009-january-pow-makes-the-great-escape

41 Slipke, D. (2014, December 3). Family, friends remember veteran Pendleton Woods in Oklahoma City. *The Oklahoman*. Retrieved January 1, 2018, from http://newsok.com/article/5372291

42 Raymond, K. (2011, June 16). Oklahoma City volunteer, POW to receive national award. *The Oklahoman*. Retrieved May 25, 2018, from https://newsok.com/article/3577468/oklahoma-city-volunteer-pow-to-receive-national-award

Chapter 6

1 Hofheinz, P. (1987, March 1). Gorbachev's double burden: Economic reform and growth acceleration. *Millennium, 16*(1), 21–54. https://doi.org/10.1177/03058298870160010401

2 Redden, J. (1985, March 11). Mikhail Gorbachev, the youngest member of the ruling Politburo,… *United Press International, Inc.* Retrieved May 26, 2018, from https://www.upi.com/Archives/1985/03/11/Mikhail-Gorbachev-the-youngest-member-of-the-ruling-Politburo/6625479365200

3 Central Intelligence Agency – Directorate of Intelligence. (1986, April). The 27th CPSU Congress: Gorbachev's unfinished business, an intelligence assessment. Retrieved May 26, 2018, from https://www.cia.gov/library/readingroom/docs/19860401A.pdf

4 Staff. (n.d.). Leningrad under Gorbachev: Perestroika and the fall of Communism (1984-1991). *Saint-Petersburg.com.* Retrieved May 26, 2018, from http://www.saint-petersburg.com/history/leningrad-under-gorbachev/

5 Vasilevskaya, I. (n.d.). David Natanovich Bell - Cruiser Varyag and the Hero City in one person. Retrieved September 26 2018, from http://lex.uni-dubna.ru/stati/david-natanovich-bell-krejser-varjag-i-g.html

6 Wines, M. (2003, February 22). Exiled American outlives Stalin's shadow. *The New York Times.* Retrieved September 25, 2018, from https://medium.com/60-days-of-impact/musical-diplomacy-and-the-history-of-la-crosse-dubna-sister-cities-9ce4f5d0d5bb

7 Wines, M. (2003, February 22). Exiled American outlives Stalin's shadow. *The New York Times.* Retrieved September 25, 2018, from https://medium.com/60-days-of-impact/musical-diplomacy-and-the-history-of-la-crosse-dubna-sister-cities-9ce4f5d0d5bb

8 Wines, M. (2003, February 22). Exiled American outlives Stalin's shadow. *The New York Times.* Retrieved September 25, 2018, from https://medium.com/60-days-of-impact/musical-diplomacy-and-the-history-of-la-crosse-dubna-sister-cities-9ce4f5d0d5bb

9 Immortal Regiment. (2015, April 23). Bell David Natanovich:

ML. Lieutenant. Retrieved September 26, 2018, from http://www.moypolk.ru/dubna/soldiers/bell-david-natanovich

10 Krivosheev, G. F. (1997). *Soviet casualties and combat losses in the twentieth century* (p. 168). London: Greenhill Books.

11 Ruben, B. (2015, July 23). Fortunate son: Dubna-La Crosse sister city founder David Bell. *American International Health Association.* Retrieved September 26, 2018, from https://www.aiha.com/wp-content/uploads/2015/07/23-Fortunate-Son.pdf

12 Ruben, B. (2015, July 23). Fortunate Son: Dubna-La Crosse Sister City Founder David Bell. *American International Health Association.* Retrieved September 26, 2018, from https://www.aiha.com/wp-content/uploads/2015/07/23-Fortunate-Son.pdf

13 Sister Cities International. (2016, July 1). Music diplomacy and the history of La Crosse-Dubna sister cities. Retrieved September 26, 2018, from https://medium.com/60-days-of-impact/musical-diplomacy-and-the-history-of-la-crosse-dubna-sister-cities-9ce4f5d0d5bb

14 Wines, M. (2003, February 22). Exiled American outlives Stalin's shadow. *The New York Times.* Retrieved September 25, 2018, from https://medium.com/60-days-of-impact/musical-diplomacy-and-the-history-of-la-crosse-dubna-sister-cities-9ce4f5d0d5bb

Chapter 7

1 Biography.com editors. (2014, April 2). Mahalia Jackson biography. Retrieved September 21, 2018, from https://www.biography.com/people/mahalia-jackson-9351242

2 Biography.com editors. (2014, April 2). Louis Armstrong biography. Retrieved September 21, 2018, from https://www.biography.com/people/louis-armstrong-9188912

3 IMDB. (n.d.). Al Hirt biography. Retrieved September 21, 2018, from https://www.imdb.com/name/nm0386707/bio

4 Biography.com editors. (2014, April 2). Fats Domino biography. Retrieved September 21, 2018, from https://www.biography.com/people/fats-domino-9276748

5 Editors of Encyclopaedia Britannica. (n.d.). Sidney Bechet:

American musician. Retrieved September 23, 2018, from https://www.britannica.com/biography/Sidney-Bechet

6   Wynton Marsalis Enterprises. (n.d.). Biography. Retrieved September 21, 2018, from http://wyntonmarsalis.org/about/bio

7   Bruno, S. (2011, March 11). A visit to Mahalia Jackson's old neighborhood in New Orleans. Retrieved August 25, 2018, from https://www.nola.com/homegarden/index.ssf/2011/03/a_visit_to_mahalia_jacksons_ol.html

8   Sutton, R. (2016, October 26). Remembering Mahalia Jackson. Retrieved September 23, 2018, from https://www.arts.gov/artworks/2016/remembering-mahalia-jackson

9   Hildebreand, L. (n.d.). Mahalia Jackson – Biography. Retrieved September 23, 2018, from https://www.amoeba.com/mahalia-jackson/artist/148271/bio

10 Whitman, A. (1972, January 28). Mahalia Jackson, gospel singer and a civil rights symbol, dies. *The New York Times*. Retrieved May 30, 2018, from https://www.nytimes.com/1972/01/28/archives/mahalia-jackson-gospel-singer-and-a-civil-rights-symbol-dies.html

11 Official Web Site of the Mahalia Jackson Residual Family Corporation. (n.d). A Childhood in New Orleans 1911-1927. Retrieved September 24, 2018, from http://www.mahaliajackson.us/biography

12 Official Web Site of the Mahalia Jackson Residual Family Corporation. (n.d). A Childhood in New Orleans 1911-1927. Retrieved September 24, 2018, from http://www.mahaliajackson.us/biography

13 Goreau, L. (1998). *Just Mahalia, baby: The Mahalia Jackson story* (p. 35). Gretna, LA: Finebird Press, Pelican Publishing Company.

14 Dennard, K. (2010, December). Entertainment profile: Mahalia Jackson. *The Informer*. Retrieved May 30, 2018, from http://www.gainformer.com/files/Entertainment%20Folder/Mahalia%20Jackson%20Entertainment%20profile.html

15 Ward, F., & Staff writers. (1972, January 28). From the archives: Mahalia Jackson, renowed gospel singer, dies at 60. *Los Angeles*

Times. Retrieved September 28, 2018, from http://www.latimes.
com/local/obituaries/archives/la-me-mahalia-jackson-19720128-
story.html

16 Biography.com editors. (2014, April 2). Retrieved September
28, 2018, from https://www.biography.com/people/mahalia-
jackson-9351242

17 Whitman, A. (1972, January 28). Mahalia Jackson, gospel
singer and a civil rights symbol, dies. *The New York Times*.
Retrieved September 28, 2018, from https://www.nytimes.
com/1972/01/28/archives/mahalia-jackson-gospel-singer-and-a-
civil-rights-symbol-dies.html

18 Official Web Site of the Mahalia Jackson Residual Family
Corporation. (n.d.) In Chicago, 1927-1936. Retrieved September
24, 2018, from http://www.mahaliajackson.us/biography/1927.
php

19 Dennard, K. (2010, December). Entertainment profile: Mahalia
Jackson. *The Informer*. Retrieved May 30, 2018, from http://www.
gainformer.com/files/Entertianment%20Folder/Mahalia%20
Jackson%20Entertainment%20profile.html

20 Bausch, W. (2013). *The story revealed: Homilies that sustain, inspire,
and engage* (p. 168). New Haven, CT: Twenty-Third Publications.

21 Staff. (1972, June 8). Galloway, the late Mahalia Jackson's ex-
husband, dies. *Jet, XLII*(11), 45. Retrieved from https://books.
google.com/books?id=oLEDAAAAMBAJ&pg=PA3&lpg=PA
3&dq=Jet,+June+8,+1972+Vol.+XLII,+No.+11&source=bl&ots
=nsWaF18dhs&sig=q_YVhF09IXnNrHdlrvLtQWnqQzg&hl
=en&sa=X&ved=2ahUKEwjB8deIxq7eAhXCoIMKHdrcCC0
Q6AEwAHoECAcQAQ#v=onepage&q=Jet%2C%20June%20
8%2C%201972%20Vol.%20XLII%2C%20No.%2011&f=false

22 BlackHistoryNow. (2011, June 14). Mahalia Jackson. Retrieved
September 23, 2018, from http://blackhistorynow.com/mahalia-
jackson

23 Official Web Site of the Mahalia Jackson Residual Family
Corporation. (n.d.). Radio, Touring, and Television, 1947-1956.
Retrieved May 30, 2018, from http://www.mahaliajackson.us/

biography/1947.php

24 Ankeny, J. (n.d.). Mahalia Jackson. Retrieved September 23, 2018, from https://www.allmusic.com/artist/mahalia-jackson-mn0000814657/biography

25 Official Web Site of the Mahalia Jackson Residual Family Corporation. (n.d.). Civil Rights, 1961-1968. Retrieved May 30, 2018, from http://www.mahaliajackson.us/biography/1961.php

26 Werner, C. (2006). *A change is gonna come: Music, race & the soul of America, revised edition* (p. 4). Ann Arbor, MI: University of Michigan Press.

27 Crockett, E. (2017, January 16). The woman who inspired Martin Luther King's "I Have a Dream" speech. *Vox*. Retrieved June 2, 2018, from https://www.vox.com/2016/1/18/10785882/martin-luther-king-dream-mahalia-jackson

28 Walker, D. (2013, August 23). Witness recalls role of New Orleans' Mahalia Jackson in Martin Luther King's "I Have a Dream" speech. Retrieved May 30, 2018, from http://www.nola.com/tv/index.ssf/2013/08/witness_recalls_role_of_new_or.html

29 Whitman, A. (1972, January 28). Mahalia Jackson, gospel singer and a civil rights symbol, dies. *The New York Times*. Retrieved May 30, 2018, from https://www.nytimes.com/1972/01/28/archives/mahalia-jackson-gospel-singer-and-a-civil-rights-symbol-dies.html

30 Younge, G. (2013, August 9). Martin Luther King: The story behind his "I have a dream" speech. *The Guardian*. Retrieved June 2, 2018, from https://www.theguardian.com/world/2013/aug/09/martin-luther-king-dream-speech-history

31 Walker, D. (2013, August 23). Witness recalls role of New Orleans' Mahalia Jackson in Martin Luther King's "I Have a Dream" speech. Retrieved May 30, 2018, from http://www.nola.com/tv/index.ssf/2013/08/witness_recalls_role_of_new_or.html

32 Stringer, S., & Brumfield, B. (2015, August 12). New recording: King's first "I have a Dream" speech found at high school. *CNN*. Retrieved June 2, 2018, from https://www.cnn.com/2015/08/12/us/north-carolina-mlk-jr-i-have-a-dream-recording/index.html

33 Rochelle, R. (2013, June 21). Aretha Franklin reflects on dad's role in freedom walk. *Detroit Free Press*. Retrieved June 2, 2018, from https://www.usatoday.com/story/news/2013/06/21/aretha-franklin-detroit-freedom-walk/2447321/

34 King, M. L. Jr. (1963, August 28). "I have a dream" address delivered at the march on Washington for jobs and freedom. Retrieved June 2, 2018, from https://kinginstitute.stanford.edu/king-papers/documents/i-have-dream-address-delivered-march-washington-jobs-and-freedom -

35 Whitman, A. (1972, January 28). Mahalia Jackson, gospel singer and a civil rights symbol, dies. *The New York Times*. Retrieved May 30, 2018, from https://www.nytimes.com/1972/01/28/archives/mahalia-jackson-gospel-singer-and-a-civil-rights-symbol-dies.html

36 The King Center. (n.d.) Get involved. Retrieved September 24, 2018, from http://www.thekingcenter.org/get-involved (Excerpted from "The Drum Major Instinct," a sermon by Rev. Martin Luther King, Jr., 1968. Available in *A Knock at Midnight: Inspiration from the Great Sermons of Reverend Martin Luther King, Jr.*)

Chapter 8

1   Staff. (2017, March 27). Study: Chick-fil-A is still the king of customer service. *QSR*. Retrieved June 3, 2018, from https://www.qsrmagazine.com/news/study-chick-fil-still-king-customer-service

2   Chick-fil-A. (n.d.). Corporate purpose. Retrieved October 25, 2018, from https://www.chick-fil-a.com/About/Who-We-Are

3   Parker, D. (2016, November 11). Humble beginnings: How Truett Cathy's love for customers grew from a Coke and smile. *The Chicken Wire*. Retrieved June 3, 2018, from https://thechickenwire.chick-fil-a.com/Inside-Chick-fil-A/Humble-Beginnings-How-Truett-Cathys-Love-for-Customers-Grew-From-a-Coke-and-Smile

4   Cathy, T. (2002). *Eat mor chikin: Inspire more people: Doing business*

the Chick-fil-A way (p. 26). Decatur, GA: Looking Glass Books.

5   Cahn, L. (2018, April 27). *Fox News*. Why Chick-fil-A
    employees don't say "You're welcome." Retrieved from http://
    www.foxnews.com/food-drink/2018/04/27/why-chick-fil-
    employees-dont-say-youre-welcome.html

6   Matthew 5:41. *Bible, New International Version (NIV)*. Retrieved
    June 3, 2018, from https://www.biblegateway.com/passage/?searc
    h=Matthew+5%3A41&version=NIV

Chapter 9

1   City of York. (n.d.). Come grow with us. Retrieved August 12,
    2018, from http://www.cityofyork.net

2   York College. (n.d.). A history of York College. Retrieved
    September 28, 2018, from https://www.york.edu/college-history.
    html

3   People to People International. (n.d.). Retrieved August 13, 2018,
    from https://ptpi.org/about/

4   People to People International. (n.d.). Retrieved September 29,
    2018, from https://ptpi.org/about/

5   Library of Congress. (1944, June 6). Retrieved June 6, 2018, from
    http://www.loc.gov/pictures/item/96522674/

6   Strobel, W. C. (n.d.). Eisenhower with 502nd airborne. Retrieved
    September 28, 2018, from http://www.historyaddict.com/
    Ike502nd.html

7   D-Day Overlord. (n.d.) 101st Airborne Division paratroopers
    composition of the D-Day airborne and airlanding serials, serial
    7. Retrieved June 6, 2018, from https://www.dday-overlord.com/
    en/d-day/air-operations/serials/serial-7

8   Rasmussen, F. N. (1999, September 5). On D-Day minus 1,
    the subject was fishing. *Baltimore Sun*. Retrieved September
    28, 2018, from http://articles.baltimoresun.com/1999-09-05/
    topic/9909140411_1_strobel-paratroopers-eisenhower/2

9   Lauder, V. (2014, June 5). Eisenhower's "soul-racking" D-Day
    decision. *CNN*. Retrieved June 6, 2018, from https://www.cnn.
    com/2014/06/05/opinion/lauder-eisenhower-d-day-anguish/

index.html

10 Rives, T. (2014). OK, we'll go. *Prologue,* Spring, 37. Retrieved September 29, 2018, from https://www.archives.gov/files/publications/prologue/2014/spring/d-day.pdf

11 Strobel, W. C. (n.d.). Eisenhower with 502nd airborne. Retrieved September 28, 2018, from http://www.historyaddict.com/Ike502nd.html

12 Lauder, V. (2014, June 5). Eisenhower's "soul-racking" D-Day decision. *CNN.* Retrieved June 6, 2018, from https://www.cnn.com/2014/06/05/opinion/lauder-eisenhower-d-day-anguish/index.html

13 Strobel, W. C. (n.d.). Eisenhower with 502nd airborne. Retrieved September 28, 2018, from http://www.historyaddict.com/Ike502nd.html

14 Rasmussen, F. N. (1999, September 5). On D-Day minus 1, the subject was fishing. *Baltimore Sun.* Retrieved September 28, 2018, from http://articles.baltimoresun.com/1999-09-05/topic/9909140411_1_strobel-paratroopers-eisenhower/2

15 Rasmussen, F. N. (1999, September 5). On D-Day minus 1, the subject was fishing. *Baltimore Sun.* Retrieved September 28, 2018, from http://articles.baltimoresun.com/1999-09-05/topic/9909140411_1_strobel-paratroopers-eisenhower/2

16 Zucchino, D. (2014, June 5). Eisenhower had a second, secret D-day message. *Los Angeles Times.* Retrieved September 30, 2018, from http://www.latimes.com/nation/nationnow/la-na-eisenhower-d-day-message-story.html

17 Simon, S. (2013, June 8). The speech Eisenhower never gave on the Normandy invasion. Retrieved September 28, 2018, from https://www.npr.org/2013/06/08/189535104/the-speech-eisenhower-never-gave-on-the-normandy-invasion

18 Eisenhower, D. D. (1944, June 5). In case of failure. *National Archives and Records Administration.* Retrieved September 28, 2018, from https://www.archives.gov/exhibits/american_originals_iv/images/d_day/eisenhower_note.html

Chapter 10

1 King, L. (2014, November 5). Children of Theodore Roosevelt. Retrieved September 30, 2018, from http://abouttheodoreroosevelt.com/children-of-theodore-roosevelt/273/

2 Meyers, C. V. (1902). *Theodore Roosevelt, patriot and statesman: The true story of an ideal American* (p. 23). Philadelphia, PA: P.W. Ziegler & Co.

3 Kryvoruka, K. (2008, November 13). Theodore Roosevelt's divided house. *The Washington Times*. Retrieved September 30, 2018, from https://www.washingtontimes.com/news/2008/nov/13/theodore-roosevelts-divided-house

4 Bunyan, J. (1678, February). Great-heart. *Pilgrim's Progress*. Retrieved June 9, 2018, from http://pilgrims-progress.net/40-Great-Heart.php

5 Theodore Roosevelt Center. (n.d.) Roosevelt, Theodore, Sr. Retrieved September 30, 2018, from https://www.theodorerooseveltcenter.org/Learn-About-TR/TR-Encyclopedia/Family-and-Friends/Theodore-Roosevelt-Sr

6 Bishop, J. B. (1920). *Theodore Roosevelt and his time shown in his own letters - Book I* (p. 3), New York: Charles Scribner's Sons.

7 The Washington Post Staff Writers. (2012, June 15). U.S. Presidents' fathers: Best and worst. *The Denver Post*. Retrieved June 8, 2018, from https://www.denverpost.com/2012/06/15/u-s-presidents-fathers-best-and-worst/

8 Samuels, P., & Samuels, H. (1997). *Teddy Roosevelt at San Juan: The making of a president* (p. 26). College Station, TX: Texas A&M University Press.

9 Renehan Jr., E. (1999). *The lion's pride: Theodore Roosevelt and his family in peace and war* (p. 23). New York, NY: Oxford University Press.

10 Samuels, P., & Samuels, H. (1997). *Teddy Roosevelt at San Juan: The making of a president* (p. 26). College Station, TX: Texas A&M University Press.

11 National Park Service. (n.d..). Mittie, Thee, and the north/south divide. Retrieved September 30, 2018, from https://www.nps.

gov/thrb/learn/historyculture/mittietheedivide.htm

12 Kelly, J.E. (1899-1902). The crowded hour. *Sagamore Hill National Historic Site*. Retrieved October 22, 2018, from https://www.theodorerooseveltcenter.org/Research/Digital-Library/Record?libID=o284532.

13 Theodore Roosevelt Center. (n.d.) Roosevelt, Theodore, Jr. Retrieved September 30, 2018, from https://www.theodorerooseveltcenter.org/Learn-About-TR/TR-Encyclopedia/Family-and-Friends/Theodore-Roosevelt-Jr.aspx

14 Theodore Roosevelt Center. (n.d.) Roosevelt, Theodore, Jr. Retrieved September 30, 2018, from https://www.theodorerooseveltcenter.org/Learn-About-TR/TR-Encyclopedia/Family-and-Friends/Theodore-Roosevelt-Jr.aspx

15 National Park Service. (n.d.). The bull moose in winter: Theodore Roosevelt and World War I. Retrieved September 30, 2018, from https://www.nps.gov/articles/the-bull-moose-in-winter-theodore-roosevelt-and-world-war-i.htm

16 Crocker III, H. W. (2014). Teddy Roosevelt's Sons in World War 1. *The Yanks are coming! A military history of the United States in World War I*. Retrieved September 30, 2018, from https://www.historyonthenet.com/teddy-roosevelts-sons-in-world-war-1/

17 National Park Service. (n.d.). The bull moose in winter: Theodore Roosevelt and World War I. Retrieved September 30, 2018, from https://www.nps.gov/articles/the-bull-moose-in-winter-theodore-roosevelt-and-world-war-i.htm

18 Sons of the American Revolution. (n.d.). Compatriot Medal of Honor recipients: Theodore Roosevelt, Jr. Retrieved September 30, 2018, from https://www.sar.org/theodore-roosevelt-jr

19 Holden, W. (2018, September 28). Who fired Terry Allen and Ted Roosevelt, Jr., the best combat generals? *Warfare History Network*. Retrieved September 30, 2018, from https://warfarehistorynetwork.com/daily/who-fired-terry-allen-and-ted-roosevelt-jr-the-best-combat-generals/

20 Military Hall of Honor. (n.d.). Theodore Roosevelt, Jr. Brigadier General, U.S. Army Medal of Honor recipient World War II.

Retrieved June 9, 2018, from http://www.militaryhallofhonor.com/honoree-record.php?id=1622

21 Astor, G. (2008). *Terrible Terry Allen: Combat general of World War II: The life of an American soldier* (p. xi). New York, NY: Presidio Press.

22 Holden. W. (2018, September 28). Who fired Terry Allen and Ted Roosevelt, Jr., the best combat generals? *Warfare History Network*. Retrieved September 30, 2018, from https://warfarehistorynetwork.com/daily/who-fired-terry-allen-and-ted-roosevelt-jr-the-best-combat-generals/

23 Balkoski, J. (2005). *The Utah Beach: The amphibious landing and airborne operations on D-Day, June 6, 1944* (p. 179). Mechanicsburg, PA: Stackpole Books.

24 Warfare History Network. (2018, September 4). Outlandish D-Day invasion tales: Teddy Roosevelt Jr's bold decision. Retrieved June 8, 2018, from http://warfarehistorynetwork.com/daily/wwii/d-day-invasion-tales-teddy-roosevelt-jrs-bold-decision/

25 Military Hall of Honor. (n.d.). Theodore Roosevelt, Jr. Brigadier General, U.S. Army Medal of Honor recipient World War II. Retrieved June 9, 2018, from http://www.militaryhallofhonor.com/honoree-record.php?id=1622

26 Bradley, O. N. (1951). *A soldier's story* (p. 334). New York, NY: Holt.

27 Atkinson, R. (2014, May 13). *The guns at last light: The war in Western Europe, 1944–1945* (pp. 126–127). New York, NY: Picador.

28 Cannon, C. M. (2018, June 6). An old soldier's valor on D-Day. Retrieved June 11, 2018, from https://www.realclearpolitics.com/articles/2018/06/06/an_old_soldiers_valor_on_d-day_137213.html

29 The Hall of Valor Project. (n.d.). Theodore Roosevelt. Retrieved September 30, 2018, from https://valor.militarytimes.com/hero/2922

Chapter 11

1 Wilber, D. Q. (2011). *Rawhide down: The near assassination of Ronald Reagan* (p. 225). New York, NY: Henry Holt & Co.

2 Taubman, P. (1981, April 3). Explosive bullet struck Reagan, F.B.I. discovers. *The New York Times*. Retrieved June 10, 2018, from https://www.nytimes.com/1981/04/03/us/explosive-bullet-struck-reagan-fbi-discovers.html?&pagewanted=all

3 Hermann, P., & Ruane, M. (2014, August 8). James Brady's death ruled homicide by Virginia medical examiner. *The Washington Post*. Retrieved June 10, 2018, from https://www.washingtonpost.com/local/crime/james-bradys-death-ruled-homicide-by-dc-medical-examiner/2014/08/08/686de224-1f41-11e4-82f9-2cd6fa8da5c4_story.html?noredirect=on&utm_term=.bdc6a32278c5&wpisrc=al_national

4 Lewis, A. (1981, May 11). In recuperation, Delahanty recalls Reagan shooting. *The Washington Post*. Retrieved June 10, 2018, from https://www.washingtonpost.com/archive/politics/1981/05/11/in-recuperation-delahanty-recalls-reagan-shooting/7f154bd5-0ecf-40a8-a62a-8372279f8ce9/?noredirect=on&utm_term=.b04817d35a1f

5 Cahalan, S. (2011, February 27). I forgot to duck. *New York Post*. Retrieved June 10, 2018, from https://nypost.com/2011/02/27/i-forgot-to-duck/

6 Crean, E. (2004, June 11). He took a bullet for Reagan. *CBS News*. Retrieved June 10, 2018, from https://www.cbsnews.com/news/he-took-a-bullet-for-reagan/

7 Schieffer, B. (2012, June 5). The Reagan shooting: A closer call than we knew. *CBS News*. Retrieved June 10, 2018, from https://www.cbsnews.com/news/the-reagan-shooting-a-closer-call-than-we-knew/

8 Farahbaugh, K. (2011, March 29). Victims recall Reagan assassination attempt 30 years later. Retrieved June 10, 2018, from https://www.voanews.com/a/victims-recall-reagan-assassination-attempt-30-years-later-118953314/174624.html

9 Crean, E. (2004, June 11). He took a bullet for Reagan. *CBS*

News. Retrieved June 10, 2018, from https://www.cbsnews.com/news/he-took-a-bullet-for-reagan/

10 NPR Morning Edition. (2011, March 11). Revisiting the Reagan shooting in "Rawhide Down." Retrieved June 10, 2018, from https://www.npr.org/2011/03/11/134429263/revisiting-the-reagan-shooting-in-rawhide-down

11 Well, M. (2015, October 10). Jerry Parr, secret service agent who helped save Ronald Reagan dies at 85. *The Washington Post*. Retrieved June 10, 2018, from https://www.washingtonpost.com/national/jerry-parr-secret-service-agent-who-helped-save-ronald-reagan-dies-at-85/2015/10/10/dabec448-6f03-11e5-b31c-d80d62b53e28_story.html?utm_term=.0a188c4fc44b

12 Retrieved June 10, 2018, from https://inthesecretservice.com/early-life/

13 Retrieved June 10, 2018, from https://inthesecretservice.com/early-life/

14 Skinner, K. K., Anderson, A., & Anderson, M. (2003) *Reagan: A life in letters* (p. 6). New York, NY: Free Press, A Division of Simon and Schuster.

15 Rothman, L. (2015, March 30). Read President Reagan's best jokes about being shot. *Time*. Retrieved June 10, 2018, from http://time.com/3752477/reagan-assassination-reaction/

Chapter 12

1 Retrieved August 17, 2018, from https://www.wunderground.com/history/daily/us/oh/marietta/KPKB/date/2010-3-23

2 Snyder, T. D. (ed). (1993, January). Years of American education: A statistical portrait (p. 55). *National Center for Education Statistics, Department of Education*. Retrieved August 18, 2018, from https://nces.ed.gov/pubs93/93442.pdf

3 Kamenetz, A., & Turner, C. (2016, October 17). The high school graduation rate reaches a record high — again. *NPR*. Retrieved September 3, 2018, from https://www.npr.org/sections/ed/2016/10/17/498246451/the-high-school-graduation-reaches-a-record-high-again

Chapter 13

1   The Appalachian Trail Conservancy. (n.d.). Retrieved June 10, 2018, from http://www.appalachiantrail.org/home/explore-the-trail

2   Heid, M. (2017, August 13). The latest Appalachian trail thru-hike statistics. *Appalachian Mountain Club*. Retrieved June 10, 2018, from https://www.outdoors.org/articles/amc-outdoors/equipped/the-latest-appalachian-trail-thru-hike-statistics

3   The Appalachian Trail Conservancy. (n.d.). Retrieved June 10, 2018, from http://appalachiantrail.org/home/explore-the-trail/multi-day-hiking

4   Emerson, B. (2010, April 17). Mountain crossings a hikers' paradise. *The Atlantic Journal- Constitution*. Retrieved June 10, 2018, from https://www.ajc.com/travel/newsmedleystory1296876/6eDOFyNNypx6Qn9PSq8uHN/Retrieved June 10, 2018, from

5   http://www.aboutnorthgeorgia.com/ang/Mountain_Crossings_at_Walasi-yi

6   Mountain Crossings. (n.d.). Mountain Crossings was named a 2014 Top 100 Outfitter in the US by Outdoor Magazine. Retrieved June 10, 2018, from https://www.mountaincrossings.com/Articles.asp?ID=1

7   Mountain Crossings. (n.d.). Get A shake down. Retrieved June 10, 2018, from http://www.mountaincrossings.com/Virtual-Shakedown-Get-A-Shakedown-s/2055.htm -

8   Mountain Crossings. (n.d.). Frequently asked questions about the virtual shake down. Retrieved June 10, 2018, from http://www.mountaincrossings.com/Virtual-Shakedown-Learn-More-s/2047.htm

Chapter 14

1   Hicks, E. L. (1994). *Sometimes in the wrong, but never in doubt: George S. Benson and the education of the new religious right* (p. 15). Knoxville, TN: University of Tennessee Press.

2   Van Zandt, E. (2012, September 23). Clifton Ganus Jr.: Harding

chancellor recalls lifetime of adventure. *Arkansas Democrat-Gazette, Three Rivers Edition*. Retrieved July 6, 2018, from http://www.arkansasonline.com/news/2012/sep/23/clifton-ganus-jr-harding-chancellor-recalls-lifeti/?f=threerivers

3   Organ, D. (1966, August 1). Looking ahead at Harding. *Harding Bulletin, 42*(4), 4. Retrieved June 12, 2018, from https://scholarworks.harding.edu/cgi/viewcontent.cgi?referer=https://www.google.com/&httpsredir=1&article=1265&context=hubulletins

4   The ARGenWeb Project. (n.d.). History of the Harding swing. Retrieved June 23, 2018, from http://www.argenweb.net/white/wchs/Harding_files/History_Of_The_Harding_Swing.html

5   Staff. (1968, July 1). *Harding Bulletin, 43*(21), 5. Retrieved July 8, 2018, from https://scholarworks.harding.edu/cgi/viewcontent.cgi?referer=https://www.google.com/&httpsredir=1&article=1282&context=hubulletins

6   Vietnam Magazine. (2009, November 25). What's Your Number? The Vietnam War Selective Service Lottery. Retrieved July 10, 2018, from http://www.historynet.com/whats-your-number.htm

7   Thompson, R. (n.d.). Memories of growing up in Beersheba. *Division of Information Technology*. Retrieved October 12, 2018, from terpconnect.umd.edu/~calmon/ThompsonRalphGrowingUpInBeersheba%20R1.pdf

8   Partin, J. L. (2009). "Can These Bones Live?"–A Talk with Albert Hugh "Hooty" Knight (p. 8). Retrieved on October 12, 2018, from https://www.grundycountyhistory.org/s/090819-These-Bones.pdf

9   Partin, J. L. (2009). "Can These Bones Live?"–A Talk with Albert Hugh "Hooty" Knight (p. 8). Retrieved on October 12, 2018, from https://www.grundycountyhistory.org/s/090819-These-Bones.pdf

10 Gower, H. (2017, October 8). Beersheba Springs. Retrieved on October 12, 2018, from https://tennesseeencyclopedia.net/entries/beersheba-springs/

11 Loyd, D. (1999). Leonard Tate: The gentle poet from Grundy

County. *Border States: Journal of the Kentucky-Tennessee American Studies Association,* 12. Retrieved October 12, 2018, from http://spider.georgetowncollege.edu/htallant/border/bs12/fr-loyd.htm

12 Retrieved October 19, 2018, from http://vcpdm.org

13 Retrieved October 23, 2018, from http://vcpdm.org/Family_Members.htm